PORNOGRAPHY
AND
SILENCE

Books by Susan Griffin

Pornography and Silence: Culture's Revenge Against Nature

Rape: The Power of Consciousness

Woman and Nature: The Roaring Inside Her

Like the Iris of an Eye

Voices

PORNOGRAPHY AND SILENCE

Culture's Revenge Against Nature

SUSAN GRIFFIN

Harper & Row, Publishers
New York, Cambridge, Philadelphia, San Francisco
London, Mexico City, São Paulo, Singapore, Sydney

Portions of this work originally appeared in *American Poetry Review*, *Bay Guardian* and the *New Boston Review*.

Selections from H.D. used by permission of John Schaffner Associates, Inc.

A hardcover edition of this book is published by Harper & Row, Publishers, Inc.

First HARPER COLOPHON edition published 1982.

ISBN 0-06-090915-3   (previously ISBN 0-06-011647-1)

87 88 89 90   10 9 8 7 6

CONTENTS

seeking what we once knew,
we know ultimately we will find

H.D., *"The Flowering Rod"*

For Kim Chernin,
who turns to look in the same direction,
with deep love

ACKNOWLEDGMENTS

The origin of one thought cannot be distinguished from the origin of other thoughts, and the ideas of many others echo throughout this work. I cannot imagine that the insights in this work would have been possible were there not a powerful feminist movement which transformed my consciousness and my experience of the world. Before this movement existed I had buried my own feelings about pornographic images. No language or way of thinking gave my emotions the shape of reason, and thus I could not see pornographic images through my own eyes.

I am able to list only a few of those to whom my thoughts owe a debt. I discussed the ideas in this book from the beginning with Kim Chernin and we read one another's manuscripts. She led me toward essential psychological insights; we shared a vision in this process. Early discussions with June Jordan and with Florence Rush shaped my thinking, as did my reading of Florence Rush's book *The Best Kept Secret* in manuscript. Michelle Cliff's reading of Simone Weil shaped my ideas in a fundamental way.

I cannot list all the books that contributed to this work, and yet I will name some. Tillie Olsen's *Silences* and Adrienne Rich's *Of Woman Born* deeply affected my thought as did Hannah Arendt's *Origins of Totalitarianism*. The work of James Hillman and Susanne Langer influenced these pages. And though I take issue with certain of Susan Sontag's idea on pornography, her work *On Photography* entered my thinking continually. I feel especially indebted to the scholarship and insights of Lucy Dawidowicz regarding the holocaust.

Both Pauline Bart and Dianna Russell generously made their research available to me. Gloria Steinem gave me some extremely helpful material. And I am deeply indebted to the organization Women Against Violence and Pornography in the Media for their compilation of pornographic images, the conference they initiated, for numerous seminars and colloquia, and for their very informative newsletter. In addition to reading the manuscript and giving me invaluable support, Linda Levitsky shared with me a collection of racist images which she compiled for a study of racist stereotypes. (This study was rejected by her thesis advisor because he claimed that, in so many words, "all stereotypes are true.")

The women in my family helped me with this work. My daughter, Becky Levy, shared her school research into images of women on television. My mother, Sally Williamson, read popular romantic novels and shared the shape of their contents with me. My sister, Joanna Griffin, lent me her collection of books about the holocaust and pointed me in significant directions.

Kim Chernin helped me enormously with her editing of the manuscript. I would also like to thank Fran McCullough for her early and very helpful editorial insights. And I would like to thank Hugh Van Dusen for his thoughtful editing and his very kind support. Let me thank the copy editor of this book, Marjorie Horvitz, for her excellent work, and Cynthia Merman for her continual good humor and intelligent support. Kirsten Grimstad read parts of the manuscript and offered invaluable insights, as did Michael Rogin, Susan Rennie, and Sandy Boucher. Deborah Dallinger kindly helped me with research, as did Barbara Christian. Kathy Moran generously contributed to work on the footnotes, and Grace Rutledge typed the manuscript; both women gave me generous support and perceptive insights.

Finally I wish to mention a woman whose name I do not know who owned a magazine stand in a city I shall not name. Despite the fact that the cover of a pornographic magazine was displayed in her store, I could not find any such literature to purchase from her. When I told her that I needed magazines for research for this work, she told me that she was forced by the distributor to sell these magazines. But since she did not like to sell them, she had formed the habit of tearing off the covers and sending them all back to the distributor as unsold. Because she liked the work I was doing, she donated one of these copies for my research. I thank her for her help and for her very canny courage, an attribute of women often slandered in pornography.

PROLOGUE

One is used to thinking of pornography as part of a larger movement toward sexual liberation. In the idea of the pornographic image we imagine a revolution against silence. We imagine that eros will be set free first in the mind and then in the body by this revelation of a secret part of the human soul. And the pornographer comes to us, thus, through history, portrayed as not only a "libertine," a man who will brave injunctions and do as he would, but also a champion of political liberty. For within our idea of freedom of speech we would include freedom of speech about the whole life of the body and even the darkest parts of the mind.

And yet, though in history the movement to restore eros to our idea of human nature and the movement for political liberation are parts of the same vision, we must now make a distinction between the libertine's idea of liberty, "to do as one likes," and a vision of human "liberation." In the name of political freedom, we would not argue for the censorship of pornography. For political freedom itself belongs to human liberation, and is a necessary part of it. But if we are to move toward human liberation, we must begin to see that pornography and the small idea of "liberty" are opposed to that liberation.

These pages will argue that pornography is an expression not of human erotic feeling and desire, and not of a love of the life of the body, but of a fear of bodily knowledge, and a desire to silence eros. This is a notion foreign to a mind trained in this culture. We have even been used to calling pornographic art "erotic." Yet in order to see our lives more clearly within this culture, we must question the meaning we give to certain words and phrases, and to the images we accept as part of the life of our minds. We must, for example, look again at the idea of "human" liberation. For when we do, we will see two histories of the meaning of this word, one which includes the lives of women, and even embodies itself in a struggle for female emancipation, and another, which opposes itself to women, and to "the other" (men and women of other "races," "the Jew"), and imagines that liberation means the mastery of these others.

Above all, we must look into the mind that I will call "the chauvinist mind," which has defined this second use of the word "human" to exclude women, and decipher what the image of woman, or "the black," or "the Jew," means in that mind. But this is why I write of pornography. For pornography is the mythology of this mind; it is, to use a phrase of the poet Judy Grahn, "the poetry of oppression." Through its images we can draw a geography of this mind, and predict, even, where the paths of this mind will lead us.

This is of the greatest importance to us now, for we have imagined, under the spell of this mind, in which we all to some degree participate, that the paths this mind gives us are given us by destiny. And thus we have looked at certain behaviors and events in our civilization, such as rape or the Holocaust, as fateful. We suspect there is something dark and sinister in the human soul which causes violence to ourselves and others. We have blamed a decision made by human culture on our own natures, and thus on nature. But instead, what we find when we look closely at the meanings of pornography is that culture has opposed itself in violence to the natural, and takes revenge on nature.

As we explore the images from the pornographer's mind we will begin to decipher his iconography. We will see that the bodies of women in pornography, mastered, bound, silenced, beaten, and even murdered, are symbols for natural feeling and the power of nature, which the pornographic mind hates and fears. And above all, we will come to see that "the woman" in pornography, like "the Jew" in anti-Semitism and "the black" in racism, is simply a lost part of the soul, that region of being the pornographic or the racist mind would forget and deny. And finally, we shall see that to have knowledge of this forbidden part of the soul is to have eros.

But the pornographic mind is a mind in which we all participate.

It is the mind which dominates our culture. A mind which speaks to us through philosophy and literature, through religious doctrine and art, through film, through advertisement, in the commonest gestures, in our habits, through history and our ideas of history, and in the random acts of violence which surround our lives. And that is why this book must be written as "we," using this plural voice, as if we were a group of beings who shared some fate. For although we are assigned different parts in the pornographic drama—myself as pariah, perhaps you as conquerer, or you as victim—we are all imagined in this mind and the images of this mind enter all our minds.

A woman's mind ought to be surprised by pornography, for most women do not read pornography. We do not even enter those places or neighborhoods where it is sold. Still, when we first see these images, this mythos, this language, we are shocked only by a shock of recognition. We knew all these attitudes before (though we did not know, or did not want to know, this mind would "go so far"). We read on the jacket of an American book that the narrative speaks of "Captive Virgins and Heroic He-Men." Another book, entitled *Fatherly Love*, describes two adolescent girls who become the lovers of older men. In the language of a French pornographer we read of a woman that "the state her heart and mind might be in absolutely doesn't matter." In a pornographer's voice we come upon the confession that "I use a woman out of necessity as one uses a round and hollow receptacle for a different need." We see a pornographic film in which women are transformed into animals, and whipped into submission by a trainer.

For the pornographic mind is the mind of our culture. In pornography we find the fantasy life of this mind. So, in a reviewer's observation that both D. H. Lawrence and Henry Miller "had a definite physical love for women and a definite spiritual love for men," we can find ourselves in equal proximity to both pornography and church doctrine. The pornographer reduces a woman to a mere thing, to an entirely material object without a soul, who can only be "loved" physically. But the church, and the Judeo-Christian culture, give us the same ethos. For we read in church doctrine that the man is the head and the wife the body, or that woman is the known, whereas man is the knower. At one end of this spectrum or another, as pornographer, in fantasy, as the beings on whom these images are projected, our minds come together in culture, as we are shaped by the force of images and through the events which these images effect.

Let us consider six lives, for instance, six lives famous to us and filled with emblematic meaning for our own lives. The life of the writer Kate Chopin. The life of the painter Franz Marc. The life of the pornographer Marquis de Sade. The life of the actress Marilyn Monroe. The life of a man who raped a young woman and cut off her arms, Lawrence Singleton. And the life of Anne Frank. We know of these lives that only accident has kept us from living out their tragedies. On some level of our minds, without thinking, without questioning, we have assumed that the shapes of these lives were inevitable, just as the shape of our culture appears to us, in our dream of an existence, as inevitable.

But let us retell these lives in a different light. And let us now consider, as we hear each brief story, that the tragedies in these histories were caused not so much by nature as by the decisions of a mind we shall call pornographic, the mind which is the subject of this book.

The painter Franz Marc was born in Munich on February 8, 1880. His father was a landscape painter and Franz studied painting at the Munich Academy as a young man. In 1903 he traveled to Paris and was moved by the work of the Impressionists. He became conscious of the problems of form. He had an empathy for the life of nature, which he sought to find an expression for in his work. He loved the paintings of Van Gogh. Later he edited *Der Blaue Reiter,* one of the great documents of modern art, with the objectivist Vasily Kandinsky, and he lived at the center of a group of painters known as the Blue Rider School. He was famous for his brilliantly sensual paintings and his allegories of the lives of animals. But gradually he moved away from natural forms and began to seek a way to dismantle the sensual, material world so that he might create a world of "pure spirit." Believing the war would purge the corruption of the material, he joined the German army in 1914 and in 1916, at the age of thirty-six, he was killed.

Kate O'Flaherty Chopin, the American writer, was born in St. Louis, Missouri, exactly twenty-nine years before the birth of Franz Marc, on February 8, 1851. She was educated at the Sacred Heart Academy in St. Louis and received "no special training that might have prepared her for authorship." She married a cotton manufacturer and lived with him in New Orleans until 1880, when he retired. Now she moved with him to a plantation in a French hamlet in Louisiana and her life was completely "given over to the rearing of a family." Her husband died in 1882 and she moved back to St. Louis. At the age of thirty-six (the same age Franz Marc was when he died in a battlefield at Verdun), "seemingly with no premeditation," she began to write of her years spent on Louisiana plantations. She published a novel and then a collection of short stories and sketches, which made her famous. She had an inborn sense of the dramatic and a capacity to make her characters "intensely alive." Yet she achieved her effects more through accuracy than by an overlay of "romantic glamour." Her last published book, *The Awakening,* was received with storms of protest because within its pages it spoke openly of a woman's sexual passion. The novel was taken from circulation at the Mercantile Library in St. Louis. And she was denied membership in the Fine Arts Club. The St. Louis *Republic* wrote that the book was "too strong drink for moral babes and should be labeled 'poison.' " And *The Nation* decided that this account of the "love affairs of a wife and mother" was trivial. Because of the overwhelming hostility of public reaction to this book, she ceased to write. And five years after the publication of *The Awakening,* she died.

Donatien Alphonse François Sade, the Marquis de Sade, was born in Paris, June 2, 1740. In 1754, befitting his class (he was the descendant of one of the best Provençal families), he began a military career. He abandoned this career at the end of the Seven Years' War, in 1763. In this same year, although he was in love with another woman, who he claimed had given him venereal disease, he followed the wishes of his father and married the elder daughter of the Comte des Aides in Paris. As governor general of Bresse and Bugey and lord of Saumane and La Coste, he led what he himself described as the life of a "libertine." Several times he was convicted of acts of violence against women. In 1772, for example, he imprisoned five girls, raped them, and gave them a drug which poisoned them. One of the girls he had kept prisoner was severely injured. And another died. For these kidnappings, he was sentenced to death. He was reprieved from this sentence, however, and then arrested again for another crime. Continually he was arrested, and continually he escaped or used his influence to obtain a release.

But only to commit the same crimes of kidnapping, imprisonment, or violence again, so that he would again be arrested. Finally, in 1777, he was arrested once more and after a trial, another escape, and a rearrest, spent six years in a prison in Vincennes. After this he was imprisoned at the Bastille and finally at Charenton. It was during the years of his life spent in incarceration that he wrote most of his work, pornographic fantasies and essays, including the novels *Juliette* and *Justine,* for which he became famous and from which the word "sadism" was coined. In 1801, when he was sixty years old, de Sade was arrested for having written *Justine.* This was the first time he was imprisoned for his writing. He was transferred from one prison because he sexually assaulted other prisoners. In the last years of his life, in Charenton, he had an affair with a fourteen-year-old girl, "who was essentially sold to him by her mother." He died in prison in 1814, at the age of seventy-four.

Marilyn Monroe, originally named Norma Jean Mortensen (and later Norma Jean Baker), was born June 1, 1926, in Los Angeles, California. She spent her childhood in foster homes and orphanages. She began her career as a photographers' model. Her nude photograph on a calendar led to a film debut in 1948, followed by larger and larger roles in films. She was publicized in her early career as a "beautiful but dumb blonde," and became famous as a "sex symbol." After she achieved this fame she began to study at the Actors Studio in New York City. In 1962, at the age of thirty-six, and at the height of her career, she ended her life by taking an overdose of sleeping pills.

Lawrence Singleton was born in July 1928 in Tampa, Florida. He was one of eight children born to a working-class family and raised in a strict Southern Baptist tradition. He quit school in the eleventh grade and began work on the railroad. Later he joined the merchant marine and worked his way up to the highest rating given by the U.S. Coast Guard, that of "unlimited master." He was certified to command any ship carrying passengers or freight. He was married twice. His first wife died of cancer. In the summer of 1978, his daughter left home because he beat her when he was drunk. In September 1978, he picked up a fifteen-year-old hitchhiker, raped her, and cut off her arms. On April 20, 1979, he was convicted of rape, sodomy, oral copulation, kidnapping, mayhem, and attempted murder, and sentenced to fourteen years in prison. In 1980, as this book is being written, he is serving his time in San Quentin prison.

Anne Frank was born June 12, 1929, in Frankfurt. She was a victim of the anti-Semitism of the Nazi regime. Her diary, written while she was hiding, "made her the personification of the martyred Jewish young." She is remembered by her teachers as a talkative, "movie-loving," "dreamy" girl. Faced with deportation, on July 9, 1942, the Franks went into hiding in the back room and office of the father's business. They lived there until they were arrested by the Gestapo on August 4, 1944. Anne Frank was sent to a succession of camps. She died in Bergen-Belsen in March 1945. After her death, her father, who was the sole survivor of the family, found her diary, in which we can still read the words: "In spite of everything, I still believe that people are really good at heart."

And now let us tell the story of pornography as if it were a part of the story of these lives, and as if, indeed, the tragedy of these lives were all our suffering. For pornography, in its intensified mythology, simply expresses the same tragic choice which our culture has made for us, the choice to forget eros.

SACRED IMAGES

Give us the strength to follow
the power to hallow
beauty. . . .

H.D., "The Dancer"

Let us begin with the erotic. The painter says that the "untouched life of animals drew out everything good in me." He was like an animal (his friend Kandinsky says of him), for he had a "direct intimate" relationship with nature; he could enter the lives of animals. In the years before the war, he appears to record human fate, in a series of painted fables, through the bodies of cows, leopards, pigs, birds, and horses—above all, horses. He has painted a large canvas dominated by great swaths of red paint, the large form of a horse's ass, round, feeling, sensuous, tail curled in an earthly ecstasy, the soft head of another horse hanging near the ass, not nuzzling but touching the thigh, surely, touching the thigh, both head and ass certainly filled, without speaking or even expressing this, with a kind of passion, that same passion which seems to shape all the brush strokes with which this close grouping of four horses is painted. To stand before this painting is to feel oneself an animal, and to be at once joyous and overpowered.

But the painter cut this painting to shreds. He was, he said, disappointed. Only later was it pieced together by others. And now when we see what he had put on canvas, we wonder if Franz Marc, the man so close to animals, could not recognize this bestiality in himself as beautiful. For often what comes through the hand and the brush is greater than the mind admits; as H.D. writes, "we are more than we know."

Thus, although Klee writes of Marc that his "bond with the earth takes precedence over" his bond with "the universe," one senses that Marc suffered from that illness by which civilized man sees himself as divided from nature. He paints a great joyous, yellow cow, who flies. And yet, of the color yellow in this painting, he writes that this is a female color, the color of nurturing, and different from blue, which he says is male, and spiritual. Red, he writes, reminding us of the red horses he had to destroy, is the color of the forces which we must fight in ourselves, the forces that must "succumb," and the color of "*matter*, brutal and heavy."

His paintings both transcend and express this conflict.* The pig, who would be known as above all a creature of appetite, above all dominated by forces, glows in his canvas with a beneficent serenity. And red—red is wholly erotic, moving, the force which seems to be the life of the painting, the very energy of life itself, and not in any way hostile to the blue, or the spiritual light which Marc's colors give off; rather, here earth and spirit are one, and matter, simple animal flesh, is holy.

But Marc records another story in this series of paintings, one of the last of which is entitled *The Fate of the Animals*.† In 1913, he paints *The Unfortunate Land of Tyrol*, in which color survives in a paler form; red is muted beyond recognition, and the landscape, the bodies of horses, the body of a vulture, are charred black. The land of Tyrol was devastated at this time by invasion and war, and warfare seemed to surround and cast a shadow over the life of this painter. But he is also suffering a war inside his soul. In 1915 he paints *Broken Forms*. Now there is no distinction at all between matter and energy. Red and blue virtually become one another. There is a breakdown of old divisions. Here culture's separation from nature, and that unholy separation between flesh and spirit, have dissolved. The life of nature and the life of culture, matter and meaning, have become one force. But the painting is violent, as if the mind which had seen this vision of wholeness had collapsed inward upon itself and, seeing, would deny what it had seen. Perhaps the painter preferred the old division. He begins to paint abstractly, saying that this is a way to escape "imperfec-

---

* In 1908 Marc speaks of his work as an "animalization" of art. See Frederick S. Levine, "Beauty and the Beast Within," *California Monthly*, December 1979, p. 14.

† This painting, which Marc emblazoned with the words "And All Being Is Flaming Suffering," was later partially destroyed by fire.

tion"; he says he translates his existence into the spiritual, that the abstract is "independent of the mortal body." When he looks on his own painting *The Fate of the Animals*, he himself is shaken: "It is like a premonition of this war, horrible and gripping. . . ."

Now he moves away from the mortal body, and seeks independence from that bestiality whose erotic and beautiful life he had captured so powerfully.* For he is drawn to the war and he calls these battles, this death, a "moral experience, . . . a preparation for a breakthrough to a higher spiritual existence." He looks to the war to sweep "the dirt and decay away to give us the future today." But this was the end of his painting. For Franz Marc became a soldier in World War I, and in 1916 he was killed.

Only a decade before Franz Marc was to cut his painting of red horses to shreds, an evocative and powerful book was published in America which occasioned the pillorying and finally the death of its author, Kate Chopin. *The Awakening* records the life of Edna Pontellier, a married woman and a mother, as she awakens to her passion for life, her own sexual feeling, and her creative vision. "She wanted to swim far out, where no woman had swum before," we read; "as she swam she seemed to be reaching out for the unlimited in which to lose herself." The novel records the heroine's rebellion against the traditional idea of a woman, her realization that her marriage is without passion, her love for another man, and her move away from her husband, and her children, into her own life, and her work. But in this novel, as in the life of its author, the heroine's passion and her creative vision prove fatal.

When Edna discovers that a passionate woman cannot exist in society, she decides to die. Throughout the novel, Edna's transformation is symbolized by her desire to swim in the ocean. The story begins as she is learning to swim and ends as she swims to her death in that very ocean which had called up her longing to live and know the

---

* In the spring of 1915 Marc wrote in a letter to his wife: "Very early in life I found man to be 'ugly'; the animals appeared more beautiful, more pure. But then I discovered in them too so much that was repulsive and ugly. . . . Trees, flowers, the earth, all showed me more of their ugly and repulsive sides with each passing year. . . . now I have suddenly become more fully conscious of the ugliness of nature, its *impurity*. Perhaps it is our European view of the world that makes it seem so poisoned and distorted. It is indeed for that reason that I dream of a new Europe." See Levine, "Beauty," op. cit., p. 14.

depths of her nature. Like her heroine, Kate Chopin succumbed to society's condemnation of her passionate vision. *The Awakening* was her last published novel. A short time later she died, and even this book fell into silence.

And what do these two lives and these two deaths have to do with pornography? Both these lives fell into silence. One fell through his own conflict and by his own choices; for, choosing to go to war, he chose to stifle the great force of the color red, which shone so brilliantly in him. While the other, because she was a woman, and thus, in culture's imagination, became a symbol for what is feared in human nature, was chosen as a scapegoat and a sacrifice, and if she was complicit in the end to this choice, in the beginning she chose to struggle with culture for her own liberation.

Here we can find the traces of two social movements and movements of the mind which find their expression in the nineteenth century, in the diverging directions of the Romantic Movement. Behind Kate Chopin's struggle to assert her political and sexual freedom, we find a political movement embracing a vision which included the emancipation of women, the abolition of slavery, the reclaiming of erotic life as a part of human nature, and the reclaiming of nature itself. This was the strain of Romanticism which began with William Blake and Mary Wollstonecraft, and included Olive Schreiner, Havelock Ellis, Margaret Sanger, Charlotte Perkins Gilman, Paula Modersohn-Becker, Rainer Maria Rilke, Elizabeth Barrett Browning.

But another strain of Romanticism—which we can see expressed in the conflicted and apocalyptic vision of Franz Marc—at the same time it sought to know the power of nature and of eros, expressed a hatred and a fear of these forces. Rather than acknowledge eros as a part of its own being, this cast of mind divided itself from nature, and then expressed a fear of the power of nature as nature returned to its consciousness in the body of women, or "the Jew," or "darkness." This was the cultural and social movement which included Byron and Schiller, the painters Segantini, von Stuck, Klimt, the decadent school of art and poetry, and which was finally to give expression to fascism in the poetry of D'Annunzio and Marinetti, and in the propaganda and the political events of the Third Reich.

"Love is a want of my heart," Mary Wollstonecraft wrote, ". . . to deaden is not to calm the mind. Aiming at tranquility I have almost destroyed all the energy of my soul. . . ." And in her life, the knowledge of the heart, of her own passion, was inextricably mixed with her struggle for political justice and the emancipation of women. That she joined the French Revolution, that she wrote for the emancipation of women, for the education of women, that she refused to marry her lover, that as a girl she stopped her father from beating her mother by standing between them—all these acts were part of one vision of liberation. And this was a vision which she shared with George Sand, the author of *Lelia*, in which she wrote: "Oh dear sister! You may deny the heavenly influence! You may deny the sanctity of pleasure! But had you been granted this moment of ecstasy, you would have said that an angel from the very bosom of God had been sent to initiate you into the sacred mysteries of human life." For George Sand, who wore men's clothing, left her husband, and lived openly with her lovers, struggled equally for the emancipation of women and against all conditions of human slavery. And in Rainer Maria Rilke, too, who was the *Dichter*, the voice of a whole age, "in whom the thousand-year-old language rises up again," this movement toward the depth of our own natures, toward eros, and for the emancipation of women, joined.

But the movement toward female liberation could not easily embrace the movement for sexual liberation. A part of the movement for sexual liberation, which included Margaret Sanger, Otto Gross, Wilhelm Reich, Havelock Ellis, and Emma Goldman, saw a release from patriarchal values as essential to human wholeness. But another voice for sexual freedom, growing from that other strain of Romanticism, saw sexual liberty as an expression of the patriarchal tradition. This was the voice and sensibility which loved men spiritually and women physically. The voice which, in D. H. Lawrence's words, saw woman as growing "downwards, like a root, towards the center and darkness and origin," and man as growing "upwards like the stalk towards discovery and light and utterance." This is the same voice we find in pornography. It believes woman ought to be mastered by man. That she desires submission. That she needs to serve him. That if her body has a knowledge which could speak to this sensibility, it is a hidden, dark, unfathomable mystery which can never come to light.

For this idea of sexual liberty and female sexuality hides a vision of the apocalypse. Within this thinking, the "darkness" of the female being becomes threatening. A man who penetrates this darkness goes into danger. He risks his life. The female voice, like the voice of Circe or Eurydice, calls him back to hell or to death. She must be silenced. And she must be mastered, for the dark forces which she ignorantly holds within her body are as perilous as the forces of nature. Now this mind, in the words of Byron, tells us that his hero "haughty still and loath himself to blame . . ." called on nature "to share the shame." Thus he "charged all faults upon the fleshly form/She gave to clog the soul and feast the worm."

Eros and nature, in this mind, are made into one force, and this force is personified as a woman. But this is simultaneously a fatal and an evil force. It "clog[s] the soul," it "feast[s] the worm." Thus eros, nature, and woman, in the synapses of this mind, bring death into the world, and desire, this mind imagines, leads one to die. D'Annunzio, the late-Romantic, early-fascist poet, draws us such a portrait of his beloved. He calls her his "perilous beauty." She is a "vessel filled with all ills, uttermost depth of anguish and guilt, remote cause of infinite strife, deathly silence." Her body is the place where "drunk with lust and slaughter, the human monster, fed upon deceit, roars through the labyrinth of the ages." But we find this portrait throughout litera- ture, in the poems of Baudelaire, in the novels of Céline, in Balzac, in Faulkner, in Wedekind's *Lulu,* in the paintings of Max Beckmann, Gustav Klimt, Segantini. Thus, when the historian Carl Schorske, writ- ing of Viennese culture, tells us, "Woman, like the Sphinx, threatens the male," he is describing a universal movement of the mind. Speaking of a painting by Klimt, he tells us, "The joyous explorer of Eros found himself falling into the coil of *La Femme Tentaculaire.* The new free- dom was turning into a nightmare of anxiety." This is the same night- mare which belongs to the pornographic mind.

And now this mind, which is so terrified of woman and nature, and of the force of eros, must separate itself from what it fears. Now it will call itself "culture" and oppose itself to woman and nature. For now culture shall become an instrument of revenge against the power of nature embodied in the image of a woman. And so now, within this mind which has become "culture," woman will either be excluded, and her presence made an absence, a kind of death of the mind, or she shall be humiliated, so that the images we come to know of woman will be degraded images.

Here this mind has made a metaphysical division. It argues that spirit, which it associates with man, and matter, which it associates with woman, are separate. It tells us that matter corrupts spirit. For instance, we hear from Schiller that "Movements which have as principle only animal sensuousness belong only, however voluntary we may suppose them to be, to physical nature, which never reaches of itself to grace." And if matter could have grace, Schiller continues, creating for matter a kind of cul-de-sac of reason, "grace would no longer be capable or worthy to serve as the expression of humanity." Or we hear from Schopenhauer that will, which is natural, and idea are at opposite poles of existence. Or we hear from Freud that culture and instinct are at war.

But this is also the metaphysics of pornography. And in this cast of mind perhaps we recognize an old familiar voice. For the separation of flesh and spirit, and the condemnation of the whore of Babylon, are old Biblical themes. And now, too, we recall that one image which was not broken in Franz Marc's apocalyptic vision which he called *Broken Forms*. There in the corner of his painting, coiled about a tree, or growing as if out of the tree, we find the serpent, the same animal that whispered some knowledge to Eve, who thereafter brought death and suffering to the world.

Transgression

> . . . all the members that had been thrust into her and so perfectly provided the living proof that she was indeed prostituted, had at the same time provided the proof that she was worthy of being prostituted and had, so to speak, sanctified her.
>
> *The Story of O*

We are perhaps surprised to find that the metaphysics of Christianity and the metaphysics of pornography are the same. For we are accustomed to thinking of history in a different light. We imagine the church fathers as the judges of and inquisitors against the pornographers. We imagine the pornographer as a revolutionary of the imagination, who bravely stands up to speak of the life of the body openly while the church pronounces on the evils of the flesh. We remember Tertullian's words that even "natural beauty ought to be obliterated by concealment and neglect, since it is dangerous to those who look upon it." And in the wake of these words, we imagine the display of bodies in a pornographic magazine to be an act of liberation. We remember the words of Saint Paul: "It is good for a man not to touch a woman," or the idea of Augustine that the sexual organs are tainted with lust. Or we go back further in time, to the Romans who preceded Christian thought with their own asceticism and hatred of the body. We hear Democritus define a brave man as one who overcomes not only his enemies but his "pleasures." We hear Epicurus intone that sexual feeling "never benefited any man." We remember the Stoics' warning against passion in marriage, or Plotinus and his student, Porphyry, who despised desire as evil, or the Neoplatonists, who practiced celibacy as a virtue. And to these voices we oppose the voice of the pornographer, who we imagine defends the body, loves flesh, worships desire, would explore all the possibilities of sexual joy. Thus we begin to think of pornography as a kind of transgression against "holy" prudery.

Certainly the pornographer is obsessed with the idea of transgression. The Marquis de Sade, for instance, finds transgression more pleasurable than pleasure itself. He tells us, "Crime is the soul of lust." He tells us that "there is a kind of pleasure which comes from the sacrilege or the profanation of the objects offered us for worship." And of his life, Simone de Beauvoir writes, "No aphrodisiac is so potent as the defiance of Good." Throughout pornography the priest or the nun, therefore, is turned into a lecherous or a prostituted figure. In Aretino's *Dialogue of the Life of a Married Woman*, a wife pretends to be near death so that she can commit adultery with the priest whom she has called for her last confession. In another classic pornographic novel, *Le Bain d'Amour*, a couple make love in a pew, and the scene of their passion alternates with descriptions of the mass. One of the more famous episodes of de Sade's *Justine* takes place in a monastery, where the monks abduct, rape, and commit sadistic acts on women. But to this we must add the enacted pornography in a brothel, in which, for example, a prostitute is asked to dress as a nun to please her client.

In his history of the creation of *Playboy* magazine, Gay Talese tells us that in the earlier years of its existence in Chicago, the *Playboy* office lay in the shadow of a great church, Holy Name Cathedral. Writing ironically of this juxtaposition, he tells us: "great cathedrals cannot be . . . maintained without sufficient numbers of sinners to justify them." But when we look at the history of pornography, and the pornographer's obsession with transgressing the morality of the church, we begin to understand that pornography, and the pornographic idea of sin, could not exist without the great cathedrals.

We begin to see pornography more as if it were a modern building, built on the site of the old cathedrals, sharing the same foundation. And if one were to dig beneath this foundation, we imagine, one might see how much the old structure and the new resemble one another. For all the old shapes of religious asceticism are echoed in obscenity. And every theme, every attitude, every shade of pornographic feeling has its origin in the church.

But this, finally, is the nature of rebellion. For to run away from the enemy is to call upon oneself the fate of one day meeting that enemy in oneself. A rebellion ultimately imitates that which it rebels against, until the rebel comes to understand himself. And no form of culture seems so blind to its own nature as pornography. The pornographic fantasy has that shape of the mind familiar to us in the madman, and in the totally naive liar, who contradict their speech with their gestures, who speak at cross purposes to their intent, and yet who tell us, even in their lies, the truth about their secret thoughts. Here we encounter the dream life of an otherwise duplicitous being.

So a veil is drawn over the real life of pornography. What advertises itself as nakedness is shrouded. What is called frankness is denial. What is called passion is the death of feeling. What is called desire is degradation. And the pornographic mind hallucinates. The two who are called lovers are really one soul divided. And what is called a transgression against the church fathers is finally loyalty. Just as Saint Jerome, in his attempt to flee from a woman's body, found the images of dancing girls intruding on his vision even when he lived alone in the desert of Chacis, so, too, perdition, sin, and hell haunt the pornographer even in his most extreme acts of rebellion.

The Loyal Son: Projection and Denial

> . . . a murderer in the moment of his murder could feel a sense of beauty
> and perfection as complete as the transport of the saint.
>
> NORMAN MAILER, *Existential Errands*

We learn from Simone de Beauvoir's account of the life of the Marquis
de Sade that nothing in the young man's character could be called
"revolutionary"; he was not yet a rebel. As de Beauvoir tells us, "He
was quite prepared to accept society as it was." He was, we learn,
even submissive. He accepted marriage with a wife whom he did not
like because his father wanted the marriage. Nor did he wish to renounce the privileges that he inherited as his father's son, as a marquis,
as lord of the manor.

And so, reading the life of this young man, one might be surprised
at the events which were to follow. For in the words of the Marquis
himself, he was to seek the "sacrilege" and the "profanation" of the
objects his father's society "worshiped." Yet, when we look more closely
at this "rebellion," at this "sacrilege and profanation," we can see that
the tradition of his father's thought determined every choice. Let us,
to begin with, identify the object of the Marquis's profanation. We
discover he uttered the word "sacrilege" to describe "the pleasure
of torturing and mocking a beautiful woman." (And let us in this light
recall that in his fantasy life, it was a woman's body, in the character
of Justine, who was tortured, and that in one scene, it was a group
of monks he imagined carrying out this torture.)

De Sade was not speaking only metaphorically of "the pleasure of
torturing . . . a beautiful woman." On an Easter Sunday in 1768, he
enacted his fantasy of cruelty and profanation on the body of a woman
named Rose Keller. He tied her up, whipped her, cut her with a knife,
and dropped candle wax into her wounds. And let us look at the meaning of this act of "profanation." Of the two roles which he gave to
himself and to this woman in the drama of his mind, he played the
religious suppliant, while she was made to play the evil one. He took
on the imagined mantle of the priest, and just as he reached the apex
of his sexual excitement, he suggested that he hear her confession.
On another occasion, famous because he was later charged with abuse,
he hired a twenty-year-old woman, a fan-maker named Jeanne Tes-

PORNOGRAPHY AND SILENCE : *18*

tarde, to serve in his fantasies. Now, with her, he played the part of the rebel raging against Christianity; he told her "he masturbated into a chalice"; he told her that he had placed two communion hosts in the body of a woman and penetrated her. Finally, he asked Testarde to whip him. And when she refused, he crushed one crucifix, and masturbated on the other.

But now this rebel demanded that Testarde carry out his own rebellion. He forced her, for instance, to crush the crucifix on which he had masturbated. He tried to give her an enema so that she would defecate on the crucifix. And at last it was again a woman whom he punished, depriving her of both food and sleep, assaulting her with cruel language through the night.

Here is the true conventionality at the heart of de Sade's "rebellion." These descriptions of his acts in every way remind us of the trials of the witches that the church fathers themselves carried out in the name of traditional doctrine in the preceding centuries, against the bodies and souls of women. His sexual fantasies and acts resemble these inquisitions in every facet. Only, in his inquisitions, he plays all the roles, becoming at one moment the inquisitor, and at another the witch; he creates and espouses an anti-Christian doctrine, and then forces a woman to act as the professor of this doctrine. Interchangeably, he plays the torturer and the tortured.

But is even this confusion between himself and his victim not, in fact, typical of the inquisitors of history? The monks who wrote the *Malleus Maleficarum* as the doctrinal justification for witch-burning clearly created their descriptions of the ideas and acts of witches out of their own psyches, and afterward attributed these fantasies to their victims. In their minds, they as freely moved from victim to torturer as did de Sade in his rituals of cruelty. We read that the witch-burners believed themselves to be the victims of the women they accused; we discover in their own accounts that they felt they were in mortal danger from the power of witches. Just as Rose Keller, or Jeanne Testarde, never existed as themselves in the mind of de Sade, but only as actresses who performed the roles he created for them, so the "witch" never existed as the church saw her; rather, the Christian idea of the "witch" was a shadow side of that religious mind.

Yet finally, that which above all gives us the key to the traditional shape of de Sade's rebellion is that he chose the same victim for his rage as had the church fathers through centuries of tradition. For the body of a woman is culture's time-honored and conventional victim. So in the end, we see this rebel is the most loyal of sons. Like his fathers before him, he reduces a woman to an object. Like his fathers, he imagines she is more evil than men. Like the church fathers of the inquisition, he punishes her. And like these same fathers, he imagines himself as her victim.

But now we see that the rebellious sons, and their fathers, not only share an ideology which conceives of women as the vessel of evil, but share a condition of the mind. For these two minds, loyal to one another in their shadow lives, move by the same mechanisms. And these are the mechanisms of projection and denial.

Denial is not mysterious to us. It is simply that means by which the mind forgets a part of itself. So we have the words "conscious" and "unconscious," and by these words we know that the mind has a knowledge of its own being which it will at times make inaccessible to itself. The mind will choose not to know what indeed it does know. But projection is born from denial. For this forgotten knowledge has a way of insisting on life. Even through the very effort we make to push this knowledge of ourselves away from us, it reappears. Thus, in *Totem and Taboo,* Freud tells us that the knowledge we wish not to know is "ejected from internal perception into the external world." We deny a part of ourselves, and deny knowledge of this part, but just as we deny this, we see this knowledge outside us as part of the world. What we detach from ourselves is, in Freud's language, "pushed onto someone else."

Both the church and pornography have chosen the same victim on which to push this denied knowledge. In these twin cultures, a woman is a blank screen. The nature of her real being is erased, as if her cultural image had been carefully prepared for a clear projection of an image, and she comes to stand for all that man would deny in himself. But she herself, as we shall later see, is no accidental victim. A woman's body evokes the self-knowledge a man tries to forget. And thus he dreads this body. But he does not understand this dread as belonging to himself, and a fear of what the female body calls up in him. Rather, he pretends to himself that she *is* evil. His conscious mind believes she is evil. As Karen Horney says, "everywhere, the man strives to rid himself of his dread of women by objectifying it." Pornography offers us a clear example of this "objectification" in the words of de Sade, who tells us that woman is "a miserable creature, always inferior, less handsome than he is, less ingenious, less wise, disgustingly shaped, the opposite of what should please a man or delight him . . . a tyrant . . . always nasty, always dangerous. . . ."

The pornographer, like the church father, hates and denies a part of himself. He rejects his knowledge of the physical world and of his own materiality. He rejects knowledge of his own body. This is a part of his mind he would forget. But he cannot reject this knowledge entirely. It comes back to him through his own body: through desire. Just as he pushes away a part of himself, he desires it. What he hates and fears, what he would loathe, he desires. He is in a terrible conflict with himself. And instead he comes to imagine that he struggles with a woman. Onto her body he projects his fear and his desire. So the female body, like the whore of Babylon in church iconography, simultaneously lures the pornographer and incites his rage.

The Virgin and the Whore

A pilgrim of eros might begin where the Christian mind stops, and traveling in an opposite direction, work his way back to wholeness. Therefore, he would start with the shame of the body, and gradually, in his mind, cast shame away and join carnal and spiritual love together again. But this is not the direction of the pornographer's journey. Instead, he travels on the same old path of morality.

In the pornographic mind, a great fissure exists between spiritual and carnal love. For the pornographer can never love one woman in both body and soul. The Marquis de Sade has told us, for instance, that he liked to be friends with "ugly" women. He could not befriend a woman whom he desired. After an act of coitus with a woman, he found her repulsive, and hated her company. The narrator of *My Secret Life* (a Victorian pornographic classic) tells us he cannot remain faithful to the woman whom he loves. Instead, he chases after women whom he calls "demireps, sluts and strumpets." He would gladly have "slain" any of his "paramours" rather than cause his beloved any pain, he tells us. Yet he pleads that he cannot control his desire. Rather, he is compelled by lust to "lascivious vagaries and aberrations."

Here we find an old and familiar duality. Now the body and the soul, which we are used to thinking of as divided, are represented by the virgin and the whore. The virgin is "pure." Her soul can be loved precisely because her body has not been touched. She is without sexual knowledge. But the whore, who knows sexual experience, is defiled. Her spirit has been destroyed by the same act which soiled her body. Only her body can be "loved." We know this thinking from the church fathers.

Indeed, were we to find in pornography a motion of the mind to liberate itself from the hatred of the body, we might expect that here the old idea of the virgin and the whore would finally vanish. But instead, the virgin and the whore are the pornographer's obsession. For through these two personae the pornographic mind finds a rich medium with which to express its own dilemma of dividedness.

The pornographer begins by reprimanding the virgin for her prudery. In his mind, he even makes her into the church inquisitor. He imagines she has shaped the cultural doctrine which denies to him a knowledge of the body. He vents a rage against her because she has rejected him.

But we must ask here: What is the vehicle of his rage? How does he express his anger against her? In the pornographic novel *The Lustful Turk*, the Dey is angry at a woman he calls haughty, who has "rejected men." And therefore, in order to punish her, he rapes her. In *Justine*, a girl who is a virgin, who typifies "modesty, decency, and timidity," whose eyes are "very soulful," is repeatedly raped and subjected to tortures of unimaginable variety. In *Behind the Green Door, Captive Virgin, Fatherly Love, Trapped and Tied Baby Hookers, A Man with a Maid*, virgins are kidnapped, tied up, imprisoned, and raped.

What we discover, finally, is that the virgin is punished by *carnality. Coitus itself becomes the vehicle of the pornographer's rage.* And as we continue to examine this act, we find that its essential element is not the pleasure that the rapist obtains from coitus itself. We discover, rather, that the satisfaction he receives is from humiliating the virgin. We read, for instance, in *The Lustful Turk* that the Dey wished revenge on the woman he captured by "attacking her modesty in the most sensible part." In *A Man with a Maid*, when the hero forces the heroine to remove her clothing, he is not obsessed with her beauty, but rather with the mortification she feels when her body is exposed. Over and over again, the pornographer's triumph, the pièce de résistance in his fantasy, occurs when he turns the virgin into a whore.

But who is the whore in pornography? We find her represented in pornographic theater as the woman who displays her body before strange men when she dances. An atmosphere of profanation surrounds her performance. (In the audience we sense the intense interest of small boys, who believe they are doing something "dirty.") In one nightclub, a woman dances seductively in a costume that reveals her breasts. And afterward she gets on her hands and knees to clean up the stage. Thus it is driven home to us that she is "soiled." In Juvenal we find this state of desecration spelled out for us. He tells us that Claudius's wife is a whore because she has received "all comers." In this act, he writes, she has brought back to the "imperial couch all the odors of the stews." And now the old Biblical notion of whoredom speaks through the mouth of the pornographer. Just as Jeremiah tells us "thou hast a whore's forehead, thou refusest to be ashamed," so Juvenal tells us that Claudius's wife is a "shameless harlot."

For shame is the essential element in the pornographic transformation of a virgin into a whore. The whore is "shameless" because she has already been shamed. She *is* shame. There is nothing in her left to sully. Therefore, when the pornographic hero rapes a whore, he tells her, "You couldn't get enough, could you?" or he says, "You give it to everybody, don't you?" He reminds her of her already fallen condition. When he rapes her he tells her that he does so because of her humiliated state, to punish her. But when the pornographic hero meets a virgin, his desire is to make her a whore. And he wishes to make her a whore precisely because he wishes to shame her.

Thus, in the pornographic drama of the virgin and the whore, we discover the old religious definition of the sexual act. For in pornography, when a man makes love to a woman who is a virgin, he does so in order to destroy her spirit. In this mind, the sexual act is an act of humiliation to the soul. It is with this humiliation, finally, that the pornographic mind is obsessed.

But of course, the virgin and the whore are part of one mind. (In de Sade's character Justine we can find a reflection of the submissive young man who obeyed a cold, controlling father. And in another of his famous characters, Juliette, who was Justine's "sister," her other half, we find a portrait of the other half of de Sade's mind. Juliette, who is the whore, is in every detail Justine's opposite. She is as cunning as Justine is submissive, as cruel as Justine is timid, as depraved as Justine is innocent.) Thus does the pornographic mind portray its own "innocence" to itself in the character of the virgin: the mind's decision to forget the knowledge of the body is projected onto the body of one kind of woman. And at the same time, the mind's knowledge of carnality is portrayed in another kind of woman, in the body of the whore, and despised in her.

Yet the pornographic mind cannot stay still within these boundaries culture has created. The mind would know itself. It is *compelled* to know itself. For the mind has about it an uncanny wholeness, and would, even through madness, retrieve all its parts. The virgin is given sexual knowledge; she is raped. But after her deflowering, this woman who had represented innocence and soulfulness must now be redefined. For culture has declared that the flesh and the spirit cannot meet. Therefore, as soon as the virgin knows carnality she must lose her soul. She becomes a whore, and now sexuality *is* her humiliation.

Yet in the pornographic mind, all along, the virgin *is* a whore. For this woman, we must remember, is a figment of the pornographic imagination. She does not stand for the absence of knowledge, the way we might suppose. She stands instead for a lie. Her image signifies the *denial* of sexual knowledge and desire which the pornographic mind has tried to forget but which it cannot forget. So in the pornographic fantasy, whenever the virgin is raped, she is told that she has always wanted to be raped. She is told that underneath her "innocence" she has the soul of a whore. In *A Captive Virgin,* for example, we read the heroine feels "delight flashing through her loins" when she is forcibly penetrated. And when he is raping a woman, another pornographic hero tells his victim, "You really wanted this, didn't you?" thus implying to her that she is already in essence a whore.

When we look, finally, at the lives of the virgin and the whore in pornography, we discover that sexuality can never be sought as a simple pleasure. In this mind, because a woman desires, she is imagined as evil through and because of her carnality. The fulfillment of her desire inevitably brings about her humiliation and at the same time implies the loss of her soul. For pornography does not present to us a new state of grace, in which the body is admitted into heaven. Rather, the pornographer gives us his own version of hell.*

The Animal

> Man is the hunter, woman is his game.
> TENNYSON, *The Princess*

Speaking of his predisposition to detest women he had known sexually, and of his preference in friendship for women he imagined as ugly, de Sade tells us: "What need for the heart to have a role in the situation in which only the body plays a part?" For in the thinking of the pornographic mind, it is the body which is the lower half of human nature, and which corrupts the soul. Yet the pornographic mind, like the doctrinal mind, denies the knowledge of its own body. By the mechanism of projection, this mind succeeds in detaching itself from its own bestiality. In this mind, the bestiality of a man's nature is expressed in a woman's body.

Thus pornography is filled with associations between women and animals. We see a film in which women become animals, who are then trained with a whip. Juvenal tells us that a woman filled with sexual desire becomes "more savage than a tigress that lost her cubs." In *Hustler* magazine, a woman is photographed surrounded by the mounted heads of wild animals and animal skins. She opens her legs

---

* Indeed, we witness a literal voyage into Hades in the pornographic film *The Devil and Miss Jones*. The film begins as Miss Jones, who is a classic virgin, commits suicide. After she awakens from her death, she finds that she is being admitted into hell. But since she has led such a virtuous life, she requests that she be allowed to indulge in one sin before her eternal perdition begins. She would like, of course, to indulge in the sin of lust. And so she is schooled by the devil in his many forms of lust, acts of coitus, fellatio, anal intercourse, and an abandoned sensuality which includes sleeping late and eating in bed. At the end of her indulgence, we discover, she has become a whore. She is in fact possessed by lust. Finally, she has become a ravening creature, wholly bent on carnality, half maddened by a consuming desire.

But the pornographic mind is not aroused by visions of sexual bliss. Thus at the end of *The Devil and Miss Jones*, the heroine's desire becomes her hell. She is condemned to live forever in a cell with a man who is entirely disinterested in making love to her, while she is tortured by her desire for him. Now her desire is her punishment.

toward a live lion and touches her own breasts. Over the photograph we read that "Lea" has shed "the veneer of civilization for the honesty of wild animal passions." "The beast in her," we are told, "is unleashed." Projecting even the mechanism of his own projection of her, the pornographer writes: "She sees in wild creatures her own primitive lusts and desires, and she satisfies them with the uninhibited speed of a beast in heat." And in the midst of several photographs of nude women who lie with their legs apart, revealing their vulvas, we find, in the same magazine, a photograph of a male lion, on his back, his legs, also, spread apart.

As common as the image of woman as beast is the image of a woman in coitus with an animal, as if, when a woman is pictured as the lover of a beast, her bestial nature is confirmed. Pornographic images of women in coitus with animals make up a secret museum of classic art. Mel Ramos, the famous painter of pinups, has a series of pinups with animals: a woman smiling serenely while an anteater performs cunnilingus on her, a woman penetrated by a kangaroo, a nude woman on the back of a walrus. In a series of offset prints by Mario Tauzin, a woman, the inevitable finger in her mouth, raises her leg to a fox terrier. In a contemporary painting by Yves Milet, a cat looks on while a man makes love to a woman, as in an anonymous eighteenth-century engraving in which a dog looks on and a cat runs from beneath a woman's skirts; in the work of Franz von Bayros, an Austrian painter, who lived his last years during Hitler's rise, a woman opens her legs to the mouth of a deer, and another to the mouth of a dog, and another to a bulldog; and in the paintings of von Stuck (Adolf Hitler's favorite painter), the coupling of women with animals, serpents, and satyrs was a major motif. In the work of Amarol, the American painter, of Frank Cierciorka, also American, in the work of the Dutch painter Melle, the Japanese artist Shozan, the French painter Yves Tanguy, the Polish artist Jan Lebenstein, or the more famous Karel Appel, women are raped by bulls, they couple with goats and horses, or strange mammalian creatures, half goat, half camel, they are made love to by birds, penetrated by the stamens of flowers; they sit nude milking cows, they become half animal, with the bodies of horses, or the heads of birds.

Yet these are not idyllic fantasies in which women realize a human unity with nature. Rather, they are portraits of degradation, filled with revulsion and ridicule. We read (in the pornographic work *Gamiani*) of a virgin coupling with a monkey, for example, that she was "bestialized, devirginized and monkeyfied." Precisely as she begins to feel ecstasy, precisely as she knows sexual joy, at the height of her "writhing and struggling," the pornographer tells us that she is "spewing out her soul." And we learn that it was the devil who urged her into the monkey's grasp.

But the idea that women are closer to nature and are therefore lacking in a spiritual dimension is not new to pornography. This idea so pervades the imagery and language of civilization that the concept takes on an air of reality. For instance, Carl Jung unthinkingly equates naturalness with femaleness, and (like the Southern plantation owner) finds the African woman more female than the "civilized woman." Sentimentally, he speaks of a tribal woman and "her own wholeness." He expands this reflective nostalgia into a world theory when, a few lines later, he asks whether the "growing masculinization" of the white woman is not connected with "the loss of her natural wholeness." And goes on to delineate the shape of this wholeness; it contains, he lists, *"shamba,"* "children," "livestock," "house," "hearth fire," "and last but not least her own not unattractive physique." Nowhere in this natural being does he mention a soul, a spirit, intelligence, art, idea! For female wholeness in this mind is equivalent only to man's idea of the bestial and of nature as mere materiality.

We encounter the same idea of the female in the mind of Schopenhauer, who wrote that women exist solely to propagate the species, and in the mind of Hegel, who wrote that women cannot comprehend abstract ideas; in the mind of a theology which reasons that women are not made after the image of God, or the mind which cautions that women's brains are so affected by menstruation that they cannot think clearly, or the mind which says women cannot learn geometry. And so from the words of Paracelsus, who wrote:

> And yet woman in her own way is also a field of the earth and not at all different from it. She replaces it, so to speak; she is the field and the garden mold in which the child is sown and planted . . .

we move through centuries to the language of Faulkner:

> Her entire appearance suggested some symbology out of old Dionysiac
> times, honey in sunlight and bursting grapes, the bleeding of the
> crushed fecundated vine beneath the hard rapacious goat-hoof . . .

to the seamy thought of Norman Mailer as he reviews Mary McCarthy's
novel *The Group:*

> Everything in the profound materiality of women is given its full
> stop until the Eggs Benedict and the dress with the white fichu, the
> pessary and the what not, set in line of the narrative like commas
> and periods, semicolons, italics and accents. The real interplay of the
> novel exists between the characters and the objects which surround
> them until the faces are swimming in a cold lava of anality, which
> becomes the truest part of her group, her glop, her impacted mass.

Mailer's figurative dunking of McCarthy's novel and her female characters in a pool of shit is part of a tradition in pornographic literature.
This tradition is perhaps most memorably captured by Rabelais, whose
famous character Gargantua uses various female objects with which
to clean himself after defecating, including a gentlewoman's velvet
mask, her neckerchief, her hood, her satin earpieces.

But here the pornographic image, beneath its literal meaning, utters
the truth. And now, in this image, perhaps we can find a whole new
significance in the endless plethora of advertisements centered about
women who wash men's clothes and men's houses and men's bodies.
A woman's velvet mask, a woman's labor, a woman's hands, are used
to clean a man's body of its own substance. And is this not the secret
content of the pornographic mind? For in this mind, a woman's body
becomes the symbol which contains all that a man finds soiled by
bestiality in himself.

We hear from Augustine that "nothing brings the manly mind down
from the heights more than a woman's caresses." But let us reverse
this statement. Let us suppose, for instance, that it is a man's body
which brings him down from the heights, and which is capable of
defiling the flesh of a woman with its touch.

Is this not a theme of both the pornographic and the traditional,
doctrinal mind? For example, in church theology, we learn that what
makes the virgin pure is that she has never been soiled *by a man*.
"These limbs," the Bishop of Poitier writes in the sixteenth century,
"unsoiled and unshared by any man." And from Strindberg we have

another account of a man's body as the instrument of defilement. In his *Inferno,* he writes of the love he felt for a certain nun, who brought him back to a love of God while he was confined to a hospital. Yet though he loved this woman, and though he wanted to kiss her hand, on the day of his departure, he was "held back by a feeling of veneration that must not be defiled." (But we have already discovered the idea that a man's body soils a woman's body in pornography. For it is the touch of a man's body that makes a virgin into a whore.)

Pornography is filled with images of a man's body as dirty. In *Hustler* magazine, all the fluids of the body—mucus, urine, feces, sweat—are depicted in fantasies whose humor revolves about ridicule. (In one cartoon, a man measures the length of another's "snot." A fly "fishes" in a toilet bowl filled with feces, whose odor is depicted with green brush strokes.) Or humor revolves about cruelty to the body. (Under the heading "Organ Transplant," a man's chest is opened and bloody while a doctor and nurse insert a miniature pipe organ.)

But now we are beginning to know why a woman's body is so hated and feared. And why *this* body must be humiliated. For a woman's body, by inspiring desire in a man, must recall him to his own body. When he wants a woman, his body and his natural existence begin to take control of his mind. The pornographer protests that he is compelled by desire. That he cannot control himself. And this lack of control must recall him to all that is in nature and in his own nature that he has chosen to forget.

For nature can make him want. Nature can cause him to cry in loneliness, to feel a terrible hunger, or a thirst. Nature can even cause him to die.

That is why wherever in his fantasy he pictures the natural, and especially the natural in the body of a woman, he also imagines himself in control. Where there is a horse, there is a rider. Where there is a lion, there is a lion tamer. And just as he imagines the natural world as chained and bonded to his will, so also he fantasizes that nature exists only to feed him. When Henry Miller describes a young prostitute with a wooden stump, he tells us: "she reminds me somehow of a goose tied to a stake, a goose with a diseased liver, so that the world may have its *pâté de foie gras.*" And in another pornographic mind, a young woman is described to us as "fresh meat."

But underneath his humiliation of nature, the pornographer feels humiliated by his own body. For underneath his fantasy of power over the bestial and power over women, we can glimpse a terrible fear. The woman who is a chick, or a chicken, or an old mare, who wears her hair in a ponytail, who is ridden like a horse, who is bridled and married to a bridegroom, is also a fox. If she lies with animals, she is also the witch who uses the bodies of animals to enchant her victims. She can instill desire and by this act turn a man into an animal. And because this mind believes she *is* nature, when she turns a man into an animal he becomes a part of nature. He belongs to her. He is in her power. And he is mortal.

The Revelation of Flesh

> Beauty stands
> In the admiration of weak minds
> Led captive.
> JOHN MILTON, *Paradise Regained*

The moment at which a woman begins to remove her clothing and thus to reveal her body is an event of high drama in pornography. It is rehearsed in the imagination. Elaborate means lead us to its eventuation, and the striptease is the pinnacle both of fantasy and of actual effort, a simultaneous realization in which culture and the material world become one. For the desire which runs through pornographic literature, to see the naked body of a woman, has about it the quality of the desire to see a miracle performed. The hero of *Le Bain d'Amour*, for example, strains with all the ardent frustration of a saint toward his holy vision:

> In his mind he lifted up the chaste petticoats of his friend Louise
> and tried with all the power of his will to conjure up an exact image
> of the dusky spot between the lily white nudity of her virgin thighs
> and stomach and that silky triangle, the mystery of which perturbed
> him so much.

In the industry of pornography, the preoccupation with an almost magical knowledge which is mythically withheld from a man's eyes by a woman's clothing takes on the aura of a search for the holy grail. Everywhere the revelation of a woman's flesh is advertised as if the true nature of a woman's body were a carefully guarded secret. Thus a film produced by the Mitchell brothers is called *Inside Marilyn Chambers.* This atmosphere of magic and secrecy informs the sale of slides of women's bodies, still photographs, calendars, magazines with fold-out pictures, fetishes of women's bodies shaped as swizzle sticks (which become nude when manipulated), endless varieties of burlesque events. It is part of the design of women's underclothing meant to titillate, veil, and reveal, or of the structure of a gesture, or of a story with a double entendre whose hidden meaning will reveal itself to the seeker. Inside this scenario of the revealed secret live all the stereotypical ideas we have of male and female behavior, of modesty and deceit, aggression and rejection, seduction and rape.

Consider the myths which surround this revelation. We believe a woman is naturally modest, ashamed of her own body, afraid by nature to reveal her flesh. And on the other hand, we believe the sight of this flesh has a transformative effect on the mind of a man. That if a woman shows a bit of her legs, or her shoulder, or even leans over so that a man may see where her breasts meet, that a man will be overcome with desire for her, and compelled almost, by this sight, to rape her. (A judge in Utah, for instance, overturned a jury's verdict of guilty against a rapist because his victim was "flimsily dressed.") Thus behind female modesty there lurks the shape of an awesome female power.

For if a woman by her beauty can make a man into a rapist, she can also transform him in other ways. Her overwhelming seductive powers can lead him into the world of flesh and the devil. Desiring her, he forgets his soul. He moves into eternal perdition. And in this eternal perdition, he loses the eternal life of his spirit. The full weight of an earthly mortality falls upon his consciousness.

But we can read in this religious scenario another language and another range of meanings, which belong to the life of the psyche. When a woman's beauty brings a man into the realm of the material, he must live in his body. He must know himself as matter. Therefore, he must give up the illusion that his mind controls his body, or that culture controls nature. Rather, inside the experience of sexual knowledge, he learns that culture and nature, meaning and love, spirit and matter, are one. And in this he loses the illusion that culture has given him against the knowledge of the vulnerability of his own flesh.

And now if we move from the language of the psyche back to mythology, we can read myth in a new light. We have a new understanding, for example, of the story of Actaeon. We see him enter the forest looking for animal prey. He is the controller of nature; he is the hunter. But by accident, or we might say through *fate,* by the natural occurrence of circumstances, he comes upon the goddess Diana as she is bathing in a pool. We know that he is stunned by her beauty. And we also know that this moment of beauty will lead to his death. For the beautiful goddess will reach her hand into the water (a pool in which, like Narcissus, he must be able to see *his own reflection*), she will splash his face with this watery face, and he will turn into an animal. Now we know the rest of his story. As a stag, he runs through the forest. But the scent of his animal body is detected by his own hunting dogs. And thus these animals, which were his own (and which belonged to his psyche), will now tear him to pieces.

The idea that the sight of a woman's body calls a man back to his own animal nature, and that this animal nature soon destroys him, reverberates throughout culture. We find it in the most ancient sources. In the Biblical story of creation, we discover Eve, who has spoken with a serpent, seducing Adam into eating an apple, the forbidden fruit of knowledge. Through this seduction, the commentators tell us, "Eve brought death into the world."

And this mythology entered the reasoning minds of the monks who shaped an ideology for the burning of witches. Thus in the *Malleus Maleficarum,* Sprenger and Kramer write that when men see and hear women, they "are caught by their carnal desires," for a woman's face is "a burning wind" and a woman's voice is "the hissing of serpents."

We meet the same idea, that a woman's beauty causes a man death (and in the same Biblical imagery), in these lines by Swinburne:

> Thou hast a serpent in thine hair
> In all the curls that close and cling
> And oh that breast flower!
> Oh love, thy mouth, too fair
> To kiss and sting!

And again in these lines by the Italian Renaissance poet Giambattista Marino:

> Black thou art, but beautiful, O thou
> Love's charming monster among nature's
> Beauties, dark is the dawn near thee.

Faulkner tells us "again and again that men are helpless in the hands of their mothers, wives and sisters." Poe writes of the dying Berenice: "And now—I shuddered in her presence, and grew pale at her approach." Balzac crafts the tale of Pauline, who, after she murders her lover by making love to him, utters the words: "He is mine. I have killed him."

And Balzac's tale is mild compared to the pornographic story we read from medieval France called "Of a Girl Who Was Ill of the Plague and Caused the Death of Three Men Who Lay with Her, and How the Fourth was Saved and She Also." Here a woman's strength is fed by the deaths of three men. Each man makes love to her while she is ill, and each man contracts the plague from her and dies. But after enjoying each lover she becomes stronger, until she's well.

Yet again, we realize that the death of a pornographic hero has more than one meaning. First, of course, it has a simple literal meaning. Even on the surface of the tale we read the old religious fear that "where there is death, there too is sexual coupling." And this death takes us to a second level of meaning, where we encounter the fear of the knowledge of the body and of the power of nature, which must lead us to acknowledge mortality and vulnerability. But beneath this level is still another meaning. For the idea of physical death, terrifying in itself, can also symbolize another death. And this is the death of a self-image. Culture imagines itself to be invulnerable to nature. A man who believes nature's illusions believes that he is invulnerable to nature and that he controls nature. But the sight of a woman's body reminds him of the power of his own body, which is nature, over his mind, which is culture. Thus, for a few moments, his self-image dies and he is *humiliated*.

In the pornographic novel *Fatherly Love,* we find a clear description of this humiliation. Here a man appears to lose control of himself. He is overwhelmed by desire. At the sight of a woman's body he begins to masturbate. And as he continues to masturbate, the pornographic heroine, who we must remember only speaks the words of the pornographic psyche itself, tells him, "Don't you feel ashamed of yourself?

Don't you feel humiliated standing there in public, masturbating in front of a girl you've never seen before?" When the hero, who angrily continues to masturbate, says that he does not feel ashamed, this humiliation continues and is equated with sexuality itself. Cunnilingus becomes a means for degradation. Telling the man she has not washed herself in weeks and that she "just took a piss," she invites him to put his mouth to her, "knowing how filthy it is." She tells him, "I can't believe any man—even your type—would be that low."

Here it is not a man who humiliates a virgin by making her a whore. Rather, it is a whore who humiliates a man. But the pornographic mind retaliates against this imagined humiliation. Participating in the church's fantasy that it is a woman's body which destroys a man's soul, now the pornographic mind takes out its revenge against that same body which has humbled it. For this is the underside and the secret message in the pornographic revelation of beauty: its purpose is to rob the female body of both its natural power and its spiritual presence. So in the striptease, culture realizes its revenge against nature. The mystery of the female body is revealed to be nothing more than flesh, and flesh under culture's control.

At once promising and giving the reader his revenge, an advertisement for a pornographic magazine emblazons these words next to the nude body of a woman: "If women have been a mystery to you," the words promise, "let *Chic* Magazine unveil their mysteries. *Chic*'s ladies have nothing to hide. . . . They know all and show all! . . . You'll know all!" Here, then, is her knowledge, her mystery, her power, her secret. Just this flesh which she reveals because she is paid to do so. Beneath her pose, one can hear the voice of the pornographer whispering, "This is all she is; she is a *thing.*"

But we need not imagine this voice of derision. Over and over, through classical culture, and through pornography, the pornographic mind tells us that woman's mysterious beauty is simply nothing. We read this in Alexander Pope's "Rape of the Lock." We discover it in these lines by the seventeenth-century poet Robert Gould:

> Strip but this Puppet of its gay Attire
> It's gauzes, Ribbons, Lace, Commode and Wire
> And tell me then what 'tis thou dost admire? . . .

Open her secret Boxes; Patches here
You'll horded find, her Paints and Washes there:
Love's artful twigs, where the chatt'ring Ape
Sits perched and hasn't the Judgement to Escape . . .

We find the same formula for the annihilation of beauty in the words of the pornographic writer Juvenal: "In good time she discloses her face; she removes the first layer of plaster and begins to be recognizable."

But the pornographic revelation of beauty goes beyond ridicule. When the pornographer models a figure of a woman, when he fashions her portrait, or captures her in his camera, he is possessing her. And now, by this possession, he controls the one who has captured him, who has ensnared and enchanted him, who causes his death and shames him. He has made himself safe from her power.

The man who stares at a photograph of a nude woman is a voyeur. He can look freely and turn away when he wishes. He can run his hands over the two-dimensional surface, but he will not be touched. He can know the body of a woman, and yet encounter a knowledge which will not change him. We read that the sight of a woman contains "the image of everything which rises up from the depths." But the voyeur, when he sees a photograph of a woman's body, keeps these depths at a distance. An invisible line separates him from the image he perceives. He will not be overwhelmed by the presence of her flesh. He need not encounter the knowledge of his own body. He can hide from the deepness of his own soul.

Of the extraordinary appeal of *Playboy* magazine's first centerfold models, Gay Talese writes:

> She was their mental mistress. She stimulated them in solitude, and they often saw her picture while making love to their wives. She was an almost special species who exists within the eye and mind of the observer and she offered everything imaginable. She was always available at bedside, was totally controllable . . . she behaved in a way that real women did not, which was the essence of fantasy.

For we must understand here again that the nude woman in the pornographer's mind is really only a denied part of himself which he refuses to recognize. But this is a part of himself which has a will to live, a will to expression, to being. This part of himself returns, and threatens to destroy his illusion of himself. If he is to entertain the existence of desire at all in his mind, desire must come to him in a form that he can control.

Yet desire always transforms us. We are enchanted by beauty. We are indeed overwhelmed by feeling. The mind's attempt to silence the soul must have another effect than silence. Part of the pornographer's mind remembers what the pornographic mind would forget. Even the desacralized and humiliated images of pornography must remind the pornographer of his lost self. Even by his means of control, the images he has created, he feels himself losing control. But this is the nature of obsession. The obsessive act must be repeated. And thus the pornographer must invent more images and fantasies, more ingenious devices through which to assert the superiority of his mind over matter.

He puts the body of a woman on a pack of playing cards, for example. And thus he can handle her with ease. He can put her in his pocket. And he is the dealer. In his hands, fate is decided. He has reversed natural order. He reprints millions of copies of photographs of women's bodies and distributes these all over the world. And he exerts his power in other ways too. In a centerfold depicting the bodies of nude women which he calls "Beaver Hunt," he displays these photographs on pink tiles, and places a man's foot next to them, so that the foot on the page looks like the foot of the man who looks at the pictures, and the toe of this foot alone is larger than each woman's whole body. But as if this display of power through size is not enough, he humiliates these images further by surrounding them with cigarette ash and stamped-out cigarettes. And in another mode of fantasy, a novel in which beautiful women are saddled, ridden, and whipped, he exclaims, "What a picture of loveliness under complete domination!"

Over and over again, the pornographer must reverse his own humiliation, his own enslavement, his own terror. Fearing that he will be transformed if he looks on beauty, the pornographer takes possession of a woman's body. Fearing that he will die of his own desire, he places her loveliness under his control. And fearing that her presence will destroy his soul, he destroys her soul and makes of her an object. And then, fearing the object he has made, he destroys her.

The Object

> That reminds me of an old joke about the female soul. Question, Have women a soul? Answer, yes. Question, Why? Answer, In order that they may be damned. Very witty.
>
> SAMUEL BECKETT, *Molloy*

At the very core of the pornographic mise-en-scène is the concept of woman as object. A woman's body forms the center of a magazine. She spreads apart her thighs and stares into the camera. Her tongue licks her lips. Her eyes reflect back nothing: she is not human. Her hands pull apart the lips of her vagina, the same way a man might pull up the lips of a horse at an auction, so that the teeth may be counted. She shows her goods. She is ornamented, fixed up, made pretty. There are no ribbons braided into her hair. But she wears white sheer stockings, white spaghetti-strap shoes, white pearls. Her hair is dyed unnatural blond. She is decorated in whiteness. In her image all the meanings of absence are realized. Her "whiteness" opens out to a blank space in the mind. She is a "blonde."

Except for her decorations, she is nude. But her face is masked in lipstick, eye shadow, eyebrows plucked and shaped in perfect arcs. Now she spreads herself out under the camera on blue satin like a jewel. Now she parts her lips, now she raises her ass to the camera, now she has arched her back.

Like a piece of furniture, she must be pictured from the side, and particular parts of her body, those intended for use—her breasts, her vulva, her ass—must be carefully examined. And yet at each turn of her body, at each face or curvature exposed, we see nothing. For there is no person there. No character, no woman recognizable as someone we might *know*. For the pornographic camera performs a miracle in reverse. Looking on a living being, a person with a soul, it produces an image of a thing. Any presence the real woman being photographed might have had has vanished in this lens. In pornography, even when a real woman poses for the camera, she does not pose as herself. Rather, she performs. She plays the part of an object. And rather than an accidental quality of pornography, this objectification of a whole being into a thing is the central metaphor of the form.

But whence does her thingness arrive? What idea in the mind of the pornographer, or the photographer directing the poses of his model, creates this illusion that a real being is an object? It is the pornographer's idea of love which creates this illusion. Read, for example, the words of Juvenal on the question of love. Rhetorically, he asks: "Why does Sartoris burn with love for Bibula?" And his answer will tell us something of the nature of the pornographic "love." For he tells us: "If you shake out the truth, it is the face that he loves and not the wife. Let three wrinkles make their appearance . . . let her teeth be black and her eyes lose their lustre: then will this freedman give her the order, 'Pack up your bags and be off!' "

For what the pornographer's mind believes he *loves* is the body of a woman and not the woman. It is her flesh alone he prizes. Her soul, if he even believes that it exists, does not interest him. He does not look for it, nor even see it. When the hero of Charles Bukowski's novel *Women* goes to the airport to meet a woman he has known only through letters, he judges each woman leaving the airplane for her physical attributes. "Oh, I hope *she's* not the one," he exclaims to himself, "or her. Or especially her." But when he finds a body he likes, he is pleased. "Now that one would be fine!" he cries to himself. "Look at those legs, that behind, those eyes." Musing to himself about his good fortune, he declares, "She was the best of the whole damn lot."

The hero's sexual life with his "object" follows exactly the contours of his "love." There is no reason or any content to his touching her except for the material act of touching, which has somehow magically been reduced to only matter. Here, the miracle in which the word becomes flesh is turned inside out. Now flesh bears no word at all. And the hero's sexual "knowledge" of this woman is knowledge of flesh alone. We can see that he prefers this; this is his choice. Wishing to copulate with her, the hero discovers that she seems "to be asleep," and he tells us that he "liked that." And when his affair with this object without a soul ends, he gives as his reason for ending it, "her pussy is too large."

Here is precisely the raison d'être of this "object." We know that a *being* exists only in order to exist. For a woman or a man exists for no *particular* material purpose. But a thing, an object, must have a reason for being, a function. And where the pornographic "woman" is concerned, that function is to please a man. She is the one to be known. To be wanted. To be used. "I love to stand before my lover and see the adoration reflected in his eyes," we read in a caption for a photograph of a woman whose legs are spread apart. "She's made for our kind of pleasure," the pornographic hero of a novel tells us. "Her thighs and breasts are as firm and lovely as any I've seen."

And in the light of this definition, we shall not be surprised to learn that the pornographer's idea of his object's pleasure is to please him. She exists for no other purpose. The hero of Nicholas Chorier's seventeenth century tale, *The Dialogue of Luisa Signia*, tells us of his wife: "She knows no other pleasure than her husband's." And for this reason, he tells us, because he does not like vulvas, she is happy to "lend him the service of her mouth." Throughout pornography, this image of a penis in a woman's mouth is among the most popular of images. And under this image we hear the pornographic voice whisper, "*She* exists for *his* pleasure."

When we hear this assertion, we are hardly surprised. Here is only an echo of what is perfectly acceptable socially. Balzac tells us, for instance, that the truest wife "will let herself be drawn hither and thither," anywhere that he goes "who is her life." Nietzsche tells us a man must think of a woman as "something predestined for service," and Byron tells us that a woman is "Made but to love." But we do not have to read these words to know this ideology. Everywhere it is manifest around us, as women dressed as waitresses, secretaries, nurses, assistants, prostitutes, orderlies serve men.

But yet another aspect of a woman's thingness manifests itself in pornography. Not only does a woman exist to serve and to please; but in this subordinate existence of hers she has no rights whatsoever, for she does not belong to herself. (Again, Nietzsche tells us that a man must think of a woman as his possession, and Byron that a woman exists to feel that she belongs to man.) So, on his wedding night, the groom in *The Dialogue of Luisa Signia* declares to his bride, of her body: "Knowest thou not . . . that this part of thy person is no longer thine, but mine by full and lawful right?" He tells her, in effect, that she must never say no to him. That he is the master of her body.

But now we are beginning to move more deeply into the pornographic mind. For this above all is why a real woman must be reduced to an object in pornography. She must be mastered. She must be controlled. After the hero of *L'Ecole des Filles* rhapsodizes "ecstatically" over the heroine's stomach, thighs, breasts, and vulva, he demands that she get down on all fours. Then he mounts her "like a rider." For in pornography, to the woman who is an object, the pornographic hero is her rider, her driver, her master.

He is, for instance, her doctor or her professor or her father, or he subordinates her through physical strength or through fear. He kidnaps her, rapes her, ties her up, gives her orders she must carry out, imprisons her. Even his sexual encounters with her are acts of dominance.

We have become so used to this way of thinking that we do not immediately recognize the contradiction here. It seems to us quite usual that a man would have to dominate an "object," a being who exists only to please him, a being that is not a being, has no rights to herself, does not belong to herself, is his possession. But there is something strange here, another of those paradoxes one finds in the pornographic mind, and that tells us of another life of that mind. For one does not feel the need to dominate a table, or a chair. Only a being with a will, who is not really an object at all, requires us to master her.

Now one might reply here that women are real and have souls. And therefore that in his obscene imagery the pornographer simply records his effort and his desire to make a woman into an object. But we must remember that the pornographic world is a world of illusion, and that in every fantasy or illusion each detail, each fact presented, must tell us something essential about the real thoughts of the mind which created it. Indeed, the pornographic mind attempts to solve the problems of the psyche precisely by creating a world of illusion. And therefore, if this mind wanted to believe women docile, it would need to represent women as docile and as objects. Why, then, must this mind show us over and over again the act of domination and subordination, which suggests to us that women are not, in fact, objects by nature, but instead must be made so obsessively, redundantly?

Because indeed, the women in pornography are not "other" than the pornographer himself. They are symbols for the denied parts of himself. And in this sense it is quite literally true that they are his possession and that they exist to serve him and give him pleasure.

But now we also know why a creature who is *owned* and who is not supposed to have a will of her own must be mastered. For in fact, she *is* will. She is a desire to be. She is a part of the pornographer's mind and body which he has denied to himself, but yet, even so, would come to consciousness, expression, and life.

So the pornographer, despite his conscious intention to make a woman an object, would give the woman he creates a will *because she is a mirror of himself.* And then in fantasy he would master that will. He is in a terrible conflict. He would let his body speak; he would let the knowledge of the body in himself live; and yet this is also precisely the knowledge of which he is terrified. And so he tries to resolve this conflict by depicting the body without a spirit. He tries to separate culture from nature. He would have what is natural in him be mute. But what is natural speaks in him. Therefore, he gives "woman" a voice in pornography, but he gives her this voice only in order to silence her.

And finally, most ironically, the pornographer, afraid of the implications of reality, would abandon reality and replace this with cultural images. Yet when he tries to do this, he puts himself in a cul-de-sac. For images and metaphors are, of necessity, wrought from reality. They always imitate the natural. They remind us of exactly what we might be trying to avoid. Even the word "culture" is derived from a material reality. It comes from the word root meaning to till the soil.

So even the route of his escape, the very material of culture, expresses his fundamental ambivalence. He would have reality and not have reality. Know nature and not know. Possess this denied part of himself and silence it forever.

We see this conflict in the mind played out most clearly around the pornographic object's most quintessential form—the pornographic "doll." Pornography is replete with images and evocations of the "doll," an actual plastic copy of a woman, made to replace a woman, and to give a man pleasure without the discomfort of female presence. In fantasy, this object appears everywhere in poetry, in stories, in novels. And in fact, we find that the "doll" is actually sold through pornographic shops and mail order houses. But everywhere that this replacement for reality is publicized, it is the object's proximity to reality that is promised.

The appeal of the doll to the pornographic mind is clear. Her vagina opens "on command," she is "ready to go, night after night," she does not talk back, she is perfectly controllable. And yet, as if this mind secretly longed for what it had to give up, and must be forever dissatisfied with this replacement, which is not in fact real, over and over again we read that the pornographic doll is almost "like the real thing." One doll is advertised as saying, "I swear I'm alive." Another advertisement, from the nineteenth century, promises that the "female belly with artificial vagina" is "designed to give the man the perfect illusion of a real woman by providing him with just as sweet and voluptuous sensations as she herself."

But the manufacture of these dolls goes beyond the simple attempt to create a realistic illusion. The attempt to reproduce material detail reaches a frenzied pitch, and takes on the air again of obsession. We hear, for instance, that the "dolls" are given the suppleness of real skin, are lubricated with female odors, have real hair; we read that contact is "regulated by pneumatic tubing." Clearly the body alone does not require such exactitude. These details speak to a need of the psyche, as do the cultural artifacts which accompany the dolls, such as lingerie sets, wigs. Some of the dolls even imitate the pornographic ideology's idea of the virgin and the whore. One doll wears bobby socks and pigtails, and another is advertised as "Susie Slut."

When we read a poem from the eighteenth century entitled "Adollizing; or, A Lively Picture of Doll Worship," we might suppose from the beginning of the narrative lines that the hero was satisfied by his doll, and longed for nothing more. Throughout the poem, the narrator's voice almost crows to us that he has won a victory over the circumstance of rejection. His lover, Clarabella, has turned him down, he tells us, but his "creative power," his own "fertile thought," has raised a "solid entity from nought." Even in the creation of this doll, the hero has vanquished nature and asserted the power of culture by matching nature's unique capacity to generate life.

And yet he has done more; he has outdone nature. For in every way, his creation bends to his own will. Thus he is both the creator and the master of the "solid entity," his doll. She is, in his own language, "unresisting and complacent," "all obsequious" to his "wanton will." And his enthusiasm over her creation contains no small amount of a desire for revenge against the natural woman who rejected him. For this doll, he tells us, is "thrice more bounteous" with those virtues that Clarabella "glories to deny."

And yet, despite the bounteousness of this doll, he is dissatisfied. Reminding us of the classic "womanizer," the man who objectifies women in his mind and simultaneously attempts to possess one after the other, the hero of "Adollizing" creates more dolls. He does not acknowledge that the first doll, being only a product of his mind, and incapable of feeling, will, or desire, is empty of what he truly seeks. Rather, his mind fastens on revenge against the real woman who left him. "A prime collection," he tells us, "will I order strait/In just revenge of Clarabella's hate." And this revenge toward Clarabella radiates out toward a whole female universe. It knows no bounds. Thus he tells us there is no "toasted beauty" that he may not "adollize with . . . ease." And now we imagine a gruesome dumb show of hostility toward the female body as he tells us that he need only "change . . . the heads" and a whole "Seraglio" of "fresh Venus's will rise."

In another pornographic tale, *La Femme Endormie*, we might suppose that the creation of the "doll" had been a mode of development in the psyche of the hero, since he progresses from a love affair with this object to a love affair with a woman. Like the narrator of "Adollizing," this hero, whom we know as Paul, has been rejected by his lover. She has given him a "brutal ride," and from her he has suffered "every possible disappointment."

Here is the same scenario again. Because nature, in the body of a woman, had disappointed him and gone against his will, the hero rejects nature and has a doll made after his own imagination, which will be totally under his control. He pays an artist to make "an imaginary will-less creature who would submit ecstatically to his obsession and his lewdness." The artist, with technical virtuosity and aesthetic genius, creates a masterpiece. Her loins are "divinely" curved. Boiling water poured through her navel makes her warm. Pushing a button in her navel makes her undulate in every part of her body. And she can be arranged into any position her owner wishes.

Before the author replaces his doll with a "real" woman, he falls in love with the doll itself. Thus, now a complication occurs in the tale, which by hindsight we might have found predictable. The artist who has made the doll falls in love with his creation. At night he steals into Paul's apartment to make love with the doll. When Paul discovers this violation of his property, he is enraged. He reacts much the way a jealous lover might, with fury at the doll. He decides her body is dirty, because it has been touched by another man's body.

Yet in his mind, he himself has soiled the doll, and the story makes this clear. In the narration of the tale, we read that after he enters the doll, he throws her on the floor and calls her a "dirty bag" of "laundry." Crying out "slut," he tells her she is a wretched whore, who, taking advantage of her body, has driven him to take her. Thus, to punish her for this act, he decides "to whack" her "bottom."

Here again we see the classic shape of the pornographer's mind. Trying to escape himself, his own natural desire, and his own nature, he creates a fantasy which replaces nature. But the metaphors of the mind and of culture must imitate culture. And thus it happens that his very replacement for what is natural inspires his own natural desire. Therefore the doll that he has worshiped calls up his rage and so he punishes her. He has named the doll Mea, which in Latin means "mine." And here, once again, we can hear a double meaning. In the word "mine" we hear that the doll is not only his possession, and not only a replica of a "woman"; she is also a part of himself.

Paul's jealousy toward the creator of the doll resolves itself when he leaves the artist a note asking him to clean the doll after he visits her. And of course, one should not be surprised to learn that he writes this note as if he were the doll, using a voice which pretends to be hers. "My darling," he writes, "the last time you visited me you forgot to wash me," and later in the note he asks the artist not to "betray a trace of male contact."

And yet here again we face one of those contradictions in a porno-graphic tale which secretly tell us the truth. For Paul continues to "seek contact" with the artist. He befriends him through a series of notes, all written in the persona of the doll, and hidden in recesses of her underwear. Now we might suppose, as do the Kronhausens (who edited an anthology in which this narrative appears), that here, "The homosexual implications are clear." And yet are they? For Paul is revolted by the idea of physical contact with a man's body. He has rejected the male body, even his own male body; he is enraged at the doll when she becomes a receptacle for this other man, or for himself. Rather, what he desires from another man is to share a fantasy. He comes to love the idea that they are both charmed by the doll. He speaks to the other man through the voice of their possession, their fantasized woman. And finally we come to see that the bond these men make with each other in every way imitates the bond men make with one another through a pornographic culture which excludes real women, and which creates an image of women that men share.

Indeed, in the shared fantasy of what a woman is, an age-old brotherhood has been formed. The female nude, painted by men, placed in museums by men, reviewed and honored in history by men, becomes the icon for a culture which is defined as exclusively male. A culture which, until the last century, would not even allow a woman into an anatomy class (or permit her to work as an artist using another woman's body as a model); a culture which has allowed the female presence to exist in its mind only as a creation of its imagination.

When Paul returns home one night to his doll, he finds a note left by the artist, telling him: "Generous master of this paradise . . . may the fairy of this home render unto you all the delights experienced in her arms." Now he has achieved a supreme and perfected state of mastery: his own fantasy is mirrored back to him by another voice.

But Paul is not satisfied with this doll. So another doll is created. However, the creator of this doll is not a character in the story. He is the author himself. And he presents this "doll" as a character. He wishes us to believe her to be a "woman" the way we believe "Paul" to be a man. And yet we discover that this doll, who is supposed to be a real woman named Lucille, does not have a voice of her own. Like the first doll created for Paul, she simply utters and enacts the fantasies of men.

When she is introduced to us and to the hero, her being is described in much the same terminology which earlier was used to describe the artist's doll. We learn about her physical proportions, her "erect carriage," her "graceful shape," her "coquettish waist." And like the doll, she has very little will of her own. Now, in a ruse designed for a person lacking both intelligence and selfhood, Paul persuades Lucille to let him make love with her in front of the doll, whom he introduces to her as his wife, in order to make his "wife" jealous. Since Lucille is clearly a doll too, she agrees. And when this ruse is finally revealed to her, she professes an admiration for the doll's creator and agrees to replace the doll by becoming his wife.

Lucille's behavior might seem wooden to us were we not wholly familiar, in the pornographic culture, with artificial behavior in women. Indeed, prostitutes are paid not only to render physical pleasure but to play roles—to, in fact, impersonate women and to create the illusion that they willingly serve, even passionately desire, the man who buys them. But the behavior dictated by etiquette for proper ladies is equally doll-like. The very posture of her body is arranged like a mannequin by custom. She must not cross her legs; her carriage must be erect. And of course, her demeanor, like the doll's, must be, if not obsequious, pliable and pleasing to men. Ibsen's choice of the title *The Doll's House* for his play about a woman wishing to be freed from this limitation was brilliantly conceived. But it is not only upper-class women who are likened to dolls. A woman who is beautiful is often called a "real doll," and we remember the words to the song: "A doll I can carry the girl that I marry must be."

Moreover, real women's bodies are often cut, molded, and reshaped so that, like the bodies of wooden or plastic dolls, they will please men. A woman's hair is dyed. A whole generation of women wear corsets. Our faces are lifted. Our eyelids are changed. Our noses reshaped. We suffer implants on our chins. Our ears are reshaped or flattened. Our breasts augmented or reduced. Our abdomens cut away and made smaller, our thighs, our buttocks, "reduced" under the surgeon's knife. With supports, clear gels, and silicone, we are made to appear like the cultural image of women.

Yet, even if we were to accept that a woman ought to so please a man, there is something futile in all these efforts. For this attempt at transformation must always fail. The doll, sooner or later, will dissatisfy this mind. For the fantasy is by nature a replacement. It is a symbol itself of an unrealized wish and a denied fear. It is a figment of the self, and this self which the pornographer hates must return to haunt him even through the very metaphors of denial and projection. Thus he must inevitably turn in loathing and rage from every doll he makes. As Paul says to the artist before his marriage, regarding his future wife: "Sooner or later the true character is revealed and spoils the voluptuous fruit."

For when the pornographic mind creates an object, it prepares the stage for the enactment of its rage against that object. It is inevitable that this object must be rejected, humiliated, punished, tortured, bound up, silenced, even murdered. But even that murder will not satisfy the pornographic mind. Because after this, it will produce another object, to desire and to hate. And with this new object it will play out the same drama and enact the same obsession. The objectification of life can never be innocent. From the moment the mind decides to deny nature through culture, it becomes committed to an ordeal of cruelty and suffering.

The Ordeal

If all the literature of pornography were to be represented by one performance, and if that performance were to move into its most dramatic moments, the scenes which have been secretly promised by all that has gone before, which will both embody the entire action and meaning of the play and give to its audience their most acute emotional experience, these would have to be the moments (which are inevitable in the pornographic *oeuvre*) in which most usually a woman, sometimes a man, often a child, is abducted by force, verbally abused, beaten, bound hand and foot and gagged, often tortured, often hung, his or her body suspended, wounded, and then murdered. But this is a drama we have all been called upon to witness, to witness and weep at beholding, taking this suffering into our hearts with our very belief in the divinity of goodness; for who in this culture can have escaped the story of Christ's martyrdom?

All the theatrical moments of the agony of Christ mirror the high drama of pronography: the arrest, the humiliating interrogation, the public ridicule, the beating, the binding to a cross, the suspension of his body from that cross, the cruel wound inflicted on his side, his terrible slow death. Cruelty, the most numinous transgression of pornography, is identical to that transgression which men played out against the body of a god who was to have redeemed the human soul from the original sin of carnality. This is the sadomasochistic ordeal.

Here is where pornography has reached an apex of the schizoid life of its mind, for on the most simple level of our knowledge of the body we find the idea that physical pleasure can be sought and found from physical pain hard to understand. And yet, in the pornographic demimonde, cruelty is treated like a rare and precious delight, a hidden voice whose commission will yield some undreamed of glory. There is almost no pornographic work without the infliction of pain, either to a vulnerable psyche or to a vulnerable body. That the pornographic plot, as it moves, in an imitation of climactic suspense, from conversation about the sexual act to the revelation of flesh to coitus, gravitates, either by realization or by implication, toward sadomasochism as a high point of narrative should not surprise us, for every pornographic device we have described as defining the form is in itself only a milder form of sadomasochism.

In an analytical study (which is still considered a definitive work), *Sadism and Masochism,* the psychoanalyst Wilhelm Stekel has described the essence of the sadomasochistic act to be *humiliation.* He tells us that no pain need be inflicted, nor even a fantasy of pain, for the condition known as sadomasochism to be present. Rather, this predilection is most typified by an experience of degradation, a degradation of the self or of another. Were we to move through the different forms of pornographic expression chronologically, we would discover in this sequence an ascending order of intensity in the feeling of humiliation.

To be made an object is in itself a humiliation. To be made a thing is to become a being without a will. But it is not the nature of a living being to have no will. Objectification of another is in itself a sadistic act, for to be made an object is to experience a pain of a loss of a part of the self: the soul. But to this degradation, the reduction of a whole being with a soul to mere matter, we must add the knowledge that matter itself is despised, and hated in its very essence. We read, for instance, in the phrase "to feel like shit," the quintessence of humiliation. For in the pornographic culture, humiliation emanates from the material.

With this philosophy framing what the eye sees, not only the objectification but the mere revelation of a woman's body is a degradation. The moment at which flesh, the material aspect of human nature, is revealed *is* humiliating to a mind which defines the body as degraded. And thus the voyeur, who appears to be a passive participant in the pornographic drama, completes a sadistic act when he watches a striptease. For without the presence of his eyes, were he not watching, no revelation would take place. As a member of the audience, he is both a witness and an actor: for his very presence has turned an innocent act into a degradation.

Moreover, hidden in the darkness of a theater, anonymous as the man who stares at a public photograph, he is in the position of power. The pornographic nude has become his object. She performs for his pleasure. He owns and masters her. And as much as she exposes herself and makes herself vulnerable, so is he also unexposed and invulnerable. Here again is the classic relationship between the sadist and the masochist.

For besides the essential element of humiliation, and an ultimate expression of violence against the flesh, the sadomasochistic ritual demands the invulnerability of the sadist and the vulnerability of the masochist. The sadist must be in power. The sadist must control. And the sadist uses this control to produce, in the words of Stekel again, "effects." He "revels in the fear" and the "anger" of his victim. And against these qualities poses his own coolness, his own lack of fear, or his cold and controlled anger, and his power. Thus the sadist is dressed and his victim is nude.

And even before the sadomasochistic ritual which is enacted in the pornographic mind creates images of violence to the body, another sadistic act occurs. Added to the countless scenes of actual violence in pornography, we must mention those scenes in which violence is simply threatened. This must include, for example, every act of rape, in which a woman's life is threatened. It must include all the stock-in-trade gestures of the "he-man" character, whose mere physical strength, it is implied, gives him dominance over women. It must include every subtly implied threat in such phrases as: "If you know what's good for you," or "Shove it," or "Up yours." It is the nature and part of the purpose of violent language to threaten.

And at any moment in the pornographic drama when a woman has given in to a threat, at any moment when she has submitted, at any moment when she has allowed herself to be mastered by fear, another sadistic act has taken place. To begin with, it is obvious that to frighten another being is in itself an act of sadism. But beyond this, when a living soul allows herself to act from fear, to be dominated by fear, another sort of suffering takes place, which is deeper than even fear itself. For a woman who does not act from her own will has by that failure again become an object, a thing. She again loses part of the sufferings of this self, her soul. Of this loss, Simone Weil writes: "Who knows how often during each instant it must torture and destroy itself in order to conform? The soul was not made to dwell in a thing; and when forced to it, there is no part of the soul but suffers violence."

But this reduction of the soul within the body, by making a whole being into a thing, is no accidental by-product of the pornographic mind. Rather, it is a central part of its purpose. The pornographic mind would separate culture from nature. It would desacralize matter. It would punish matter with image. Pornography's revenge against nature is precisely to deprive matter of spirit. And so in one act, pornography humiliates woman's body, by reducing her soul. And in another act, by terrifying her, pornography pits a woman's physical survival against the needs of her soul, and drives her soul thus to destruction.

Yet here we must remind ourselves once again that in pornography a "woman" is not a *woman*. She is a symbol. She is a denied self that is human. As we look more deeply into a culture which has fashioned itself after the pornographic mind, we will find that sadism and masochism have not been derived from the biological behavior of men and women, as some theorists have supposed; but rather that the ideas of masculine behavior and of female behavior have been shaped by culture to embody sadomasochism. We should not be surpised, for instance, to discover that both words, "sadism" and "masochism," were derived from the names of male pornographers. We know that the word "sadism" comes from the Marquis de Sade, in whose works the bodies of women were punished. But the word "masochism" also originated from a man's, and not a woman's, imagination. For Leopold von Sacher-Masoch, after whom the word was coined, wrote a famous novel, *Venus in Fur*, in which a man is whipped, humiliated, and tortured by a woman. And it is Masoch's hero who cries, "Whip me . . . I implore you."

In Stekel's study, he makes clear to us that sadism is no more an expression of masculinity than is masochism an expression of femininity, and that a woman can take on a sadistic role just as a man can play a masochist. Because above all, what his clinical work demonstrates is that the sadist and the masochist are one person. In the midst of the sadomasochistic ritual, we discover that the sadist imagines himself in the body of the masochist and the masochist imagines himself in the body of the sadist. The two halves of this ritual represent one self divided and at war with itself.

Thus, throughout pornography, we discover a reversal of the sexual roles. In *Fort Frederick*, a novel published in Paris in 1957, we find that this reversal of roles exhibits the true sadomasochistic meaning of culture's idea of the male and the female. In this novel, Jean Gedeon, who is the hero, begins as a rapist. Because he is fugitive, however, he falls under the power of a woman when he hides on her estate. And now the tables are turned. She makes him simultaneously her victim and a "woman." Under the threat of exposure, he becomes her servant, and later her willing servant. The heroine, Anne, uses the cultural meaning of female labor to degrade her captive. He is made to do dishes and make beds, all as part of a pornographic humiliation. "I'll make you work quite hard at any job I choose, anything at all. And . . . I won't pay you," she says. Thus his position becomes equal to that of a wife.

Now she verbally insults him by criticizing his work. "Get on with your dishwashing," she says. "You're not making any progress." For she has become the master and the judge of all that he does. And when she makes him wear a dress, it is an expression both of humiliation and of his submissiveness (which is also a humiliation). As he becomes passionate toward her, she expresses her disdain for him, for in the pornographic mind, rejection is also part of the arsenal of sadism. But the content of her disdain is the same content with which the pornographic mind condemns a woman. She associates him with animals. Thus, when he wants to kiss her, she says, "What are you thinking of, Jean Gedeon? Your mouth is only fit for my sandal, which is not very new and probably still smells of the stable."

In pornography, sexual roles exist as forms for the expression of sadomasochism. Thus we can read the obscene tale *Miss High Heels* as a parable whose moral reveals that the idea of the masculine and the feminine originated in the sadomasochist's imagination. In this underground novel, written in 1931, we discover the story of the creation of a woman. And this story is all the more dramatic and clear to us because in this novel it is a person with a male body and not a female body who is made to be "feminine." In the novel, Denis, who is dominated by two female relatives, becomes gradually more and more like a woman, and is, at the same time, more and more the victim and recipient of sadism. Each stage of his feminization is a humiliation. One of the heroines of the tale tells him:

> For two years you have been mincing in petticoats in a girls' school. You are a young gentleman, are you? Nobody would believe it. Your hair reaches down below your waist. You have the figure, the face, the soft limbs, the hands and feet and the breasts of a girl.

Denis responds, "I was dreadfully ashamed at Phoebe's outburst. I could not deny a word of it."

In becoming the pornographer's idea of what is a "female," Denis relishes his shame: "I had dreamed . . . of a world in which ladies, to punish me, dressed me as a girl in the most exquisite of frocks and then high-heeled shoes, gloves and corsets, and then laughing at my pretensions to a career, kept me in bondage and subjection as a toy for their amusement." And part of this shame is contained in the pornographic idea that women are inferior beings. One of Denis's female relatives taunts him, "You are a very great person, I suppose . . . with a great career in parliament . . ." and as if to prove to him his social inferiority, threatens to lace his corset one inch tighter.

But now this "femininity" is punished. Because Denis is narcissistic, and loves the lavish clothing, white kid gloves, and white satin shoes he is dressed in, his mistresses prepare a "punishment" for him in order to "correct" his vanity. In front of a guest, who voyeuristically enjoys this enactment, Denis is strapped to a chair, while his hands and feet are trapped in glass and mirrored boxes. Into these boxes his masters introduce a swarm of fleas, which drive him to madness with their "ravenous" bites. "Oh! Oh!" he protests, "the torture is excruciating. . . . I am being eaten up."

But he is also being taught the female virtue of silence, for this outburst is answered with a more terrible punishment. Worms are introduced to the glass boxes, and they crawl over his hands and leave "slime on the dainty slippers."

His mistress makes the moral lesson of this scene clear: "If you were wearing high boots and thick stockings, you would not mind the worms," she tells him, and thus warns him that while he wears female clothing he must be careful to be "obedient and modest."

In other tales, male and female characters trade roles freely, so that now the male is the master and then he is the slave, now the female the driver and then the driven animal. In *Le Club des Monteurs Humaines,* for instance, an obscene work about a "horse" club in which the "horses" are played by human beings, men and women take turns at being horse and rider. At one moment a "Madame Weinberg" rises. She wears the predictable patent leather boots. A young man kneels beside her. He lowers his head and gazes into the leather of her shoes. Finally, in a trembling voice, he asks her, "Madame, before I have the honor of feeling your weight upon me, will you allow me to pay homage to the lovely feet which I will soon have the good fortune to hold in my hands?" But later it is a woman who performs the part of the horse and is ridden.

Finally, as we explore the behavior of men and women in pornography, we must remember that these are not men and women in actuality, but only figments who belong to a fantasy. And in the deepest sense, this fantasy is an illusion society has given to men exclusively. We know, of course, that a woman can participate in the pornographic mind. She can harbor the same illusions; she can read pornography; she can model herself after its images. And yet the world of pornography is a world of male gestures and male language and a male ethos. It is an atmosphere which belongs to men's clubs and locker rooms, to the lobbies of brothels, to the private male conversation, to fathers and sons. Pornography is written largely for men and largely by men, and the women who have recently entered this audience or this trade enter a tradition already defined and shaped by men.

Thus the male and female characters who play out the roles of sadist and masochist in pornography are simply representations of one mind, and of a mind that has been shaped as "male" in this society. Yes, in actual life women have acted as sadists or masochists. But here we do not examine actuality. Here we examine illusion. We want to find the origins of certain lies in the mind, for we suspect that behind the stories told in pornography are still other stories, which may be closer to the truth. Once we reveal to ourselves the essential being who hides behind the pornographic mythology, we know this must be *human*, and, at the heart, neither male nor female. Yet let us understand that the fantasy figures in pornography are not "women," and that "the female masochist" of pornography is simply a part of a socially male mind.

But the pornographic fantasy itself tells us this more clearly. For obscene culture is filled with images of men whipping men, men humiliating and debasing men, men mastering, driving, and possessing other men. In the pornographic mind, the "woman" is simply a mask. When this mask is dropped, we find a man. The content of the pornographic drama does not change when we find this man. Perhaps, when we see two men play out this ritual called "male" and "female," our own illusions about who men and women are will drop further away, as in turn we see further into this mind.

Scenes of flagellation in which a man or a male child is beaten by another man make up a whole school of pornography. In *Ernest*, for instance, the hero, Gernand, forces the boy under his care to commit sexual acts. And just as the pornographic "male" makes the pornographic "female" into a possession, so does Gernand possess Ernest. He declares to the child, "You are going to get used to the idea that your nudity and every part of your body belong to me—and perhaps to quite a few other people besides, if I so choose!"

Gernand forces Ernest to masturbate in various postures, including standing at military attention. He "enslaves" the boy. He speaks to him of "deflowering" him through his anus. In every way, Ernest resembles the pornographic female. Like the "female," he is systematically "overpowered" and "broken." And he even takes on the "female" response of modesty; he is "half choked with shame and pain."

But now we begin to hear another tone in this pornographic dialogue. We read about the "smallness" of the boy. We read such phrases as "obey my orders" and "as I told you"; we read the word "punish" over and over. We read that Gernand slaps Ernest on his "bottom." All these details remind us above all of parental discipline. But "discipline" is the word used in pornographic literature to describe the sadomasochistic ritual. Slowly we begin to recognize that another couple has entered the pornographic fantasy besides a man and woman, and this is the parent and the child.

And now this couple melts into yet another couple. For a whole school of pornography depicts sadomasochistic relationships between teachers and students. In a long poem, "The Flogging of Charlie Collingwood," originally published in the Victorian pornographic journal *The Pearl,* the birching of a schoolboy is described with obsessive detail. We learn Charlie Collingwood is whipped five or six days out of seven. And the poet tells us almost ecstatically that "From the small of his back, to the thick of his thighs, is one mass of red weals." Just as Romantic poetry listed and sighed over the beauties of nature, this poetry sighs over the ravages of the body:

> There are weals over weals, there are stripes upon stripes, there are
> cuts after cuts
> All across Charlie Collingwood's bottom, and isn't the sight of it nuts?

What fascinates and holds the eye of the poet, beyond his gravitation to the mere marks of pain, is not only the thoroughness with which the master attacks the boy's body but also the coolness with which the boy receives this attack. The poem describes the schoolmaster as picking out the most sensitive places to hit, whipping Charlie as if he wishes to "cut" him "to bits." He tells us Charlie is "covered in blood." But though each blow from the master brings blood to Charlie's forehead and "makes him bite through his lips," he walks from the flogging with an air of nonchalance, like a victorious hero. And a "crowd of boys" dogs "the heels of their hero."

Here, the boy becomes a hero because he succeeds against the feelings of his own body. His victory is that he does not cry out, does not respond as the body might naturally cause one to respond to pain. Thus Charlie has not been humiliated, or "femininized." He may even be said to have become "manly." For this poem is a parable of the formation of the masculine character in pornography.

Now one begins to understand the real identity of who we call "the man" in pornography, and of who we call "the woman," or of those pornographic couples, the woman and the man, the parent and the child, the teacher and the student (or the doctor and the nurse or patient, or the rider and the horse, or the master and the slave). All these couples represent one being divided into a mind and a body. Like the man and the woman, or the parent and the child, or the rider and the horse, one appears to suffer and the other does not. (Charlie's body bleeds, but in order that he not express the feelings of his body, he bites his own lip.) Here is the essential couple in pornography, that couple which appears in so many disguises and so many familiar social modes—it is that part of the mind which belongs to culture pitted against the body.

But it is not simply dead flesh which is punished by this cultural mind, the mind of pornography. Rather, this mind would deaden flesh which is not dead, but is alive and feeling. It is the body in its capacity to feel, to cry, to love itself, to suffer grief, desire, shame, or mortification of the spirit, which must be made to suffer.

Thus Charlie Collingwood becomes a hero because he does not feel. And thus the pleasure which Ernest gives to his master is not a pleasure in the body so much as the pleasure Gernand takes in the pain of the boy's submission. And Severn, in *Venus in Fur*, would hardly experience pain were he not in love with the woman who treats him "cruelly." The masochist must have a capacity to feel in order to suffer, for it is the feeling of the masochist which is punished. Not women, but feelings, are the object of sadistic fantasy.

Above all, what makes a sadist recognizable is that he does not feel. He glories even in his unfeelingness. His very coldness gives him power. He cannot be humiliated by rejection because he does not love. He never woos; he takes. His passion is not for union or for closeness, but for dominance. He wants to control the other. He wants to humiliate the will of the other. He wishes to demonstrate over and over his ability to make the other carry out his will. This is the pleasure above all pleasures which he seeks.

Yet Gernand and Ernest, Severn and his lover, spring from one mind. They are figures from the same psyche. On the deepest level of this drama we see that the sadist seeks to dominate, humiliate, punish, and perhaps even destroy a part of himself. And this part of himself is his feelings, which come from his body, and his *knowledge* of those feelings.

Here again, we find that opposition of culture and nature, now in one being, in one mind. And now the meaning of humiliation in pornography takes on a new significance. For what causes "shame" in pornography is always nature. Denis is humiliated because his white gloves are covered with worms. In *The Dialogue of Luisa Signia,* it is the physical nature of sexual pleasure itself which shames. "You should not degrade me so far as to make me drink a man in liquid form?" the heroine asks. In *A Man with a Maid,* when the hero "appreciates the mortification" of his victim, we learn that he has mortified her by looking on her body.

And what makes the Don Juan and the femme fatale of pornographic culture both cruel and victorious is that they are in control of nature, particularly the nature of their own bodies. *They are unfeeling.* And it is this very unfeelingness which causes so much suffering in their lovers. They abandon their lovers callously. They have no tenderness. No concern for those who love them. They know none of the vulnerability of love. They do not weep. They make love without feeling love. What makes them "libertine," what makes them powerful and free, is that they do not know eros. (For what is eros but a consciousness of feeling, culture revealing nature?) The loss of eros is the source of their pride.

The Marquis de Sade exhibits this same strange pride in the death of feeling; indeed his whole *oeuvre* can be taken as an obsessive ridicule of eros. In a work published in 1872, early in his career, and thus not blatantly pornographic, de Sade argues by example that innocent love is doomed. *Ernestine, A Swedish Tale* is both a tragedy and a romance. In this story, a maiden, her lover, and her father are subjected to every kind of indignity, every sort of grief bearing on loss and death, every kind of suffering imaginable short of the classic whip and chain.

The novel begins with a heartening pledge of love between Ernestine and the man she plans to marry. But from this point onward, the narration of events proceeds to destroy any hope of the realization of the love. Ernestine's lover is executed. She is kidnapped and raped. And finally, through a series of masquerades, her father inadvertently causes her death. Here the Marquis's cynicism is not so much spoken as it is played out in events, as if natural acts themselves prove that love is doomed.

In de Sade's later and more famous work, *Justine,* his cynicism and his cruelty become more bold. When the parents of Justine and Juliette die, Justine cries and feels great sorrow at their death. But Juliette feels nothing. Predictably, as the plot proceeds, it is Juliette who succeeds in life, while it is Justine who suffers. Juliette coldly uses the sexual feelings of men to advance in the world, until she becomes a wealthy and respectable woman. But Justine, who continues to experience feelings throughout the novel, is made to suffer over and over an almost ingenious list of punishments and depravities.

The Marquis tells us he writes to demonstrate that virtue is never rewarded. And by this he probably means the virtue of virginity. But besides integrity, the virtue which Justine displays most often, and which most often causes her trouble, is compassion. When she rescues a man called St. Florent from thieves, he canes her on the head and rapes her. When she finds a man by the side of the road and takes pity on him, he takes her to his castle and shows her into his private torture chamber. Even her death is eventuated by her sympathy. At the end of the novel, Juliette has rescued her sister and taken her to her castle. Here, in the midst of the storm, when Juliette is frightened by the sound of thunder, Justine runs to shut the window and is at once disfigured and killed by a bolt of lightning.

But feeling must be murdered again and again in pornography. Always in new ways. For in truth, feeling comes to life again, over and over. This is the denied part of the pornographer's mind, that knowledge of the body he can never banish from himself entirely. Feeling wants to live in him, despite a decision he must have made long ago. And feeling keeps urging its presence into his consciousness. He does not seem to be able to exist without it. And yet he wishes to destroy it. So the sadist seeks out the masochist and in his own way depends on the masochist.

Yet the masochist seeks out the sadist, too. For feeling itself, within this man, is in a state of indecision. He can never really decide not to feel. The sadist and the masochist are one being—one being who feels and who would not feel. Remembering feeling, this being goes back perhaps to that painful moment when he decided to murder feeling within himself. There he stands at the crossroads again. There once again he can make the old decision. And he does. Over and over, he hates himself. Over and over, he murders himself. For a few moments, feeling has returned to his consciousness. Feeling must make an appearance in order that he may murder it. And so, in one moment, he is able to murder feeling and he is able once again to feel and to know he feels. For of course, the feeling in him wants to live. But now, as he murders this feeling in himself, his suffering has yet another purpose. With this suffering he propitiates that angry god in himself who would annihilate feeling. For a few moments he knows his own feeling again. And he offers his pain like a sacrifice.

No wonder this ritual has become such an obsession for him. In this moment of pain, the crucial trauma and irresolution of his life is played out, and at least at this moment, through this ordeal, he becomes real. He is no longer a figment of his own denial. He is at the heart of himself, his rage and his suffering, and all that lies buried in him, every subdued response, every impulse which his body and his heart have silently memorized, even if his mind has silenced them, can now be expressed. But there is such a stockpile of furious feeling in him he is afraid he will lose control. He fears the power of his own feeling. So the whip which returns him to an earlier state of feeling now serves another purpose. It can punish him for feeling. It can discipline feeling. Now we can see finally why this masochist (who is his own sadist) looks with gratitude to the one who holds the whip, and why he regards this torture as that which saves him. In the hell which is his mind, this lash brings a moment of relief and of resolution that must be bliss.

Stekel tells us that the sadomasochistic patient comes to him complaining of numbness, complaining that only the infliction of pain will make him feel. And we learn from Stekel, too, that in his mind the sadist enters the psyche and the body of the masochist, and he cries out, and he trembles, and he feels. While, in his mind, the masochist enters the sadist's soul, and in his imagination rages at feeling.

No wonder, then, that the pornographer tries to convince us that women want to be punished. For there is a being within him, whom he calls "woman," who would be punished. In the assumed voice of a "woman," the pornographer tells us that to be threatened with a knife or to be slapped excites him. In an obscene novel, he poses as a woman who secretly wishes for her rapist to "ram his . . . cock right between my bruised and whiplashed thighs."

And then he becomes the rapist. And playing the part of the rapist, he tells this woman inside him, "Relax and enjoy this; this is the kind of action your keeper ought to be giving you." Speaking to that part of himself he wishes to shame, he promises, "I'm going to treat you like something that crawled out of the sewer."

One discovers the same movement of a mind captivated by feeling and the desire to murder feeling at the same time in a passage from *The Villa Chigi* by the poet D'Annunzio. As the hero stands with a woman, they begin to hear the sound of an ax, until the repeated blows echo all around them. Now the woman begins to cry, "as though wounded"; she bursts into sobs, "into desperate tears." As he watches her weeping, a fantasy is born in the poet's mind. He tells us:

> I saw her in my mind, as though in a lightning flash, . . . humble and bleeding, humbly gasping, prostrate in a pool of blood, and raising suppliant hands from the lake of red; and she said with her eyes, "I did you no harm."

And what is it in this pornographic mind which would seek revenge against feeling?

We find the beginning of an answer to this question in the pornographer's description of his hero's motives. Jack, the hero of *The Skin Flick Rapist*, has felt himself humiliated. He has been rejected by women. He has been left in a state of desire, a state of wanting which he could not satisfy or control. He wanted to "perform" sexually. But even his own body deserted him. For his "cock had played tricks all too many times." His own body has humiliated him.

Such is the power of the body. The body and our capacity to feel must always humble us before the images we have of ourselves. The life of the body precedes any image we have of ourselves. Therefore, our pride, our desire to believe an image of ourselves which our bodies might prove untrue, must be simply a defense against some truth, some knowledge we have chosen to forget. But what would this knowledge be?

Let us imagine for a moment that under all humiliation, that of rejection and exclusion, of powerlessness, of shame, is one ultimate humbling, and this is the humiliation of *being* flesh. Of being vulnerable and helpless, unable to care for oneself, dependent on the love of another, without control, so that we might be covered with substances from our own bodies which burn and cause pain, so that we might be overcome with hunger, so that we might be beside ourselves with fear of being abandoned, or with fear of the power of the one who feeds us to withhold nourishment, presence, love, or even with fear that she might harm us. And this being, moreover, is one with whom we are so close that we, in our infant minds, confuse her body with our own, confuse her mind with our own, so that, like the pornographer who projects what he cannot accept in himself onto a woman, we do not know where she begins and we stop.

Do we not discover this very mechanism of the mind to confuse one's own body with the body of one's mother in the pornographer's projection of his own denied self onto the objectified image of a woman? The pornographer is obsessed. He is chained and enslaved, not to a real woman, nor to a body, but to the past and his image of the past, which he must recreate again and again. For his re-creation has a purpose which he can never accomplish. He must be forever frustrated. He desires a Biblical justice, an exact revenge for all that he has suffered in body and in mind. This is why pornography is so filled with reversal. Behind every pornographic fantasy which has reversed reality is the infant's wish to turn the tables on his parents. Here is the child's desire to have the power his parents had, to inflict upon them the longing, rejection, frustration, pain, and humiliation that the infant once felt.

Again and again in pornography, for instance, we find the image of a woman sucking a man's penis. And this image can be a door for us into an understanding of the obscene reversal. Here, fellatio, which in itself is a simple act of pleasure between mouth and penis, becomes more than itself. It takes on the aura of an obsession; its performance begins to appear to us as compulsive. For it is emblematic of another situation. We can guess this immediately from the style in which it is always portrayed.

In the film *The Devil and Miss Jones,* for example, when the heroine is taught oral lovemaking, she begins to desire this act with an unrealistic avidity. She seeks this act as if her life depended on it. She becomes a nymphomaniac of the mouth. She appears to us like an addict frenzied with need, almost maddened by her wanting. Her eyes take on a lurid and a frantic quality. The men she makes love to in this manner, however, are calm and almost indifferent, lying back, without any urgency of their own or any expression of need. So we see her beg for this pleasure, as if it were hers alone.*

One sees this image over and over in pornography—a woman driven to a point of madness out of the desire to put a man's penis in her mouth. So that finally, by this image, we are called back: this image reminds the mind of another scene, a scene in which this avidity to put a part of the body into the mouth is not a mystery. Here is a reversal again. For it is the infant who so overwhelmingly needs the mother's breast in his mouth. The infant who thought he might die without this, who became frantic and maddened with desire, and it was his mother who had the power to withhold.

Now this reversal becomes, in and of itself, a humiliation. The mother is punished. She herself is made into an infant, and the hero can coolly grant or deny her frantic infant desire.

That pornography which is explicitly sadomasochistic only shows the hidden motive of this reversal more clearly, for now the rage of the hero turns fellatio into an act of aggression, a "forced feeding." In *Apartment House Sex Killer*, we read:

> He slipped his huge dagger-like dick inside her mouth. He slammed it relentlessly inside her, driving it with forceful energy. He slammed it hard until it was pushing all the way to the back of the throat.
> ". . . I'm gonna slam this thing down your throat, slam it until I shoot off all my pecker-juice," he said.

This is no rare passage in pornography. Like a neurotic drama, it is played out again and again. So it is repeated in another work, with another hero and a different female victim:

> She gulped several times, barely able to breathe, as he rocked his body back and forth, shoving that huge pecker into her as deeply as it would go. . . .
> "I'm gonna fuck this mouth of yours until my hot juice explodes inside you."

Again and again we read the same language of rage and revenge. "His cock was whistling in and out of my mouth as he suddenly shouted

---

* The entire humor of *Deep Throat* hinges on the observation that many women do not even take sexual pleasure in fellatio. Thus the hero, who is a doctor, discovers that the heroine has a clitoris in her throat.

out at the top of his voice, 'Shit, yes, now, suck on it you smelly shit! Drink me, feel it!" we read in one passage of *Teenage Sadism*, and in another:

> Kurt rammed my head cruelly down against his penis, stuffing every last thick inch of his huge cock right inside my mouth. It banged against the back of my throat and I gagged.

Just as the obsessed mind must repeat fantasy in a kind of mental enslavement to old images, so, too, the fantasy of the obsessed mind always includes clues, details which will bring one back to the original scene for which the mind seeks revenge. In the pornographic depiction of fellatio, the heroine, under threat of punishment, must always drink the semen of the hero. He is obsessed with her drinking of his white semen (which of course reminds us of milk from a mother's breast). So the hero in *Apartment House Sex Killer* intones:

> "Get ready, swallow every drop of this juice. You'd better eat every drop of it. . . . If you spit this stuff out you're in real trouble. You'd just better eat every drop of my hot cum. . . . Taste every bit of this hot stuff . . ."

evoking for us at once the infant at the breast, or the small child told to "eat every bite," who is told if he spits he is "in trouble," who is forced by his parents to finish his meal.

The demand that a woman drink semen is repeated throughout pornography. Volume after volume presents such scenes as this which we find in *The Skin Flick Rapist:*

> Maria gagged on his juice. It made him so angry that he reached out with his right hand and pulled at her hair.
> "I don't want any of that shit, you little bitch, eat every bit of that juice," he said threateningly.

Or this scene from de Sade's *The 120 Days of Sodom*, in which a "Father Superior," having welcomed a brother and sister into his monastery, enacts this rape on the girl:

> "Pretty face," he gasped, "pretty little whore's face, how I'll soak it in my fuck, by sweet Jesus."
> And therewith the sluices opened, the sperm flew out and the entirety of my sister's face, especially her nose and mouth, were covered with evidence of our visitor's libertinage.

(The girl tells her brother, "You've just seen one of his favorite stunts. . . . He's mad about discharging in girls' faces.")

Yet these scenes do not contain the rage of the pornographer's mind. And so, often, at the same time that the woman is made into the infant, or a few moments before, or afterward, the pornographer turns his rage on the breasts themselves. In *The Story of O*, for example, just before Sir Stephen penetrates the mouth of O (it was not the caress of her lips the length of him was looking for, but the back of her throat), he grazes her nipples with his fingers while holding a burning cigarette and flicks an ash between her breasts. Or in *Apartment House Sex Killer*, as the hero forces fellatio on another victim, he "turns . . . sharp fingernails loose on" her breasts.

In *The Skin Flick Rapist*, the hero pinches and "abuses" the breasts of one of his victims. The narrator tells us: "the ripping stabs of his fingernails had produced a series of tearing cuts around her breasts." Later in the book, again followed by another scene of forced fellatio, the hero focuses his sexual passion on a woman's breasts:

> From the very beginning, from the very first time he had seen her, Jack Henson had been infatuated by Wanda's stunning breasts.

And these breasts become emblematic of all that he has wanted and been denied:

> Now, as he stared down at the firm, jutting globes of flesh which were peering directly toward him, he got an idea. He could give vent to his angry, sexual passions by punishing that creamy flesh which she no doubt held in high esteem.

Now he is enraged directly at these breasts, which as a man he wanted and as a child he wanted, and which a woman had the power of withholding from him. So Jack bites into her breasts, and "When he saw the blood penetrate" her skin, "he almost experienced an orgasm." In *Apartment House Sex Killer*, the fascination of the hero with a woman's breasts leads to the same violence against her body: "her tits continued to fascinate him and he wanted to see them bloodied and shattered." And he murders this victim by slashing her breasts with his knife.

And now the breasts take on a double significance. For at the same time they represent power, they also represent vulnerability. They are sensitive. They feel. They are defenseless. They manifest sexual desire. Their nipples harden. And the flesh around them is soft, yielding; to touch them is to evoke at once tenderness and need.

Pornography is not entirely ignorant of itself. Thus, in the benign voice of the scientist and doctor, the author of *Teenage Sadism*, "A Documentary Casebook," tells us: "Sadism among teenage boys is usually an extension of an original hate for the mother figure." In this "case," the hero (who is the narrator's patient) has pulled the bra from his cousin and pinched her nipples "viciously," so that when she screamed he was able to force his penis into her mouth, "trying to stuff it down her throat." (And like other heroes of these pornographic books, who urinate in the faces of women, shit on them, or call them "Shit," the hero of this "case study" enters his victim anally, in order to torture her, and then humiliates her by spreading her face with her own feces and blood.) He describes his pleasure:

> Her very defenselessness appealed to me. I enjoyed her helpless condition. Enjoyed the fact that she was suffering just as she had made me suffer.

Here, in this scene which rests at the apex of sadomasochistic ritual, in which a woman is tortured and reduced to the level of an infant, humiliated by her desire, her helplessness, and materiality, the issues of control and revenge mingle in an obsessive repetition of the crucial drama of infancy.

In *The Story of O*, the voice of the narrator tells us: "O hated herself for her own desire and loathed Sir Stephen for the self-control he was displaying." And: "a big grin" spreads itself over the face of the hero of *Apartment House Sex Killer*, because he enjoys having women "in a subservient position." In *Teenage Sadism*, one of the patient-heroes announces he will teach his victim "discipline, more discipline than she learns at school. We'll show her who's boss around here."

Just as the pornographic hero relishes the subservience of his victim, so does he also glory in his own control. Sir Stephen in *The Story of O* is cold and without response. He even withdraws from O before the point of orgasm. He never, even in sexual response, appears to lose control. The hero of *Teenage Sadism* boasts of being "in full control of the situation." In *The Skin Flick Rapist,* after raping and torturing a woman, Jack ruminates:

> . . . Suddenly a feeling of peace surfaced inside him. It was strange how in the aftermath of a series of violent acts, he could remain so calm.

And yet, inside the calmness of the sadist there exists a hidden aspect of himself: he longs for hysteria, fear, the uncontrolled. This aspect of himself which he has sacrificed is lived out in the body of his victim. "Judy was crying and thrashing about," the hero of *Teenage Sadism* tells his "doctor," "but I was in full command of the situation." Thus when he declares, "I was giving it to her, showing her that I wasn't a piece of shit, that I wouldn't take the crap she'd been dishing out at my own expense," we hear the voice of a soul split in two and divided against itself. That Jack's grievances against his cousin "Judy" were mere figments, illusory grievances, is not clear in the text of Jack's fictional account itself. He is portrayed as believing his denunciation of his cousin. He believes that she has been cruel to him, and though his cruelty to her far exceeds what he imagines she has done to him, we are led to agree with his description of her. But in the fictitious doctor's analysis of Jack's story, we learn that Jack is "paranoid." Thus again, pornography, like the compulsive liar who compulsively gives himself away, reveals the shape of its own delusion.

But now this "doctor" who has been created in the pornographer's mind simply lifts the moral battle between his patient and his patient's victim from a microcosmic to a macrocosmic plane. No, he says, Jack's cousin did not injure him. No, he says, of all the "cases" he "studies," the girls these boys torture do not deserve their punishment. But, he tells us, their mothers are the true criminals, the ones whom the boys must punish in their compulsive enactments of this ritual. For the mothers have rejected their sons. Thus, from a more lofty and philosophical plane, the pornographic "doctor" has given us the same formula. A woman sins against her son, a female against a male, and the male punishes all women in retaliation against one woman. For this "mother" of the pornographic imagination has been found guilty of rejecting her son.

But this rejection has another meaning. For in the infant's mind, his mother is a part of himself. And with this understanding, now let us reverse the story the pornographic "doctor" has given to us. Let us say that the sadistic boy is angry because he rejected his mother. But in this rejection of his mother, he has rejected a part of himself. He has pushed away from his own mind the natural part of himself. He has tried to forget that he suckled at his mother's breasts. He has tried to forget his own vulnerability. The one desire. The knowledge of his own body.

And thus the pornographic hero rejects himself. He excludes from his conscious idea of himself that part of his soul which pornography calls "feminine." But this is precisely what society in reality does. Culture excludes women. Yet if culture has successfully rejected the feminine, then, we must ask, why must pornography continue to humiliate and punish the feminine? Why is such a prodigious effort, such a massive amount of paper and print and celluloid, dedicated to this task, when the feminine has already been made silent?

Because—the answer is so simple—this self cannot die. She remains alive in all of us. We cannot forget her. She comes alive with every desire, with every breath. She lives in our bodies and in circumstance, in our nature and in the unpredictable works of nature about us. We try to exclude her, but she always returns.

Even though we have created an image of ourselves which we call "man" (by our very name excluding the feminine), the female continues to enter our consciousness. And thus, whenever she does enter our minds, especially when we think of her with sexual desire, or with any kind of wanting, we must punish her. For our wanting is the way she exerts her power over us. Thus our torture of her is a self-defense.

But what is the weapon which we choose to use against this powerful adversary? We use our minds. We use our imaginations. We fantasize. And through our fantasy, we invent the perfect revenge. Thus, in fantasy, the pornographic mind gives itself power and diminishes the power of nature. It opposes itself to nature. And it erects culture as an act of revenge against nature.

Yet in order for this revenge to be powerful, the mind must believe in culture's power. The mind must begin to believe, in fact, that words are more powerful than sticks and stones. And inside this mind, this belief becomes true. For this mind has rejected the natural realm and attempts to live exclusively within its own images. Therefore, inside this mind, to attack with an image is the most powerful form of attack. And that is why over and over again, as if he were commanding a devastating force, the pornographer humiliates and degrades his imagined victims. Because he lives in his world of images, and since his victim *is* an image, to humiliate this image is to annihilate it. For humiliation by definition implies the *destruction* of an image, either of a self-image or of a public image.

But in this war of images, the pornographer finds himself in a terrible dilemma. He finds himself in a cul-de-sac of his own creation. For by the very images he has created to humiliate nature, he recalls nature to his consciousness. All images, all metaphors, are imitations, at their origins, of nature. The image of a woman's body which he uses to contain and punish his rage against nature has a certain power, therefore, in his mind. This image he has wrought to humiliate nature now works a power over *him*. He is overcome once more. Vanquished once more. Nature is like a many-headed dragon. For every head he cuts off, more heads grow. And now the very device, the very image he uses to silence nature rises up to speak to him.

This is why his images must accelerate in their violence. They must indeed accelerate in intensity until they become actual enactments. And then these enactments themselves must also become increasingly more violent. For never does he succeed in murdering the real object of his rage.

And so pornography does not end with the pornographic fantasy, but returns to our lives.

Yet should we be surprised with this return? Every time we raise our eyes from the page of the pornographic book, we find the same images in the culture which surrounds us. We even begin, like the pornographer himself, to confuse these images with reality.

The cold, manipulative glint schooled into the eyes of fashion models, cruelly spiked high heels, the heavy leather jacket of the motorcycle rider, steel-studded pants, the cultivation of sharp fingernails. The punk rock titles, "The Wounds," "The Pointed Sticks," "The Dead Kennedys," "The Zeroes," a singer named Sid Vicious, a film which begins with the identification of a female corpse, a film which advertises itself as terrifying, in which young women are murdered by a psychotic and cruel rapist, countless such films, images of female bodies chained, beaten, to sell record albums, an advertisement for a perfume which shows an overturned chair, part of a woman's naked body, and a revolver, a film in which homosexual men are sadistically murdered, an advertisement for a film, *In Search of Historic Jesus* which reads: "2000 years ago on a hilltop near Jerusalem a man was brutally whipped, repeatedly tortured and finally crucified. His name was Jesus . . . WAS HE THE SON OF GOD?"

In our imaginations, by which we tell the story of our own culture, we might, as others have done before, name the story of Jesus Christ as the origin of culture's torture of the body. All the elements of sadomasochistic ritual are present in the crucifixion of Christ. And the Christian religion itself labors to deny the body. "Imitatio Christi" means to be selfless, to be virgin, to renounce sensual pleasure. The early church fathers labored to prove that Christ's birth did not eventuate from earthly coitus, and one scholar of the Gnostic tradition even argued that Christ was not born of Mary but materialized fully formed, so that the son of God would not be supposed to have been made up of flesh.

And yet Christianity did not originate these attitudes toward the body. Rather, the Christian tradition, and the story of Christ's death, became a perfect vessel to contain the mind's image of itself as free from the body. The cross on which Jesus is crucified again and again in culture's imagination bears this meaning. For a cross represents a crossroads, and a choice. Let us imagine that one arm of this cross goes in the direction of culture, and its image of itself as free from nature, while the other arm of the cross stands for the body and for nature, and all the meaning nature yields us.

Within the story of Christ we find another tradition, in which culture and nature are not opposed, in which there is not a crucifixion but a transformation, in which matter has meaning and flesh has spirit. In this version of the story of Christ, he was not the son of God, but a son of God among many daughters and sons of goddesses and gods, who was divine simply because he admitted his own divinity into his idea of himself. And that he knew himself to have spirit within his body was the blasphemy for which Christ was crucified. For if he had denied his own divinity, he would have gone free from the sentence of death.

But the mythological presence of Christ which culture worships today, the emblem which we are asked to kneel before, and which has become our culture's image of "man," is Christ crucified on the cross— the spirit in the body sentenced to death. It is this death, a death promised to deliver us from the original sin of knowing flesh, that we are asked to imitate.

The Sacred

We must, in pornography, sense the weight of a morbid mind. In this mind, the hope of a marriage between spirit and flesh is replaced by a longing for death. For it is only dead flesh that the pornographer controls. Only a body without life, which has no desire or will. Through humiliation, enslavement, and torture, the human body is made into a living thing. In the obscene mind we enter a kind of Night of the Living Dead, in which the human soul has vanished from all present, and the human being is represented by a corpse which walks and talks and impersonates the living. Here the arc of culture's war against nature is completed.

The Marquis de Sade, who is famous to us not only as a pornographer but as an ideologist of pornography, gives us the real meaning of the form. In his *Philosophy in the Bedroom*, as the heroine, herself an ideologue of the obscene, anticipates the arrival of a child to whom she is to teach this philosophy, she promises:

> Be certain I'll spare nothing to pervert her, degrade her, demolish in her all her false ethical notions with which they may already have been able to dizzy her; in two lessons, I want to render her as criminal as am I . . . as impious . . . as debauched, as depraved.

She wishes to stifle "within this young heart every seed of virtue and of religion planted there by her tutors."

Yet, as we have discovered, this is not an elaborate attempt to free flesh from Christian hatred of flesh. The Marquis does not speak ironically when he speaks of turning a child into a criminal. For in his vision of the world, nature is criminal. Thus he writes to us: ". . . those murders which the laws punish so rigorously, those murders which we assume to be the greatest outrage which one can do to Nature, not only . . . do her no wrong; they become useful to her." And elsewhere in de Sade, we read: "Nature lives and breathes by crime," or "hungers at her pores for bloodshed"; we hear that "Nature is weary of life."

We do not rise up with love for the world from de Sade's vision. He tells us nature's eyes are "sick of seeing, her ears heavy with hearing," and we sicken as she sickens, grow heavy as she does. Nature is not, in de Sade, bent on joy, but rather she "yearns for cruelty." And spelling out for us the pornographic ideology which would turn eros into death, he writes: "she kindles death out of life, and feeds with fresh blood the innumerable and insatiable mouths suckled at her milkless breasts."

Here is an ideology which appears an exact mirror image of the miraculous initiation which seers experienced from the goddess Persephone at Eleusis. For at the apex of this transforming ritual, when a sheaf of grain was held up to the open eyes of the initiate, the initiate was supposed to have understood that there is no death, that life and death are one, the soul is immortal, and thus to have taken into herself (or himself) the secret of rebirth. But where this mystic vision sees life, de Sade sees death; where this vision sees rebirth, de Sade sees an interminable cycle of meaningless cruelty. And where the Eleusian mystery embodies a vision of both woman and nature, in the figure of a goddess, as sacred, in de Sade's mind woman and nature are embodied by a figure of cruelty who mocks every idea of the sacred in the human imagination with her avid and terrifying hunger for death.

In his symbolically conceived universe, de Sade as philosopher plays precisely the same role that "Dr." Copeland gives himself in his pornographic novel about the sadism of teenaged boys. His metaphor is larger and more fantastic, his language richer. He uses the richest metaphors culture uses to describe existence. But the mechanism of his mind is the same. De Sade has blamed the cruelty of the characters which his own mind created on "the mother." Only, in this instance, he has lucidly described for us the structure of his own mind: he says the mother *is* nature. It is this mother which his vision profanes.

Through all pornography, and behind every profanation, then, we can find a different vision of the world, glimmering, just out of reach, at times not even visible, but always present—this silenced presence of the idea of a marriage between spirit and matter, the forgotten knowledge that culture might embody nature for us rather than deny her; and that where we are terrified by the force of nature, where we suffer loss, or are overwhelmed by desire, culture might mediate nature's power for us, and might make of our own minds and bodies the sacred vessels which transform experience into meaning.

Behind the static object which the obscene vision calls woman is a sacred image of the goddess, the sacred image of the cow, the emblematic touch of divinity in the ecstasy of the sexual act, and behind all these the knowledge that within matter and not outside the material is a knowledge of the meaning of the universe.

Here lies the answer to why it is so essential to culture that the image of divinity be male, that Christ had to be a "son" of God, and not a daughter. And here is why the idea that earlier cultures might have worshiped a Great Goddess remains to some minds shaped by this culture absurd and unthinkable. For the proposition that woman, who *is* nature, could be sacred is not a possible concept in a culture which is by definition above nature. We catch a glimpse of pornography's profanation of the Great Goddess in this passage from Juvenal:

> Well known to all are the mysteries of the Good Goddess, when the flute stirs the loins and the Maenads of Priapus sweep along, frenzied alike by the horn-blowing and the wine, whirling their locks and howling. What foul longing burns within their breasts! What cries they utter as the passion palpitates within! . . . O would that our ancient practises, or at least our public rites, were not polluted by scenes like these.

Here Juvenal records the pollution of his own mind. He presents himself to us in his vision of passion at a temple of the Goddess.

The obscene mind makes an alliance with the Judeo-Christian vision of the world. Both render death to the things of the material world. For they are two heads, two faces belonging to the same sensibility. And thus from one mouth they implore the virtuous with the threat of eternal death not to worship an image of a golden calf—the cow an aspect of the Great Mother, the nourisher and procreator, celestial and chthonic at once, the primordial, sacred-first-creator-of-flesh. And from the other mouth this two-headed mind makes of the body of a woman a dead object without a soul.

Yet behind the obscene object and the sacrilegious icon exists the power of the image, the image as the manifestation of the idea of spirit and matter together, the image of nature as the place where mind and body, culture and the natural, meet as one, and breathe. This breath that the sacred image contains fills the seer with breath. (As John Blofield writes of Tantric mysticism, by seeing the deity in an image, "we actually do become the deity.") This image to which, in our seeing, we have given both sacredness and life in turn gives us the sacred and gives us life: "The worship, the worshipper and the worshipped, those three are not separate."

So the material nature of the world, which pornography degrades, is transformed in this presence of the sacred. "Recognize everything around you as Nirvana," we read from Tantric Buddhism. Earth, water, fire, air, skin, fish, vulva, penis, ear, wasp, ant, dog, horse, monkey, leaf, bird, stone, feces, rain, apple—all these, in this now buried understanding of the world, become not only filled with spirit but capable themselves of awakening the spirit in our minds.

And indeed, it is precisely the animal nature of the image, its sensual presence in this world, which awakens in the seer her own spirit. When the shaman wears the mask of a deer, she is filled with a knowledge the deer has. Entering the body of the deer gives her a way to discover the knowledge of her own body. What a different philosophical vision this is which understands that when an elephant bathes at the river he invokes the heavens! What a different way of experiencing the world! In the human imagination, in this culture and in others which we know about and perhaps would wish to enter more deeply in our minds, the animal has two aspects, two opposite poles of meaning. And so in the pornographic imagination, a woman is spoken of derisively as breeding like a rabbit, but at another moment, when a shaman wears a rabbit skin, he or she becomes the rabbit and learns humility before the Great Spirit.

Here in these two images of the animal world we confront face to face the two images we have of ourselves: the sacred and the profane.

And yet can we understand this simply as a difference of opinion? The Marquis de Sade's vision of the world after all does not differ in matters of factual detail from that of the mystic seers Heraclitus or Empedocles, nor by virtue of fact from the ecstatic vision associated with Dionysus and worship of the goddess. What separates these two visions of the world is not a rational differentiation, but rather a *feeling*.

On the one hand, in the case of both pornography and religious asceticism, we encounter a profound distrust. The sensual world is dangerous. Women, Nietzsche tells us, are nature's most dangerous playthings. A woman, Saint Paul tells us, ought to have a veil on her head. The beauty of women, and even the beauty of flowers, the Christian theologians warn us, can lead one to hell. The revelation of beauty is dangerous.*

Yet when one no longer takes Christian theology literally, why should beauty be dangerous? To the Christian mind, the danger of beauty leads one to hell. To understand the sacred meaning of the revelation of beauty, we must then understand the deeper meaning of perdition in the psyche. (And so our questioning after the sacred meaning behind pornographic thought leads us again from revelation to transgression, for to the Christian mind, hell was the place one arrived at through transgression.)

But here we find a kind of tautology, that sort of hellish circle which must be terrifying to a mind which would escape the reality of its own nature. For hell is the dominion of the devil. All that is in hell is defined by his law and his nature. And what is his power? He can transform men into animals. He inflicts pain and loss such that a being in his sway is entirely at the mercy of his own physical nature. Trapped and imprisoned, the devil's victim experiences the opposite of freedom. His body is tortured by frustrated desire. We recognize this desire in the form of the flames which lick his flesh. The devil makes the human soul a victim of the human animal nature.

---

* This fear of beauty did not die with a belief in God. It is, as Mario Praz has told us, an intrinsic part of the Romantic obsession with beauty. Thus, after quoting Victor Hugo's lines *"La Mort et La Beauté sont deux choses profondes/Qui contiennent tant d'ombre et d'azur qu'on dirait/Deux soeurs également terrible et fécondes . . ."* he tells us: "In fact, to such an extent were Beauty and Death looked upon as sisters by the Romantics that they became fused into a sort of two-faced herm, filled with corruption and melancholy and fatal in its beauty." *The Romantic Agony* (London, 1978), p. 31.

And should we be surprised to find that in the Christian imagination, it is women who lead men to the devil with their *beauty?* Thus, in his book on nightmare, Ernest Jones reminds us of the Abyssinian proverb: "When a woman sleeps alone, the devil sleeps with her." Now we should not be surprised to discover the etymology of the word "glamour"—for this word, which refers to a woman's beauty, in an earlier time was the term used to describe that power a witch has over men to transform them.

But the devil, Jones tells us, bears about his person the fragrance of an older, a sacred meaning. For earlier than the idea of the devil, and sharing many of his physical attributes, there was, we must remember, the figure of Pan, Pan with cloven feet and horns, who played on pipes, who was a god of nature, who celebrated sensual feeling. And Pan, Jones tells us, was "the equivalent of Euphrates, the spirit who provided us with what was till recently the scientific name for nightmare."

So again, we discover that in the devil, as in the animal, we find ourselves. This is that other self, that disowned self. Here is the self Freud called "subconscious," a self accessible only through dream, or poetic raving, or madness, or perhaps through the experience of ecstasy in the spirit of the body. And here is *beauty* again. For this ecstasy arrives through that window into the soul, and the body, which is opened when we feel an overwhelming beauty.

In his book *Shakti and Shakta*, which describes the experience of revelation in Eastern religion, Arthur Avalon writes: "As she thus reveals herself, she induces in him a passionate exultation and that sense of security which is only gained as approach is made to the Central Heart of things. For as the Upanished says, 'He only fears who sees duality.'" In this vision, nature and culture come together through an experience of the beautiful, which opens the soul, and transforms being.

And beauty also leads us back into a memory that we would wish to forget. For who is this soul that beauty opens us to, who lives in us, and whom we have forgotten? This is the child. The child who originally saw the world as enchantingly beautiful. Who saw her mother as beautiful. Who accepted all nature as beautiful. And when pornography punishes the vulnerable, when pornography punishes our memories of infancy, when pornography punishes the breast, and humiliates our body's knowledge of this world, pornography punishes this child. This is the deeper meaning behind pornography's obsession with the rape of virgins. And with the molestation of children.

But hidden within pornography's degradation of the child is another sacred knowledge. For the child is an almost universal symbol for the soul's transformation. (So Christ declares that one must be like a little child to enter the kingdom of heaven.) The child is the innocent whose vision of nature has not been clouded with culture. The child is whole, not yet divided, and is, therefore, a being who can see eros. (But of course, in our cultural imagery, we see Eros as a child.) When we would heal the mind, or when we would return to what we remember as an original state of bliss, we ask this child to speak to us. And it is beauty, above all beauty, which gives this child a voice.

The German Expressionist painter Kokoschka, a contemporary of Franz Marc, in his verse "The Dreaming Boy" (published in a series called *Eros*), has given us these lines: "And I was giddy with ecstasy when I came to know my flesh/And I was a lover of all things when I spoke with a girl . . ." And yet this same man, who here celebrates the transformative power of beauty and the childlike joy of the body, had also within his imagination a darker vision of this part of the soul we call the feminine. Kokoschka also wrote the play *Murder, the Hope of Women*, and he spoke, in a journal, of "the bliss of self-mutilation until one found oneself again." What we find in this man, and what we found in Franz Marc, is a division in the self; an attitude which is both for and against the body and the feminine; two parts, one which would have wholeness, and perceives the sensual world as filled with ecstasy; and another, caught in duality, which sees that world as dangerous. This may well be the central conflict of this culture. Certainly it is this conflict, within the self, that has created the preconditions for the warfare against the body which we call sadomasochism.

But if the objectification of the female body, and the likening of woman to an animal, the hatred of flesh, the revelation of beauty, and transgression, all have a sacred meaning which pornography hides, then must not humiliation, which is the core of sadomasochism, and the theme of all pornography, also have another meaning? Let us consider first what it is that is humiliated in the obscene mind. The child is humiliated; beauty is humiliated; the body is humiliated; the feminine and the animal are humiliated. And of all these we can say: Nature is humiliated by culture. And now suppose we were to reverse this situation, to humiliate culture with nature? In his *Philosophy in the Bedroom*, the Marquis de Sade speaks through his heroine's mouth, boasting that they will degrade a young girl and destroy in her any ethical notions with which her teachers have already made her "dizzy." Let us here for a moment forget ethics and Christian morality, then, and instead concentrate on the word "dizzy." For we are made dizzy with feeling, beauty makes us dizzy, sexual ecstasy makes us dizzy, above all love makes us dizzy. To be dizzy makes us lose our balance. We suddenly see the world differently. We do not know where we are going. We lose control. We give ourselves over to fate, or to the hand of divinity, to the goddess. Dizziness was the state of the initiates at Eleusis. It is the state of a dreamer. Of one who contacts a deeper knowledge than her conscious mind had supposed existed. And above all, this dizziness destroys the ego, the ego which is made by culture, a culture pretending to be reality, a culture that demands that the self remake itself after the image of culture.

If we see behind the death which occurs in so much pornographic literature, this death that is the death of a woman, and of the vulnerable, feeling self, we can glimpse another death which might have taken place, which sexual feeling itself might have brought about, and this is the death of the ego. A death of the part of the self that culture claims as its own.

In his classic study of eros and death, *Love in the Western World*, Denis De Rougemont sees the coupling of death and love as the psyche's expression through culture of a profound ambivalence toward union. Now one does not want so much to argue with this vision of De Rougemont's as to shift the axis of his vision so that it is colored with a different feeling. For De Rougemont's view is like de Sade's pessimism. He perceives a love of death, for instance, in the myth of Tristan and Iseult. And yet there is another meaning here, which he does not grasp. He fails to note that culture has threatened eros with death. This is the meaning of Franz Marc's life, of Kate Chopin's life and the life of her work. Eros, which contains the child and the woman, the animal and the body, and unites these with meaning, with a longing of the spirit—eros, which unites nature and culture—is dangerous to a culture conceived as revenge against nature. The very force of eros, the very brilliance of vitality, the irrepudiality of feeling, that eros cannot be reasoned out of existence, at once humiliates and threatens to annihilate a culture which would attempt to place itself above and separate from nature.

In the myth of Tristan and Iseult, and in so many other Romantic stories, including *Romeo and Juliet,* two lovers are threatened with death. They have transgressed a law of culture. To love with body and mind together is a cardinal sin. And this is why, when we see the ending of these dramas, though we grieve at the loss of lives, the loss of one lover to the other, still at the end of these stories we feel what we call exultation. We sense that these deaths have made us larger and more ourselves. And why should we glory at death? Because in these stories we have witnessed courage. A hero and a heroine have been threatened with death by culture. They have been met with force and told not to feel what they feel. They have been asked to violate the soul's knowledge in their bodies and yet *they have refused to obey.* They have said to this threat of death: We will live as whole beings. We will not allow the threat of death to make us into living corpses. We will love.

And with this refusal, they have escaped the humiliation of the body and the soul. For there must be a part of our beings that would rather die than live as we have been asked to live by culture, to live as enslaved and partial beings.

This, then, is the sacred meaning of humiliation: If we humiliate the false, cultural image of ourselves, which is not ourselves, we free our real beings. And it is by the false image of ourselves, expressed and given a life by pornography, that we are enslaved.

For we are whole beings. We know this somewhere in a part of ourselves that feels like memory. And thus, despite the fact that we can find no culture living today which does not express a profound hatred of the bodies of women, and a fear of human nature and natural life, we have within us a longing. Perhaps we know or perhaps remember that meaning and instinct, rather than being separate, were born together. We know that every natural being has spirit. Every culture recorded has expressed this longing in some form. One encounters it as an idealized vision of the past, or as conjecture about the nature of past societies, as a utopia or an idea of heaven. And as if we knew that when we attack the other we attack some unexpressed part of ourselves, we have, in our imaginations, given a saintly wholeness to those societies we have destroyed. Thus the American Indian becomes for us a symbol of wholeness with nature, for a wholeness we have lost.

Within our own culture, we witness the rebirth of a vision of wholeness as deviation. We call it by names which hide and distort its real meaning. Thus we say that artists are eccentric, or androgynous—and fail to question the effect of convention or of social and sexual roles on human creativity. As if we knew we were being persecuted by convention in our real nature, we take the real persecution of others as symbolic of our own suffering. We ask for the deliverance and the freedom of others. And yet we know in our hearts that there is much more than altruism in our rage, for example, at the oppression of a people with darker skin. For within this rage at the oppression of a "dark" people is a knowledge of a dark and beautiful part of ourselves which has been silenced.

Nature has written this knowledge into our very existence. Even the persecutors have this vision. They see what they secretly long for in themselves written over the faces of those they persecute. Hidden within the racist's description of another being we find this: a fear of and desire for the secrets of his own heart. When one reads, for instance, through the description of witches, written by the men who burned "witches," we discover a pornographic picture of women: the witch is imagined to have the power to incite desire and cause impotence. But we also find in the mind of the witch-burner a fantasy of ritual practice, and an idea of a religion which worships nature and gives to the material world a spiritual meaning. We find this eros which the church has lost.

Thus the witch both steals eros and threatens us with it. And where does she get the power of eros? Every doctrine tells us that she conceives her power when she fornicates with the devil. And who is the devil? He may be the King of Death. But he is also the Prince of Nature. And we know he invades natural forms.

It is in the witch-burner's version of the witch's sacred ritual that we see most clearly the content of the church's nightmare.* For here is a vision of nature degraded, nature severed from spirit, with even the very stuff and substance of the body used as an agent of humiliation.

This doctrinal nightmare begins with a flight. It is a flight which brings the witches to their sacred meeting. But flight, we learn from Jones (who takes this from Freud), is an unconscious symbol of erotic excitation. And so, in the witch-burner's mind, eros brings the witches to the sacred. But what is the witch's ritual? The witch-burners imagine that at the sabbat the witches kiss the devil's face, his navel, his penis, and his anus. And this "devil" whom the witch-burners saw the witches kissing was often a dog, or a goat, or assumed the shape of some other animal (or when he looked like a man, he dressed in black). The water the devil used to anoint his worshipers, the witch-burners imagined was urine; and they said he lit the candles of holiness with a fart. Of course, the worshipers eat a very large banquet. For they indulge in all the sensual pleasures. And they express, too, in their imaginary existence, all the witch-burners' revulsion and fear of the physical world. The banqueters are thus foul and unclean and give off a stench. And as we might imagine, these devilish nightmare figures who peopled the minds of the pious church fathers celebrated a mass. But how like a pornographic drama was this mass! For the altar is a woman's body. And upon the buttocks of this altar, a mass of feces, urine, and menstrual blood was kneaded by the devil. And then, of course, as is inevitable in the obscene plot, this imagined ritual ends when the devil fornicates with all who attend the sabbat.

Here, then, we have come full circle. In this pious nightmare, we have found a clear definition of pornography and the pornographic sensibility. For above all, pornography is ritual. It is an enacted drama which is laden with meaning, which imparts a vision of the world. The altar for the ritual is a woman's body. And the ritual which is carried out on this altar is the desecration of flesh. Here, what is sacred within the body is degraded.

And we should not, if we are to find in the imagined ritual a definition of pornography, forget what ensues upon this nightmare. For after

---

* See H. R. Hays, *The Dangerous Sex* (New York, 1972), pp. 138–48; H. R. Trevor-Roper, *The European Witch-Craze* (New York, 1969); Jules Michelet, *Satanism and Witchcraft* (New York, 1939); Rossell Hope Robbins, *The Encyclopedia of Witchcraft and Demonology* (New York, 1959).

the witch-burners desecrated flesh in their minds, they tortured flesh in reality. Were there two million or nine million witches burned? Whatever the number, we must imagine a conflagration, a mass terror, the constant odor of burning flesh, whole villages massacred, children whipped or thrown on the flames with their mothers. And these deaths were only the climax of a series of events. For the witches were arrested first, and then put on trial, they were bound up and tortured and told to give evidence against themselves. They were made to utter the hallucinations of their persecutors and made to repeat the pornography of their accusers as if this vision were their own. And before these confessions were wrought out of them, they were hung upside down, beaten with whips and mallets, their fingernails were pulled out, they were put on a rack which violently stretched the body, a *tortillon* squeezed the "tender parts," a pulley jerked the body violently in midair, a leg screw squeezed the calf and broke the shinbone in pieces. They were put on beds of nails, they were grilled, fingers and toes were crushed, needles driven into the quick of nails, and they were deprived of sleep, they were not allowed to dream, to rest. But we know these instruments of torture: the whip, the pulley, the various screws, the leather devices necessary to carry out such a regime. They are a part of sadomasochistic ritual. They have all been described to us over and over in the pages of pornography.

And we know, too, from our understanding of pornography, that culture does not stop at images which degrade nature. We know that culture must move from these images and begin to actually torture nature. For this culture, as we know it, seeks revenge from a criminal that will not be still. A criminal which lives in the body, and rises up from the body, and which possesses a dangerous knowledge. It is this knowledge which Franz Marc could not let live within himself, this knowledge which society condemned in the soul of Kate Chopin, this knowledge which pornography would silence: the knowledge of eros.

♡

Let me never utter
words less than heart beat
H.D.

Heart, we read in the book of symbols, a presence at the center. As in *Unto whom all hearts are open*. The heart in the body defined as the vital function, the seat of life. *Man with the head,* the place of lifeblood, *woman with the heart*. The heart as the essence, the heart of the matter, of winter, of the artichoke, of all things. And the inner being (the sage has even orifices in her heart, all open). My heart was not in it, she said. The soul described as the eye of the heart or the heart's vision. Heart, the place between head and sex, partaking of both. Heart knowledge. The authority of the heart. And the place of joining. Defined as the center, the seed, the flowering place. She took heart, we say, she was lionhearted, brave. And we say *Nature's mighty heart.* Heartbeat. Pit-a-pat, as in Dear heart, Sweetheart. She is all heart, we say, I poured out my heart to her; he lost his heart. The place of longing. (Where the heart is in flames, we read, we find great ardor.) As in the inflamed heart of Venus. The burning heart, we say, to be loved, to be filled with light, to love, to illumine. As in her tears pierced my heart, or my heart, the place of compassion, we say, went out to her. Or my wild heart. *Wild nights,* she said. As in the secrets of the heart. (In my heart, I know, she said) and the heart's language.

THE DEATH OF THE HEART: FROM FANTASY TO EVENT

> All great simple images reveal a psychic state.
> GASTON BACHELARD

We know the heart to be the center. The place where body and soul meet, where reason gives way to passion. And the trembling of desire we feel in our bodies, which comes from the heart, is also the spirit's trembling. In this trembling, the body expresses the soul, and perhaps it is this trembling that tells us the body is captured and ruled by the spirit's longing.

But where is this heart in the pornographer's vision of ourselves? The heart is here, but she is held captive. We find this shape of the red valentine, for instance, depicted on the cover of a pornographic magazine for February, the month of Valentine's Day. Before a glistening red background, a woman in a glossy photograph kneels before us. She wears red glasses in the shape of hearts. And she is in chains. But this is the task of pornography—to chain and imprison the heart, to silence feeling.

Two tales come down to us from a long history of a civilization and they both tell the story of a civilization's sacrifice of innocence and vulnerability in the body of a young woman. Yet one, Euripides' *Iphigenia,* is a great tragedy; the other, *Justine,* is pornography. What separates the two is feeling.

To watch Agamemnon send his daughter to death is almost unbearable. We are outraged. We hope. With Clytemnestra, we pray and plead for her life. And when she dies we weep, as if one we loved, or a part of ourselves, were lost. But one never weeps as a witness to pornography. No death in pornography touches us with sorrow. Justine's suffering fails to move us. We cannot imagine loving Justine, and we let her die with no protest, because as we enter the mind of the Marquis de Sade, our own hearts are silenced.

All death in pornography is really only the death of the heart. Over and over again, that part of our beings which can feel both in body and mind is ritually murdered. We make a mistake, therefore, when we believe that pornography is simply fantasy, simply a record of sadistic events. For pornography exceeds the boundaries of both fantasy and record and becomes itself an act. Pornography *is* sadism.

This sadism has many forms. A woman who enters a neighborhood where pornographic images of the female body are displayed, for instance, is immediately shamed. Once entering the arena of pornography, she herself becomes a pornographic image. It is *her* body that is displayed. And if she is interested in pornography, this interest becomes the subject of pornographic speculation. If she is shocked and turns away from the pornographic image in disgust, she becomes the pornographic "victim." She cannot escape pornography without humiliation. And we know humiliation to be the essence of sadism. It is thus that pornography exists as an act of sadism toward all women.

But now let us add to this that there is nowhere in culture where a woman can evade pornography. She cannot have come to age without seeing at least one of these images. And, we know, when images enter the mind, they remain there forever as memory.

Yet pornography (which appears to know its own cruelty to women) is also cruel to the souls of men. In the pornographic mind, women represent a denied part of the self; in this mind a woman is a symbol for a man's hidden vulnerability. Here disguised in a woman's body are his own feelings, and his own heart. When Agamemnon sacrifices his daughter, he also gives up his own tenderness. And as part of this choice, he takes on the armor of a warrior. But when we witness Agamemnon's choice, we regret it. In *Justine,* when feeling is slaughtered, it is slaughtered twice. Once in the ritual portrayed to us. And a second time within us. For this second sacrifice of feeling is accomplished through language and imagery which horrifies, disgusts, and finally numbs us.

Now one learns why it is that pornography is so often ugly. One of its functions, one of its reasons for being, is to offend sensibility. We find the ugliness of obscenity in a magazine such as *Hustler,* for instance, in which the publisher writes of the need to "dig . . . turds" out of another man's "rectum." (Without making a conscious connection between cruelty and ugliness, we understand that these two qualities belong together.) In the same magazine, a cartoon appears which depicts a man about to be executed. We accept the crude caricature of his features, his body, the way he is made repulsive to us. We know without knowing why that this style is appropriate to the message of the cartoon. The man stares at two electric chairs, one of which reads "Regular," and the other, "Extra Crispy." This is the language of the sadist; ugliness is his style. We are shocked, but shocked away from feeling. For while beauty evokes feeling, ugliness numbs us. The pornographer's art is meant to dull our feelings, and his own.

Even where the language or style of pornography takes on the skill and superficial grace of great art, even where it *is* artful, it never partakes of that quality of beauty which makes us *feel*. Thus de Sade's language is elegant and skillful, but through another means, it creates the same effect on us as ugliness. In *Justine*, a Monsieur Rodin, who has been the headmaster of a school for children, decides to put his daughter to death for "the progress of science." But unlike the evocative language of Euripides' tragedy, this language works to deaden any response we might have to this sacrifice. Thus her father speaks to us of the death of his daughter:

> Anatomy will never reach its ultimate state of perfection until an examination has been performed upon the vaginal canal of a fourteen- or fifteen-year-old child who has expired from a cruel death; it is only from the contingent contraction we can obtain a complete analysis of a so highly interesting part.

In her essay on pornographic literature, Susan Sontag writes that this flatness of tone we discover in obscene writing is not an "index of principled inhumanity." And yet de Sade, through a self-portrait of the artist as sadist, which he draws in the words of his character Rodin, tells us exactly the opposite. Defending the murder of his daughter for the progress of science, Rodin argues: "when Michaelangelo wished to render a Christ after Nature, did he make the crucifixion of a young man the occasion for a fit of remorse? Why, no: he copied the boy in his death agonies. But where it is a question of the advance of our art, how absolutely essential such means become!" In *The Story of O,* another "artful" example of pornography, where we find the same flatness of language, we discover the same attitude toward feeling. When a character named Jacqueline is horrified and upset by the scars the heroine has received from her floggings, O first ridicules her, and then vows to punish her. And this logical argument against compassion, this ridicule, and this threat are equally intended for the reader. For when one reads pornography, one enters into a sadomasochistic relationship with an author in which one is punished, humiliated, and terrified through language.

In the sadomasochistic ritual, the sadist must appear to have no feeling. Projecting his feeling onto his victim, he tries simultaneously to elicit and destroy feeling. In his mind, he is both actor and acted upon, writer and reader. Wilhelm Stekel, in his massive study of sado-masochism, writes:

> The sadist pictures to himself what is happening in the mind of his object, whose resistance he calls forth and breaks. Only this feeling of himself into the affective life of the object brings him the expected pleasure. But this object is merely a reflection of his different psychic and sexual components, and the scene represents a play with himself.

Thus fantasy lies at the very heart of any sadistic event. And at the center of pornographic fantasy lies a real event. The reader plays the denied self of the pornographic writer and the writer plays out the denied self of the reader, and for both, feeling is destroyed.

In *The Past Recaptured,* a work which is not pornography, but is instead a profound portrait of the sadomasochistic dilemma, Marcel Proust describes sadism as it is performed within a male whorehouse. His hero, M. de Charlus, has paid to be beaten and humiliated, but he is dissatisfied with his treatment. The young man who whips him appears to be insincere when he tells him, "No, you worthless trash . . . since you bawl and crawl on your knees, we're going to chain you to the bed. No pity!" As the young male prostitutes stand in the reception room of the brothel, in an effort to appear sadistic they impersonate "Belleville toughs." They must give the impression to their clients that any of them would "do it with his own sister for twenty francs." As part of their performance, they speak of brutal sexual exploits, boast of murder and theft, brag about life as soldiers in the trenches ("some days a hand grenade goes right through you"). Above all, the aesthetic which they must create for their patrons is one of hardness, unfeelingness, invulnerability. (And M. de Charlus is disappointed again when he hears the young man speak of his parents as "dear old mother and father.")

The house of prostitution is in itself an illustration of pornography's transformation into reality. For the whorehouse is simply an obscene illusion acted out in space and time; it is four-dimensional pornography. Here the "client" (as does the patron or the reader of pornography) asks to be brutalized. He complains at the presence of sentiment or softness. He wishes his sexual partner to act out coldness and harshness. And in this one can sense the shadow of a whole culture. Outside explicit pornography, culture has created "hard" heroes, in the writer, the actor, the public persona. We expect Norman Mailer to shock and offend our sensibilities. We celebrate Charles Bukowski for what we label crudeness. We seek the imperviousness of Brando. And all this "toughness" is part of an aesthetic which we believe to be sexually exciting.

Of the flatness of language and the absence of emotion in pornography, Sontag writes that the "arousal of a sexual response in the reader *requires* it." Yet now we must begin to question this conventional idea of sexuality. For perhaps, like the statement of the sadomasochistic patient—made over and over in clinical studies—that he *seeks* feeling, this may be one of those unconsidered thoughts we accept as canon whose real truth is revealed to us when they are reversed. Let us remember, for instance, that it is extremely difficult, perhaps next to impossible, to experience any sensation without an emotion. Memory attaches itself to smell, to touch, to color. As Stendhal tells us: "Each time the soul is moved by two affections at the same time, then, in the future, every time it feels one of them again, it feels the other also." A therapist who attempts to heal the mind through the body uses this knowledge. The body holds memories of feelings from the past. To be touched, to move, to breathe, all these experiences of the body bring intense feelings to consciousness. A woman is touched on a certain place on her back, and she remembers an old grief from her childhood she had forgotten. After moving and breathing, sinking deeper in the knowledge of his body, a man begins to weep and scream as he relives an incident from his youth. In his analytical work, Wilhelm Reich found that the emotional amnesias, called "blocks," and muscular tensions were in fact, to use his language, "functionally identical." Freud's first patients were "hysterically paralyzed." Their bodies were literally paralyzed with unexpressed emotions. Thus paralysis in the body was a metaphor for an emotional paralysis.

Nothing brings the soul to feel so much as physical sensation, for emotions live in the body; we know a whole physical language of emotion. The body cries tears in sorrow, convulses with laughter in mirth, becomes flushed and hot in anger. The pornographer argues to us that pornography gives him back his sexual feeling. But the truth is more complex. In truth, what has made a man impotent *are* his feelings, because *he is afraid to have them*. He would avoid knowledge of himself. And in the language of the body, this fear and denial of a part of himself is expressed as impotence. For he is literally afraid to experience sensation, especially sexual sensation, which is an intense physical feeling, and therefore an intense emotional feeling. This is the real history of his impotence.

If "the arousal of sexual response" requires the deadening of feeling, this fact does not belong to the nature of sexuality. It is the nature of sexuality to arouse feeling, and of feeling to arouse sexuality. Rather, "the arousal of sexual response" requires the deadening of feeling in a man who is already impotent, and who has already chosen to "forget" his emotions. This man might instead have chosen to remember. He might have sought to be healed by memory. (Or his culture might have offered him this choice in its very idea of sexuality.) But instead, driven by his own ambivalence, wanting and not wanting his feeling back, his own body still expressing the desire for eros, he solves his dilemma through brutality. He is brutal to all that might be emotionally sensitive in himself. He destroys the emotional part of himself, in himself or in a projected image of himself. For he is terrified of what he denies.

In one who is afraid of feeling, or of the memory of certain emotions, sexuality in itself constitutes a terrible threat. The body forces the mind back toward feeling. And even when the mind wills the body to be silent, the body rebels and plagues the mind with "urgency." And the body, seeking to be open, to be vulnerable, seeking emotional knowledge, is threatened, punished, and humiliated by the pornographic mind. All these acts are intended to deaden the heart. To make the heart retreat long enough so that the body, which perhaps has reached a fever pitch, can "release" sensation. And yet we must not be too quick to believe that this "urgency," and this "release," this fever pitch, this demandingness, belong to the body alone. For the separation between body and mind is unnatural. The body speaks the language of the soul. In the body's fevered longing is perhaps a deep desire for that part of the self which has been sacrificed, a desire for that self to come to consciousness, to be remembered. For an experience of the heart is also an experience of the mind. The body and heart cry out like a long neglected child, pleading, "Pay attention to me." But the pornographic mind, hoping for silence from the heart, responds with punishment. And now, if the body is "relieved," it is because at least the mind has given some sign that it is aware of the body's existence. Like the neglected child, the body is glad even for this destructive gesture from the mind.

But the real intent of sadomasochism and of sadomasochistic pornography is to sever the connection between mind and body. And it is precisely because this severance is unnatural that it must be violent and terrifying. Because the body, in its desire to become a part of consciousness, is persistent. Like any living thing, it would survive, and survive in consciousness also. Just as the sadomasochist tells us he seeks feeling, when indeed he is afraid of feeling, so also the pornographer, who says he would bring sexuality into consciousness, and who says that he desires the freedom to speak of sexuality, in fact wishes to suppress and silence sexual knowledge. This is the message of the brutality of pornography: the pornographer is a censor.

Liberty and Liberation

Pornography is filled with heroes who are seeking liberty. But the meanings of the words "liberty" are not simple. Within the range of meanings this word has, one discovers two definitions completely opposed to one another. The first reference to liberty listed in the *Oxford*

English Dictionary speaks of an "exemption or release from captivity, bondage or slavery." But from this definition the word "liberty" evolves into an entirely different concept. It soon becomes "the faculty or power to do as one likes," and then freedom from the control of "fate or necessity," then "leave, permission," then "an unrestrained use of or access to," then "license," and then "to take liberties or be unduly familiar" (as, for example, when "the poor man had taken liberty with a wench"), and then the word "liberty" comes to mean a privilege granted by a sovereign, and then it means privilege over one's domain,* and finally, "at one's power or disposal." And giving us an example of this usage of the word "liberty," the dictionary quotes: "I nowe had her at my liberte I sholde make her to deye a cruell deth."

In the pornographic mind, "liberty" moves through all of those meanings. The pornographer begins by telling himself that he wishes liberation. To himself and to the world, he poses as a man who would simply liberate his sexuality from an imprisoning morality. And yet it is his own mind which holds him captive. And this is a mind which would have a power over nature which exists only in fantasy. The pornographer wants the power to "do as he likes." But in order to have freedom from natural limitation, the pornographer must obtain privileges which do not exist in nature; this mind must be given power by the authority of culture, which it holds sovereign. And now, by the right of this power, the pornographic mind conceives of nature as part of its domain and makes nature at its power and disposal.

But in the pornographic mind, woman *is* nature. She represents natural fate. And so, in the name of freedom, the pornographer imagines he must control her. And to control her he must take away her liberty. He must imprison her. He may even take the "liberty" of murdering her. But above all, this man, who pleads to us that he only wishes for "freedom of speech," must silence "woman."

Pornography expresses an almost morbid fear of female speech. A pornographic magazine publishes this poem next to an illustration of a pornographic "device" in which to encase a woman:

> It sculptures her breasts and it narrows her waist
> And it shows off her gorgeous behind

---

* And here we might remember that in the sixteenth, seventeenth, and eighteenth centuries, a white man's "domain" included his wife, his children, and his property.

> And the helmet which over her head has been placed
> Keeps her deafened and silent and blind

An advertisement in another magazine promises a doll as the "bed-partner that doesn't talk back—just obeys." Even the sexual act, in pornography, seems to exist less for pleasure than to overpower and silence women. Hands, feet, penises, are thrust like weapons into women's mouths. Orgasm itself becomes a retaliation against a woman's words. From a novel by Henry Miller, for example, we read this scene:

> "Shut up, you bitch," I said. "It hurts, doesn't it? You wanted it, didn't you?" I held her tightly, raised myself a little higher to get it in to the hilt, and pushed myself until I thought her womb would give way. Then I came—right into that snail-like mouth which was wide open.

And to this list of pornographic fantasies we add a series of still photographs which appear in a pamphlet published in Amsterdam. Here a woman is strapped to a table. She is naked. And a man in the uniform of a doctor stands at her side. He places a tube in her rectum, and a tube with a funnel in her mouth. But we have seen these postures before. We recognize them as history, as actual events. In the nineteenth century, women in the female suffrage movement were strapped down to tables with tubes thrust into their mouths. And this force-feeding took place as a retaliation and punishment against the political movement for a woman's freedom of speech and equal social power.

Inside and outside explicit pornography, a woman's expression of her will to freedom is met with violence or a threat of violence. In 1850, an editorial in the *Saturday Review* argues against female suffrage, that as a means to recover "the lost rights of man," men should resort to the "argument of the black eye." And this recommendation is enacted in the pornographic novel. In *The Skin Flick Rapist*, for example, as she is being raped, a woman begins to protest. ". . . you men," she says, "aren't really concerned about women. You're only concerned about what you can drag out of their bodies. You're not concerned about them as total entities, as human beings." The hero responds by taping her mouth. And then he beats her.

But we can find a deeper shade of the meaning of the pornographic silencing of women in this scene. Just as she is protesting against his treatment of her, and pleading for her own beingness, the heroine accuses the hero of being a "mama's boy" who is "weak-kneed" and "gutless." When the pornographer creates a female character, he creates a "doll" through whom he himself speaks, and thus we know it is his *own* fear that he is weak, that he is tied to his mother. Nature terrifies him. Therefore, when a woman declares to him that she is human, her very beingness evokes his fear. Thus, when a woman asks to be treated as a human being, as an equal, he imagines that she is calling him "weak." And when she protests that he doesn't care about her feelings, he imagines she wants to reduce him to the powerlessness he felt as a child with his mother.

Throughout Western literature one finds a tradition of male struggles against the female attempt to weaken men. This is the story of Ulysses and the Sirens; it is the story of Samson and Delilah; of John the Baptist and Salome. In each of these legends, men are not only weakened— their very lives are endangered. In this mythos, not only is male freedom based on female silence, but a man's *life* depends on the death of a woman.

That male freedom and vitality require the death of women is a major but hidden theme of the modern novel. We find it in *Crime and Punishment,* in *Native Son,* in *An American Tragedy,* in *An American Dream,* and countless other works. In *An American Tragedy,* as the hero, Clyde Griffiths, watches his lover drown, he calls out to himself: "You desire to *live!* And her living will make your own life not worthwhile from now on!" And Norman Mailer expresses this theme when he writes, in *An American Dream:* "Deborah had gotten her hooks into me . . . living with her I was murderous; attempting to separate, suicide came into me." As he murders her, he describes himself to us as a victim who acts only in self-defense: "It was as if killing her, the act had been too gentle, I had not plumbed the hatred where the real injustice was stored. She had spit on the future, my Deborah, she had spoiled my chance, and now her body was here." His hands on his wife's throat, moments before her death, he glimpses the promise of heaven beyond her existence, "some quiver of jewelled cities shining in the glow of a tropical dusk."

Mailer's novel *An American Dream* is virtually a reversal of Dreiser's

An American Tragedy. In Dreiser's book, because the hero wishes to marry the daughter of a rich man and rise in society, he feels entrapped by his promise of marriage to a woman in his own social class. While in Mailer's book, his hero is married to the daughter of a rich man, and feels himself to be under her power. After he murders his wife, he becomes the lover of a woman in the lower classes. Dreiser's novel comments on and grieves for the corruption of Clyde Griffiths' soul. And the hero's intention to murder his lover inevitably causes his own death. But in Mailer's work, the murder of a woman bears no consequences. His hero escapes punishment victoriously. We are left with the impression that he committed a *just* murder.

In the pages of pornography, one finds a mechanism of the mind, through which the victim becomes the murderer. The Marquis de Sade even describes this mechanism for us through the plot of his novel *Justine*. Over and over again, Justine, who is the victim of every kind of crime, is accused by her persecutors of having committed *their* crimes. In each instance, their word is believed over hers and she is found guilty, imprisoned, and prepared to be executed. Justine even takes the identity of the criminal into herself, for by these accusations she feels herself to have been "dreadfully humiliated."*

Yet when we remember that the "woman" in pornography is simply the pornographer's dark self projected onto a female character, Justine's dreadful humiliation takes on a symbolic meaning. For it is the female aspect of the self who is punished in pornography—punished and then blamed for her own punishment. The pornographer's fear of his own sexual feelings is written implicitly into every scene in which a man binds and silences a woman. When the pornographer murders a woman, part of himself dies. That place in his body dies where gentleness sings, where the child's fear hides, where the heart lives. And as he is committing this ritual murder, the pornographic hero turns on his victim and blames her for this death. He calls her frigid. He claims she has rejected him. She has driven him to this

---

* We find the same reversal of moral order and of shame in rape (that event which is surely pornography enacted). The woman who is raped is often accused of perjury in a courtroom. Her word is not believed. Moreover, part of the defense of a man accused of rape has been to accuse a woman of being a "whore," of being licentious or amoral. Even a woman who has been raped but who has not gone through a rape trial feels ashamed of what has happened to her, as if this violence against her revealed something of her own nature.

act. In the same way, as the pornographer himself ritually murders his own feeling by doing violence to the *image* of a woman, he turns on the woman who is horrified by this violence and he calls her a prude. He cries out that she threatens his liberty. That it is she who would silence his sexual feelings, and who would enslave him. For he is a man at odds with himself, who cannot recognize the prudery he fears as his own prudery, who does not see that he is his own master, nor that he is his own slave.

Catharsis

Yet the pornographer denies that pornography deadens feeling. He argues to us that pornography actually prevents violence against the bodies of women because it has a cathartic effect. He even shows us data that "prove" this. For example, he says the legalization and there-fore the surfacing of pornography in Denmark actually reduced the rate of sexual crimes. But on a closer look, one finds this research not as conclusive as was supposed. For the Danish method of recording sexual crime changed at the same time the study was done, and there-fore the actual increase in rape was hidden. And alongside his data, another study can be produced which shows that in a county in Austra-lia where pornography was introduced, sexual crimes increased signifi-cantly. But let us momentarily leave off this statistical debate and descend to another level of the mind.

What is the subtext of this speech the pornographer gives us? Under-neath his "reasoning," what are his reasons? *Catharsis.* Catharsis, he implies in a grim voice, saves us. Were it not for his fantasies, there would be more rape, more mutilation, more random sadistic attacks on the bodies of women. The very argument conceals a threat which is in itself sadistic. We must have our photographs of men beating women; we must have our stories of the rape of little girls; a papier-mâché chorus of imaginary men is made to choir, or else beware the apocalypse.

If there is a cruelty in the threat implicit to this argument which mirrors pornography, we should not be surprised; for in every way, the defense of pornography mirrors pornography. In the pornographic drama, the hero experiences a fictional catharsis, much like that his reader is supposed to feel: relieved after he has beaten his victim, renewed after he has raped, unburdened after he has murdered.

The pornographic hero pictures himself as bridled by an uncontrollable lust for sexual violence. He imagines he is the victim of a feeling which he can conquer only by acting it out. In Mailer's *An American Dream* (in many ways an artistic realization of the pornographic novel), the hero cries out release as he murders his wife:

> . . . and *crack,* I choked her harder, and *crack* I choked her again and *crack* I gave her payment—never halt now—and *crack* the door flew open and the wire tore in her throat, and I was through the door, hatred passing from me in wave after wave, illness as well, rot and pestilence, nausea, a bleak string of salts. I was floating.

Now, at the death of his wife, Mailer's hero tells us he is "as far into" himself as he has ever been; new possibility appears to him, "universes wheeled in a dream," and when he opens his eyes he is weary, "a most honorable fatigue," he says, "and my flesh seemed new."

What a strange argument the pornographer gives us. He claims his fantasy will release the mind from an obsession with violence. And yet his fantasies promise that only violence will give the mind release. We are accustomed to hearing this argument, an argument which on the surface makes no sense, because it exists inside a mythology we have come to mistake for truth. This is the mythos which has as its act of revelation and its essential ritual the murder of a woman by a man, and which rests on the belief that men are inherently and by nature violent.

For why else, except that men have some intrinsic need for violence, would a violent catharsis be necessary? The pornographer's argument for catharsis rests upon a philosophy which describes the male human being as filled with an innate rage which must from time to time be alleviated. We are familiar with the philosophy, for example, of Lionel Tiger, who despite his "scientific" approach, appears almost to be answering a religious question when he tells us that the equivalent of childbirth for the male perhaps includes "the violent mastery and restriction of others." But Tiger's thinking is part of the tradition of scientific and philosophical thought.

What the pornographer's argument for catharsis conceals above all is his secret worship of the image of himself as violent, and his desire for some redemption, some entrance into a mystery within himself, through violence. The pornographer himself argues the opposite. He claims that his animal nature, his own body, desires violent acts. But indeed, the quality of violence in pornography is that of violence in service of an image. For these acts of violence are not pure. They do not have the aura of blood lust, of one animal springing out of hunger to devour another. Rather, they are conceptual murders. One hears the rapist speak throughout his rape of his revenge against all the women who have rejected him. The boy beating his cousin boasts to her that now she will not see him as weak, as a victim. Every murderous gesture, every infliction of pain, is accompanied by a humiliation of the one who is murdered, and at the same time, an aggrandizement of the image of the murderer. Mailer's hero tastes a victory, not only of the body, but of the mind.

The nineteenth century was obsessed by the idea that man is competitive and violent. Darwin, Spencer, and before them Hobbes, and also Adam Smith and Marx and Engels, believed that the laws of nature and society and history are laws of struggle, which determine that violence is inevitable.*

Wilhelm Stekel, writing of sadomasochism, insisted that hatred is a more important human impulse than love. He argued that culture represses the instinct for hatred, and therefore exaggerates it. Freud, too, in his later years, decided that an instinct for death exists, and that this instinct makes human behavior destructive. And finally, later, Konrad Lorenz added to the pessimism regarding basic human nature by defining human nature as aggressive and cruel.

The thought of all these men implies that indeed culture is basically a hypocritical and dishonest attempt to make a pragmatic peace among beings whose basic natures are rapacious and hateful. Yet what they fail to recognize is that they themselves are the makers of culture, producing, in the name of scientific knowledge, culture's pronouncement on the nature of human instinct. Moreover, they do not see that in making such a pessimistic pronouncement, they are not at odds with their culture, but are indeed rather expressing its most fundamental reasoning. For it is the bias of our culture to find human instinct

---

* As Ruth Hubbard has pointed out in her essay "Have Only Men Evolved?" science describes only "masculine behavior" as such.

evil. In our civilization, humankind is described as "fallen," and flesh is described as the province of the devil.

As Ruth Hubbard has written of Darwin's thought: "There is no such thing as objective, value-free science. An era's science is part of its politics, economics and sociology: it is generated by them and in turn helps to generate them." In short, science is not fact: it is culture; and so science's definition of instinct can perhaps tell us more about culture's will and belief than about the natural limits of our behavior, more about our minds than about nature.

And indeed, a large body of scientific data exists to disprove the ideas of Freud and Lorenz and Stekel and Hobbes and Spencer regarding human nature. In his massive study of both instinct and our culture's biased view of nature, *The Anatomy of Human Destructiveness*, Erich Fromm writes: "The anthropological data have demonstrated that the instinctivistic interpretation of human destructiveness is not tenable. While we find in all cultures that men defend themselves . . . destructiveness and cruelty are so minimal in so many that these great differences could not be explained if we were dealing with an 'innate passion.' "

Regarding Lorenz's hypothesis, Fromm points out that primates show "little destructiveness" and that all other mammals, whether or not they are predatory, "fail to exhibit aggressive behavior" such as might prove Lorenz's theory.

Yet Freud's assumptions are accepted generally and the work of Lorenz and of his inheritor, Lionel Tiger, remains popular; these ideas have a place in the imagination; they seize the civilized mind, because this mind, which has been fashioned of this culture, wants to believe in the violent nature of the body. But when we remember that in the psyche which has been shaped by pornographic culture, a woman's body symbolizes nature and the feelings of the body, and her death means the death of those feelings, we discover that this pornographic victory is a victory of the mind over the body. For here, in this murder of a woman, and in every murder in pornography, feeling is sacrificed to an image of the self as invulnerable.

This may perhaps let us understand more deeply the hysterical nature of the pornographer's arguments. For he contradicts himself at every turning. The very definition of his expression is "that which moves his audience to sexual arousal." He poses images of the body before us to make us want, to cause us to desire. But in regard to those images of violence to the body which he also shapes, he denies the intent to arouse desire. These images, he argues, do not make us want violence; but instead, he claims, they make us want violence less.

To untangle what he is telling us about his own nature, we must turn his words around, and reverse them again. For in the normal human physiology the feeling of fear acts to prevent feeling, especially desire.* A trauma, some buried terror in the psyche, can sometimes so diminish feeling that a woman or a man can actually become paralyzed.

Here, once again, as we enter the territory of the pornographer's defense of himself, we see this mind take the same shape we discover in pornography itself: a profound ambivalence toward the body and the feelings of the body. Despite this ambivalence, the body continues to desire, wants to touch, desires to feel, to hold, to enter and be entered. Yet the pornographer fears the power of nature; he cannot decide to admit his own feelings into his knowledge of himself. Therefore he is caught. And like a trapped animal, trapped by his own body, he becomes violent. He punishes that which he imagines holds him and entraps him: he punishes the female body.

This is precisely what Mailer's hero tells us as he murders his wife. He has imagined himself to be trapped by her, by his own longing for her. That is why he must kill her. This is a familiar refrain in pornography. The hero feels himself trapped by his own desire. Thus he makes a doll as revenge against the women who rejected him. Or he kidnaps a woman and keeps her in bondage. Or he murders. Or he rapes and mutilates.

But the pornographer asks us to believe that this pornographic hero, who frees himself from desire through a violent act to a woman's body, will not be imitated. The pornographer argues that this ritual murder, this ritual rape, frees the reader of pornography from the need to author violence. Thus, perhaps we are to believe that if, for instance, Lawrence Singleton had read certain pornographic novels before Sep-

---

* Wilhelm Reich, among many others after him, has recorded this correlation. The fear of orgasm, which can cause impotence or frigidity, is often a fear of death.

tember 29, 1978, he would not have had to rape Mary Vincent, or cut off her hands (as he did) after he raped her.

And yet let us look for a moment at the mind of Lawrence Singleton. For in his mind was a distortion which was not authored by his body. He believed fervently, and offered as his own defense, that it was he who was kidnapped, "who was threatened, who begged to go free," whose life was in danger, and that his persecutor was the young woman whose body he mutilated. Like the pornographer, he felt himself to be trapped by a woman's body. Whether or not he ever read pornography, his mind clearly reflects and was shaped by a pornographic culture. When the pornographer argues that fantasy might free Lawrence Singleton from his need to enact violence, he is arguing essentially that by belief in delusion, a belief in delusion is healed.

For in the pornographer's argument for pornography as catharsis, he has confused what would heal with the symptoms of the disease itself. If we see sexual violence as part of an illness of the mind, then we must understand that pornographic fantasy is itself another manifestation of that illness and is, in fact, part of its genesis. For the violent act follows from the delusion and is generated by it. The mind projects itself on another; the mind imagines aggression from another; imagines danger; the mind makes others into dolls which speak out its own torments; the mind imagines itself imprisoned. And it is in this world of delusion, a pornographic world created by the mind, that violent sexual acts take place.

Indeed, pornography exists in the service of an obsession, lends language and image to the construction of a fantasy world, weaves a sensual imitation of a nightmare which the mind chooses over reality. "Obsession is, of course, one of the prime motivations for characters in erotic fiction," Michael Perkins writes, in a book written in defense of the literature. And de Sade himself tells us that the men who live out sadistic fantasies are like addicts, who must always have more, for whom the fulfillment of desire, on any level, only excites more desire.

What the pornographer calls catharsis is not at all a catharsis. Rather, it is an attempt to defend a belief in illusion. The pornographer's argument is really his illness arguing for its own continued existence. This defense is what a healer of the mind might call *resistance*. The mind at war with itself wants to be healed, but still clings to the old damaged way of being. And underneath resistance one always finds a reversal of the truth, another story, a hidden feeling, or a hidden experience. Resistance *is* the attempt to deny knowledge of the self. But this is why a real catharsis heals us. For a real catharsis takes place beyond resistance, and can only be experienced past resistance. It is that state of mind where illusion and defense have broken, and true feeling lives again.

A patient of Freud has fits of choking. Another has a morbid fear of snakes and her arms suffer a paralysis which is not of the body. Another woman suffers attacks of dizziness and fears heights. A man has a morbid fear of wolves. A young woman will not eat or drink. What makes each of them well is her or his own memory, and inside that memory, the experience of *feeling*. The death of a friend who was never mourned is now lamented; a father who died and was hated is now hated openly; a daughter remembers her mother forcing her to eat food two hours old. Feelings which could not be owned, recognized, or named are now lived through in consciousness, confronted, accepted, and thus they cease to distort body and mind.

The mere experience of choking or dizziness or fear or paralysis did not heal illness. These symptoms by themselves were only part of an illness. As symbols, they contained a meaning which might heal. But as symptoms they worked to hide knowledge. In each case, the meanings of these symptoms and the feelings they contained had to be acknowledged, and owned and experienced. For such knowledge is what heals the mind.

The pornographer argues that pornography pulls back the veil drawn over violent impulses and by revealing these impulses, heals in the same way. But what the pornographer does not see, because he himself speaks for the illness, is that pornography *is* the veil, *is* the false paralysis, *is* the obsession with a delusion. And *part* of this delusion is the belief that man is a violent creature who must purge himself of his violence by acting violently, or by imagining violence. This delusion serves the deluded by arguing (to whatever in him may abhor violence) that his fantasy of violence actually heals him. And moreover, through this delusionary image of himself as intrinsically "violent," he continues to imagine himself as invulnerable and powerful. Arguing that he is "overwhelmed" by desire to be violent, he escapes the fact that he is indeed "overwhelmed" by other feelings: by fear, or by desire.

In this sense, we can render the false meaning of catharsis which occurs in pornography with a different meaning than the catharsis we associate with Aristotle's definition of tragedy. For in tragedy, we weep, grieve, and feel pity. We are brought to *feeling*, we experience both meaning and sensation at the same time, tremble in our bodies and our souls. Thus we weep over the death of Iphigenia, of Tristan and Iseult, of Madame Bovary. In experiencing these feelings, we have tapped a part of ourselves which had perhaps been quiet for some time. Which indeed, in this stillness, we were not certain was even there. Or had even forgotten. And thus, when we weep at this tragic playing out before our eyes of a drama which touches our hearts, a part of ourselves we had left in shadow comes back to us and is named and is lived. But pornographic catharsis moves from altogether different needs. For, we know, one does not weep over the death of Justine. One does not feel at all. Rather, one experiences only *sensation*, and mastery. If there is a vulnerable part of oneself that would weep, this vulnerability is projected onto the body of a woman who is punished, and is destroyed there. And so we cease, in this projection, to recognize this vulnerability as a part of ourselves. We *believe* we are punishing a woman. And rather than reclaim a feeling, or own a part of ourselves once more, we disown ourselves. What pornography calls "catharsis" leads to denial and not to knowledge.

In this sense, too, the rage we feel at this object we imagine is not ourselves is a shadow rage, a rage which covers an inordinate fear, a terror, even, of the power of our own nature. The discovery of rage, which is indeed a vulnerable feeling, is often healing. If we have been angry from our childhood at a mother or father, and tried to conceal this rage from our consciousness, in our attempt to deny it, our rage grew. But if we discover the original cause of our anger, and who it was meant for, and if we express this rage, we find that it has a natural end. And that after we express a rage, we are capable of forgiveness. But to discover the rage which pornography describes is to discover nothing. To discover only air. A phantom self whom we encounter during our flight away from ourselves.

For consider: as part of his defense, Lawrence Singleton constructed a pornographic picture of the young woman he mutilated. He claimed she was a prostitute who offered herself to him and to other men. He gave to her a kind of nymphomania which only men imagine women have. He said she liked to "suck men's cocks." From this picture he moved to a picture of her as *his* kidnapper, saying that she had wanted to castrate him. But this man was a seaman, and proud of his "fearlessness." (As a captain, he said, he never showed fear to his men.) Yet now he describes himself as feeling in mortal danger from a fifteen-year-old girl because she threatened him with a stick.

And why would a man who is so fearless in the presence of the real danger of the sea be so terrified of a young woman? Because in his mind she has become a disowned part of himself, and one cannot escape from the self. Above all, one cannot escape from knowledge of the self.

Just as in one pornographic novel after another, the hero responds to a woman's speech by brutalizing her, here, in this violence conceived by a pornographic mind, when the woman Singleton had bound and raped and sodomized asked for her freedom, he cut her hands off, telling her, "Now you are free." Because indeed, as long as one resists feeling, one must be haunted and tortured by the body. The mind, perhaps, can shut out feeling, but the body keeps reminding us. The touch of skin, an odor, a certain slant of light—the body remembers and will not let us be free of ourselves. And so to be liberated from a part of himself, a man—believing his own desire lives in the body of another—mutilates that body. This, too, is the essence of pornographic catharsis.

For the man who enacts violence does so in defense of an illusion which his mind has created; an illusion which is identical to pornographic fantasy, and which, like that fantasy, keeps him safe from knowledge of himself. All that is natural in him he projects on the body of a young woman. Describing her as a nymphomaniac, he denies his own desire. Against her body he enacts his rage. And in the court-room his protestation of innocence reflects back to all the statements of the pornographic mind in defense of itself. He says all he did he did for his own survival. And in this we hear the echo of the apologist who says that pornographic cruelty is a need of the body. We hear the strange reversal of this mind which calls a man a "libertine" who

binds and gags and imprisons women. We see that the fantasy of silencing women masquerades as a cry for freedom. We recognize the mind
of the Marquis de Sade, and of all his defenders, who protested that
de Sade, who was jailed for the torture and kidnapping of countless
women, was the victim of social injustice. And we must see, finally,
that these defenses do not exist for the courtroom alone. For the arguments go deeper and exist beyond the power of any legal systems.
They are arguments of the psyche with itself, the soul in a lonely
dialogue with illusion.

Of the obsession which is the core of pornographic experience, Michael Perkins writes that it causes the characters "to go to any lengths—
debasement, even death—to satisfy their needs." These needs, contrary
to the pornographer's idea of human nature, spring not from the body
but from obsession, from a distortion in the mind. It is the nature of
bodily needs, and material wants, that they can, in fact, be satisfied.
A real thirst can be quenched; a real hunger filled. But a symbolic
need of the mind perpetually hungers if in reality that need is a need
to silence the body. Such insatiability arises precisely because the mind
contrives against nature. If an obsession is meant to change and replace
nature, it must always and inevitably fail. Thus each stage of the mind's
defense of its own delusion must become more desperate, more terrified, and more violent.

Far from reflecting human nature, or acting to deflect natural violence with fantasy, pornographic catharsis feeds the mind's hunger
for illusion. When it encapsulates madness, culture tells the madman
that his delusionary vision of the world is real. Now, if something in
his own nature, or in the nature of the world, contradicts culture,
culture presents him with a stage upon which to revenge nature. On
the stage are dolls who do not have a soul such as he has. Engraved
into the scenery behind him are countless shapes of violent acts inflicted
on women's bodies. Just as in the works of de Sade, where a woman's
body is used as a table, the furniture on the stage has been made
from women's skin and teeth, from the skeletons of victims. The very
floor of the stage has been built with words which describe women
as hateful and monstrous beings. In his mind, he begins to exist on
this stage. Here his madness is justified, his mad fantasies are real.
Finally, like the hero of the novel in which a man rapes women after

he watches pornographic films, or the hero of the film who murders women while producing pornographic pictures of them, no longer satisfied to sit before this stage and imagine himself on it, he enters the theater as an actor. And he acts.

Image and Event

> There was a child went forth every day
> And the first object he looked upon, that object he became
> And that object became part of him for the day or a certain part of the day
> Or for many years or stretching cycles of years.
>
> WALT WHITMAN, "There Was a Child Went Forth"

We are told that pornographic images do not affect our lives. Whether or not these images vitiate violence through catharsis, the pornographer tells us, his images are harmless. If we believe, for instance, that the rape and murder of a young woman we read about in the newspaper may have been inspired by a pornographic image, a scientific study is quoted to us which is said to *prove* that pornography does not cause rape, or any other violent act.

Yet indeed, no study has ever *proved* or ever claimed to prove that pornographic images do not cause violent events. Instead, when we encounter arguments in favor of the existence of pornography, we discover that numerous studies and experiments have been conducted by social scientists in order to discover whether or not a correlation exists between a pornographic image and a violent event. To say that no such correlation can be found to exist does not prove that this correlation does not exist.

A researcher might construct an experiment designed to prove the existence of subatomic particles. If his experiment fails to discover these particles, it does not tell us that the particles do not exist. In fact, we know they do exist. Rather, we have simply learned that *his* experiment could not reveal these particles to us. In some experiments, social scientists have not found a correlation between pornography and violent behavior. And in other studies such a correlation has been found.*

---

* See also a study by Dr. Edward Donnerstein, University of Wisconsin in Madison, in which it was found that men who watched sexual violence were more likely to administer electric shocks to their partners in an experiment to test the effect of images on

In one study, for example, 39 percent of men convicted of sexual crimes said that pornography had "had something to do with" the crime they committed. From another study we learn that masturbating in association with certain fantasies "provides the critical reinforcing event for the conditioning" which leads to behavior. In still another study, the authors concluded that "one exposure to pornography is the strongest predictor of sexual deviance among the early age of exposure subjects."

In a study by the sociologist Diana Russell, which was conducted in San Francisco, women were asked if they had ever been upset by someone trying to force or persuade them "to do what they'd seen in pornographic pictures, movies or books." Ten percent of the women studied answered yes to the question.*

In addition to these studies, other social scientists have criticized the methodology of those experiments which found no correlation to exist between violence and pornography.† The sociologist Pauline Bart, for instance, tells us of another study (which reportedly found no correlation between pornography and violence), in which, in fact, pornographic images were not distinguished from simple, explicit depictions of sexuality. (Thus such a study declares it finds no correlation between pornographic imagery and violence when, in fact, it has only failed to find a correlation between *sexual* imagery and violence.)

But of course, here we have uncovered the difficulty with social "science." For even more than physical science, social science is shaped by the values, the ideologies, and the *perceptions* of the culture from which it is born. So a social scientist who studies the effects of pornography makes no distinction in his mind between the degrading images we call obscene and the sexual body in its material life. And perhaps

---

violent behavior. Also see a study by Neil Malamuth and James V. Check, University of Manitoba, in which men subjected to violent films which tended to justify violent sexual behavior tended to score higher on a questionnaire that measured their belief in the myth that women want to be raped.

  * The acts which upset these women included pouring champagne on the woman's vagina, forcing a woman into coitus with a dog, binding a woman's body, gagging her, beating her, and torturing her.

  † Victor Cline has suggested that the conclusions of certain studies within the famous *Report of the U.S. Commission on Obscenity and Pornography* distorted the data. Hans Eysenck has written of the same commission that "the majority report suppressed information that goes against the recommendation."

he cannot *see* this difference. Perhaps, like the culture he lives in, he is blind to this difference.

The feminist thinker Julia Stanley (using the words of Italo Calvino) has likened language to "a hardened shell, in perpetual self-repetition, of which we are all prisoners." But this is also true of culture. Culture, which includes language, shapes the way we see, our choice of scientific methodology, our idea of what is "biased" and what is "objective," and even our notion of what is truth.

Indeed, the overwhelming effect of culture upon the decisions of our lives has been the very subject matter of much of anthropology and sociology, of the sociology of knowledge, of social science itself. But here we come to a strange contradiction in this "scientific" thinking. For social science itself tells us that images shape human behavior.* And thus, if the social scientist makes the argument that pornography has no effect on human behavior, we are faced with a strange and mysterious phenomenon. For in order to argue that pornography does not reach into the lives of the audience and change their behavior, we would have to say that pornographic images are different from all other images, both actual and cultural, and that the mind, when confronted with the pornographic image, suddenly acts differently than it does when confronted with any other image.

If the social scientist who found no correlation between violence and pornography believes his studies to have proved that pornography does not cause violence, then we must wonder why he does not begin to examine pornography as a strange and extraordinary exception to all other imagery. For in this case, if he has discovered a form of culture which does not affect behavior, he ought to study this form to discover what is exceptional in it, and what it might tell us about the mind.

---

* Both the social scientist and the pornographer collaborate on the assumption that pornographic imagery *does* in fact affect behavior. Millions of dollars are spent on research, which not only documents but discovers techniques by which an association between sexual desire and any activity encourages behavior. This research is financed by an advertising industry which used pornographic photographs of women and subliminally embedded images of penises and breasts in the belief that showing these images in proximity to a given product, a kind of Scotch, or a brand of cigarettes, will cause the viewer to buy these products. Here research suggests that the pornographic image has such a powerful effect on behavior that it is worth millions of dollars a year. See Wilson Bryan Key, *Media Sexploitation* (New York, 1977) and Vance Packard, *The Hidden Persuaders* (New York, 1957).

And yet he does not examine pornography in this light, for he does not argue that pornography does not affect behavior. Of course it affects behavior, he tells us. Pornography is *intended* to affect behavior; it is *expected* to affect behavior and it does affect behavior. We read, for example, in the *Harper Dictionary of Modern Thought,* under the heading "Pornography," that this is a medium "designed primarily to arouse sexual excitement." And indeed, the pornographer himself, just as he denies from one side of his mouth that pornography causes certain events, defends pornography as a necessary stimulus to another event. He tells us some men need pornography in order to be able to participate in any sexual act.

The pornographer and his apologists argue that pornographic images *do* cause some events. That is, he tells us his images will cause only benevolent events. Just sexual pleasure comes from pornography, he says, never violence. And yet, is this not the voice of delusion again? (Earlier the pornographer has described his art as the expression of eros; he has claimed to wish to liberate the body into pleasure. But in fact, when we explore his imagery, we discover a movement of the mind against eros; we find the body is punished. In his mind, he has substituted the actuality of desire with a fantasy of violence. In the name of pleasure, he has given us images of humiliation and pain. All along he has denied to us what his real purpose is.)

For the pornographic mind is a mind without self-knowledge. Just as the pornographer denies a part of himself, so also he denies his own purposes to himself. But he is also capable of speaking from two sides of his mouth. All that he hides from himself in one moment he can reveal in the next, for he speaks to us through masks and personae and disguises. (Thus, at one moment, the pornographer tells us he loves the sexual body. And an instant later, through the mouth of a character he has created, he articulates the desire to mutilate that body. He writes of the "hideous pain" he imagines his character inflicting, "and inflicting gleefully . . . with complete awareness," on a woman's body.) Just as one of his apologists tells us that his images have nothing to do with events, one of his admirers takes pornography as evidence of the future. Thus we read in *L'Express* of *The Story of O:* "A woman has finally decided to admit, 'I like being beaten.' . . . *The Story of O* is woman's future."

The pornographer fantasizes that his images become events. And he publishes this fantasy. In the novel *The Skin Flick Rapist*, the pornographic hero is inspired to commit rape after he sees pornographic films. Again and again, the pornographer depicts his hero as leaving the theater, entering the world, and enacting real murders. (And the hero, Jack, is named after a real murderer; he is called "Jack the Ripper of Los Angeles.")

For pornographic images do not stay in the past. We do not know what personal experiences influenced the mind of Lawrence Singleton. He must have read pornography. Yet every man who has read pornography does not behave as he did. If a pornographic image affected his behavior, it did so by activating and shaping a rage with a more private origin.

Yet private griefs are given public forms for their expression. Human behavior is not universal, as is animal behavior, precisely because different cultures give us different forms through which to live our lives. Through culture, we learn what modes of behavior are acceptable expressions of our internal existences. Culture therefore becomes a determining cause of human behavior.

One might say that we can choose to reject cultural forms of behavior, and we can. But we have reason to accept these forms. When we speak or act through these forms we are understood. We are taken into the circle of humanity. And this is true even when it is rage we would express. For each culture has a range of "criminal" or "deviant" behavior which it offers as a way to express rage. In this culture, rape is one of those forms. We know that cultures exist where rape is unimaginable. These cultures do not offer this form of deviance to the mind. And even in deviant behavior, the mind clings to culture, feels comforted by image.

For the power of images over human behavior is a property of the human mind. As Susanne Langer has written, symbols and images *are* the modality of thought, "the instrument of thought." An image of food draws hunger from us. If we see a sleeping body, we are reminded of our tiredness. Any expression of rage will evoke our own anger. Through the image, we think. Through the image we make associations of cause and co-relativity and purpose. It is through the image that we *decide*. For the image and combined images comprise in our mind the very form of the process of choice whereby feeling becomes action. An image which combines sexual desire with violence cannot affect us selectively: we take the whole association into our minds. And if sexuality has about it an intrinsic violence simply in the intensity with which it overwhelms us, we learn through pornographic images to deal with this feeling of violence by enacting violence. Our inward violence is now contained by an image which directs it toward a woman's body.

One cannot overestimate the effect of images on our lives. In the Buddhist tradition of meditation, we are told that we become what we see. If we meditate on a river, we become like a river. But this is no magical thought. The human mind has a capacity beyond our conscious understanding to take in and imitate what it sees. The body silently memorizes all that it sees and the mind can accurately reproduce any image. (It was by these eidetic images that the famous cave paintings, so accurate in their depictions of animals, were made.) And no image we have ever seen leaves our minds. What we see does become part of us.

But now as we consider the intermingling of culture and event, we must take into account even one more property of the human mind. In the mind, we do not distinguish between a cultural image and a natural image. For the mind can reproduce each accurately, and in the mind, all images have an equal power regardless of their origin. And since this culture that we live in would dominate nature, gradually we replace natural images with cultural images of ourselves.

The anthropologist Lévy-Bruhl, writing of tribal cultures, describes a state of mind which he calls *participation mystique*. In this state, the tribal mind does not experience a separation between itself and nature. Thus a woman or a man does not know herself or himself as separate from plants and animals and seasons and rainfall or sunrise. But Lévy-Bruhl fails to note that our culture has created a participation mystique also. Except that we do not participate with plants or animals, and we do not confuse our identity with nature. Rather, we participate in culture and we confuse who we are with the cultural images of who we are supposed to be.

The fact is that if we believe ourselves to be something, we become what we believe. A group of athletes, for example, who are injured, and must therefore rest, imagine themselves doing daily exercises. When the time for competition comes, they play as well as athletes who have actually exercised. A group of schoolchildren are told that they are bright and capable. Another group hears of themselves that they are terrible students. In fact, both groups of students begin as equals. But the group that believed itself bright did very well, while the other group, as it had come to believe of itself, did poorly. (So the child who believes she is "good" becomes good, and the child called "bad" becomes a "bad" child.)

We enter the theater to see a play about a terribly deformed man. First we are shown pictures, photographs of a man with a disease that has covered his body in a fibrous tumor. We are repelled, moved, and terrified by the photographs. Now the screen dims, the photographs fade. And an actor appears to us. He is introduced to us as "The Elephant Man"; he will play the part of the man who had this awful disease. But he is well! His face is not covered with a tumor. His head is small. He is, in fact, quite beautiful. Yet he himself has seen these pictures. And he has taken this image into his mind. So he slightly twists and distorts his body, with the inward feeling of *being* that outward image we have all seen. And quickly we accept his suggestive movements, the illusion he offers us. Now, when we see this beautiful young man, we feel a terrible pity; we feel fear and nausea; we feel repelled; we feel like crying for ourselves and him.

Images work a powerful effect on the mind. If we question in our hearts who we are, our minds throw up to our vision an image of ourselves. We seek a picture, a word, a *name*. We feel we do not know our own feelings unless they are named. And we inherit through culture the very names we give to feelings.

This power of culture over our lives is a power we study and recognize. Kenneth Boulding, a philosopher in the sociology of knowledge, writes: "persons themselves are to a considerable extent what their images make them." And he follows this with another insight, which should be terrifying when we consider the images of men and women in pornography and in the pornographic sensibility. He writes: "people tend to remake themselves in the image which other people have of them."

The philosopher of language Wittgenstein gives us a similar insight. He writes: "The child learns to believe a host of things, i.e., it learns to act according to these beliefs. Bit by bit there forms a system of what is believed, and in that system some things stand unshakably fast and some are more or less liable to shift. What stands fast does so, not because it is intrinsically obvious or convincing; it is rather held fast by what lies around."

This relationship between culture and event has tragic consequences in our lives. In 1972, for example, the surgeon general's report on images of violence on television suggested that a causal relationship exists between an exposure to television violence and a child's participation in more aggressive behavior. For culture and event become one another. In the early twentieth century, a magazine publishes a photograph of a real event, a photograph of a woman political activist being tortured by the czarist police. Now this event, through its publication as a photograph, has become culture. And a young man buys this photograph. He stares at it. He becomes obsessed with it. Later he imagines that he is torturing a woman who has rejected him in the same fashion as this photograph depicts. Finally he actuates these fantasies in ritual tortures as a sadomasochist. (We read of his life after he becomes a patient of Wilhelm Stekel.) He makes culture actual.

By this transformation from image to act and act to image, we become imprisoned in a world of mirrors. For we cease to be able to tell illusion from actuality or to distinguish our own natures from the nature we are imagined to have. Thus if we are unhappy, we can find no way out of our dilemma, no door leading us into another world than this world of mirrors. In one mirror we see a photograph of a woman who is tortured. This may be a fictional pose. Or it may be a newspaper reporting an actual event. Or we may witness this event in our own lives. So, gradually, we cease to be able to imagine ourselves as otherwise. Every reflection we see tells us that only cruelty is possible. That violence is inevitable. We are trapped by our own minds.

In this way culture becomes like a web that is invisible to our eyes, made up strand by strand of image and word, each strand becoming more powerful through the existence of the other strands. But we do not see any of the strands. We do not examine our assumptions, our choices, our decisions. Rather, they fade into the background for us. And we confuse them with ourselves and with nature.

So if an image turns into an act, we do not perceive this transformation as having taken place. Rather, we say to ourselves that the image
has accurately predicted the future. And if a pornographic fantasy
becomes an event, we say that pornography has truthfully portrayed
sexuality. And finally, when we read that a man is convicted of kidnapping and "brutally" murdering an adolescent girl "to fulfill a bizarre
sexual fantasy," we do not come to understand that the pornographic
imagination can lead to actual murder. We do not suspect, as we ought
to suspect, that pornography endangers our lives.

Pornography as Sadism

> Ridicule, to a woman of sensitive mind, is a powerful weapon.
> DR. F. C. SKEY, *Advice on controlling hysteria in women*

Another truth looms over this dialogue about causation, a truth so
simple and blatant we wonder what has blinded us to it. For whether
or not pornography causes sadistic acts to be performed against women,
above all *pornography is in itself a sadistic act*.

Let us remember again that the central experience of sadomasochism
is humiliation. The actual images of pornography degrade women.
This degradation is the essential experience of pornography. It can
be argued that for a woman to be disrobed in public at all, given
the values of this culture, is a degradation. And yet such a nakedness
could be a defiance. For instance, there is the posture of an Isadora
Duncan, a woman who declares the body is beautiful, who refuses to
hide herself; she reveals her body as part of a protest against the pornographic culture. But the model in a pornographic magazine is not
defiant. She has been paid to take off her clothing. And she has about
her posture the attitude of one who has been paid to move in a certain
way. She is chattel. When she is chained, her chains are redundant,
for we know she is not a free being. The whole value, the thrill of a
"peep show" or a centerfold depends on a woman's degradation. In
this way she plays the whore. For she is *literally* for sale. Her image,
printed on a newspaper, is reproduced countless times, and lies flat
under a plastic screen, to be had for twenty-five or fifty cents by any
passing man.

And now, as her likeness shines out onto the public sidewalk, she has become all women: any woman walking by this image may feel the urge to turn her head away in shame. For this picture of the body of one woman has become a metaphor, in its anonymity (and in the general anonymity which belongs to women), for all women's bodies. Each sale of a pornographic image is a sadistic act which accomplishes the humiliation of all women.

One cannot overestimate the effect of this sadism in women's lives. Just as the image of cruelty can make a man become cruel, so the image of a degraded being can make a woman into a degraded being. Perhaps we can see this more clearly in the lives of those who produce pornography, whose lives are surrounded with these images every day and whose minds are involved in the making of these images. Indeed, the real lives of those who create pornography mimic the obsessional dramas they portray.*

Even within the world of pornography there is a class system which reflects levels of degradation. An actress who has worked in "hard-core" pornographic films finds it impossible to return to "legitimate" modeling, because her reputation has been spoiled. *Playboy* magazine, wishing to retain a "virginal" quality in its images of women, will not hire women who have modeled for "hard-core" pornography. A former pornographic model tells us bitterly, "They were very picky about the flesh they exposed."

This degradation does not remain on a conceptual level. The life of the pornographic actress would not change if she were to suddenly become socially "acceptable." For after her first birth as a human being, the pornographic actress suffers a second birth: she becomes a humiliated creature. In her autobiography, *The Ordeal*, the pornographic star Linda Lovelace has documented this transformation. Even her entrance into this identity was a humiliation. For she was beaten and literally imprisoned by her lover,† and thus forced to act in pornographic films.

---

* Because the filmmaking pivots around male tumescence, for example, on the set of a pornographic film, women who are called "fluff" girls are required to manipulate and suck the penises of the male actors.

† Chuck Traynor, who later became her husband in a marriage which took place in an atmosphere of force, held a gun to her nephew's head, and threatened to murder her mother and father and her sister, when she tried to leave him.

In the life that Linda Lovelace had with this man, she became other than herself. He forced her to give herself to other men, both as a prostitute and as a favor he extended to his friends. He forced her to dance topless in a club, to commit sexual acts with him that repelled her, to put objects in her vagina (including the candy "red hots"), to swallow his penis, to pose nude for still photographs, and finally to make pornographic films.

His desire was not simply to exploit her so that he could make more money or become more powerful. Even in their private lives, in their private sexual encounters, he created her after his own image. He dreamed of new humiliations for her. He longed to see her copulate with animals. Made her perform as his puppet in front of friends. Actually produced his own pornographic street theater, forcing her to lift up her skirt and expose herself to a group of men in a public restaurant, or lift up her sweater in order to shock truckdrivers and strangers on the road.

In order to become a pornographic image, she had to erase her self. Frequently when she was forced into sexual acts she did not want or found shameful, she would cry. But whenever she cried, or even showed tears in her eyes, he would beat her. She learned to place a permanent fake smile over her face. She replaced her real feelings with a mask, and eventually became that mask. The people who met her remarked that she seemed hardly alive.

Traynor's desire to erase her will went to even more extreme degrees. He loved to hypnotize her. (He hypnotized her so that her throat would not "gag" and thus she could take his whole penis into her mouth.) When even in a state of hypnosis she resisted his will, he would beat her again. Thus she learned to imitate a trancelike state so that she could pretend to carry out his orders, or otherwise divert his attention from the fact of her rebellion.

Even before she performed in pornographic films, she had become an object. Of the first night that Traynor sold her for prostitution, she writes:

> They were so into getting off their rocks that they wouldn't have cared if I was an inflatable plastic doll, a puppet. They picked me up and moved me here and there; they spread my legs this way and that; they shoved their things at me and into me.

To endure an almost constant state of pain and depression, she began to take drugs.

Her life with Chuck Traynor prepared Linda Lovelace to be the ideal pornographic actress, not only because she was introduced to every kind of sexual fetish, but because she became accustomed to acting as if she had no will of her own. She learned to do things she did not want to do. She became resigned. During the filming of one of her first roles, the director ordered her to urinate on another actress. (When she had difficulty doing this, she was told that unless she performed, she would have to play the part of the other actress.)

The pornographic plot in which a woman is raped or in some way threatened with violence is repeated in many ways in the actual production of pornographic films. When Lovelace refused to make love with a dog for one film, Traynor threatened her with death. She acquiesced when she was led back into the production room and saw a gun resting in the middle of a table surrounded by the director, cameramen, and producers.*

When we hear the simple details of Linda Lovelace's life with Chuck Traynor (though we know that her life and the lives of those she loved were threatened), we wonder how she allowed this state of imprisonment to take place in the beginning. But to ask such a question is to be blind to pornographic culture. The society we consider to be "normal" helps to teach women acquiescence. It is the accepted feminine role to be submissive. A woman is taught that she is helpless, both physically and with regard to her ability to support herself. Many women have become pornographic models simply because they felt they could not find other employment. Here we see how a cultural idea works to reinforce a cultural event. Because of her cultural conditioning, a woman believes she is not capable. And at the same time, since culture also believes this, it is actually harder for women to find well-paying jobs in which we do not have to prostitute ourselves.

Let us add to the idea of femininity two compelling stories which

---

* Since Linda Lovelace has left Chuck Traynor, we read, he has become the "manager" of another pornographic film star, Marilyn Chambers. And one is led to imagine that her life with Traynor may duplicate the condition of nonbeing which Lovelace has described. In a recent interview, the questions directed to Chambers were answered by Traynor. When she asked if she could leave to go to the bathroom, Traynor refused, telling her, "You stay right there." See Gloria Steinem, "Linda Lovelace's 'Ordeal,'" *Ms.* magazine, May 1980.

Linda Lovelace tells us about her early association with Traynor. He began to court her by buying her clothes. But it is culture that has given women the desire, the idea, even the necessity of dressing beautifully. We are told we must look attractive for men, that we must please lovers, husbands, possible husbands, employers, in this way. Moreover, we are not given any other value, except this value as a beautiful object. It is true that not everyone in society feels this way. But this is culture's prevailing attitude, and we have reason to believe that Linda Lovelace's parents accepted the traditional idea of what it is to be a woman. For here is the other revealing incident Lovelace tells us. Very early after her marriage to Chuck Traynor, she tried to escape. She went to visit her mother and then refused to return to him. She even told her mother about his violence and his pornographic desires. But her mother told her, in so many words, "He is your husband." And because of the sanctity of marriage, which carries with it the provision that a wife should obey her husband, she was returned to a more extreme servitude.

The conditions in the lives of pornographic film actresses are often only more desperate versions of the conditions of ordinary women's lives. One woman becomes a film actress to buy drugs for her husband. Another is herself a drug addict. Another comes on the set bleeding, and wears tampons despite the fact that she has just given birth and against her doctor's orders. She earns money to pay the hospital bill so that her newborn child will be released to her. Another woman makes films so that she can feed her children. Another supports herself this way while she is going through school. Another does this work to please her lover, not because he beats her, but for fear of losing his love, or simply his presence.

Whether or not she comes to this work through desperation, the pornographic actress becomes humiliated through what she does and is reduced to less than herself, because it is her body that she sells. Very little acting is required of her, in the real sense of acting. Instead, she must pretend to be a papier-mâché character, a being less than herself. Even a pornographic film actress who claims that she is not ashamed of her work tells us that she does "not want to end up like Linda Lovelace or Marilyn Chambers, porn queens forever." She knows she is not valued for any capacity except her capacity to resemble an object. "I don't just want people to come see me fuck. I want them to come see me act. I'm an actress."

A woman who enters an agency for pornographic acting and modeling is immediately catalogued according to her physical dimensions. We are told by a woman who screens applicants that most of them can be "eliminated" over the telephone when they reveal their height and weight. Another applicant is rejected because her "bustline" is not "firm" enough for the *Playboy* aesthetic. One agency keeps a special catalogue of the names of women with large breasts, which they call a "tit rag." A former pornographic model tells us that while she worked in these films she had to stay away from the sun to avoid tan marks, and worry about every scar and wrinkle.

And it is not enough that a woman is reduced to flesh. The actress is humiliated and abused in other ways during the making of the film. New women who enter the trade are referred to as "fresh meat." A woman's breasts are called "tits," their vulvas "cunts." The actresses are referred to in the third person while they are present, as if they were deaf or beneath contempt. The film actress is required to work for very long periods, until she is exhausted, for twelve and fourteen hours at a time. One model speaks of having thrown herself repeatedly onto a hard mat, without breaking her fall, so that she could be photographed in midair. Another woman lost the top layer of her skin after she was painted. Another suffered rope burns. Actresses and actors are asked to wear costumes encrusted with semen and other secretions. They suffer constant infections.

But the line between pornography and event, between imagination and enactment, is completely erased in the "snuff film." In Los Angeles, a woman hired through an agency is murdered, and filmed during this murder. The man who hired her photographed his torture of her. A film is advertised nationally as recording the real murder of a woman. A whole trade in such films goes on underground, and men pay huge sums of money to see a film which, it is said to them, has captured a real death of a real woman.

Again, the line between culture and reality vanishes in the production of child pornography. In Kathy Barry's book on female sexual slavery, we learn that another writer, investigating boy prostitution, discovered that he recognized boys in several pornographic pictures to be children "he knew from his research on the street prostitution scene." We learn from the California Attorney General's Committee on Obscenity and Pornography that most often, those who produce child pornography are themselves molesters of children, "who take photographs of their victims." Moreover, for the child pornographer, the photograph of his act is not simply a way to make a profit from his perversion; it is part of an act of molestation.*

Pornography and the production of pornography reflect one another in still other ways. For example, the pornographic fantasy that women enjoy being made into objects, dominated, and brutalized is often expressed through the idea that the film actress enjoys her work. Not only must she appear to enjoy hours of sexual posturing for the camera; she must also dissemble enjoyment for her fellow actors. A pornographic model, Rene Bond, tells us that in order to "keep the actor hard you have to make them think that you like it." Even the sociologist who interviewed this woman wanted to know if she could, or did, in his words, "enjoy the balling." She answers that she does not enjoy this work, explaining to him that "for a woman . . . emotions are essential to sexual experience."

Another actress, who had been ordered by her director to "make love to the camera," tells us that she prefers work in which she can sit still and "be photographed." She would like to remain detached, for emotion to her in a pornographic film is always a violation of and a deeper alienation from her own feelings than is total silence.

This detachment at the core of experience is another aspect of the creation of pornography which reflects the essence of the pornographic sensibility. A man who worked as a writer in a pornographic "factory" speaks of the process of storytelling as a process of alienation. ". . . we hated the unending sex scenes," he writes, "not because of the subject matter but because of the numbing boredom." For him, his experience went beyond numbness when he was assigned to write a novel on the subject of child molestation. The formula for this work instructed him to emphasize the "innocence of children" and the "lechery of adults." He was to depict "boys from six to thirteen and girls

---

* Often a man who rapes or molests children will make photographic records of his acts for his own pleasure.

from six to fifteen," calling attention to "hairlessness, tiny privates, lack of tits." Since he was not allowed to refuse this assignment, he resigned. Had he remained, in order to write this book he would have had to do violence to his own feelings. (But, he tells us, above all he refused this work because he felt himself incapable of creating such fantasies.)

If the men who produce, create, and distribute pornographic films do violence, in some forgotten region of themselves, to their own feelings, they also act out physical violence among themselves. (In this way we see that violence has a way of radiating out beyond the intended victim and returning to its author.) A partner in the production of *Deep Throat* sold his share in the film for far beneath its real value. When he was asked why, he answered, "Look, do you want me to get both my legs broken?" A murder is reported in the newspaper. We read that this act is reputed to have been a Mafia murder, and subsequently one discovers that the victim was involved in the sale or distribution of pornography. A man named Jacob Molinas is murdered in his backyard. The newspapers tell us that he was involved with organized crime in the distribution of pornography. A man named Bernard Gusoff is beaten and strangled to death. He, too, was involved in distribution. Joseph Torchio dies when he is hit by a car on the Las Vegas strip and we learn he, too, was part of "the business of pornography."

This violence to body and soul extends beyond the producers of pornography, even to the pornographic audience. The attitude of the man who makes pornography is one of pure exploitation. He uses both the medium of his expression and his audience with the same callousness. He is not the artist who loves what he has made. Rather, he loves the great power which pornography gives him over his audience. The consumers of pornography, because they feed an obsession, are like drug addicts. Therefore, the producer of pornography can charge exorbitant prices for his product. But his control over his audience extends even further, into a sadistic humiliation of other men.

One needs simply to walk in a district which sells pornography to feel this degradation. The buildings, the streets, the men walking the streets, the signs and placards, all contribute to a feeling of humiliation, a sense of debasement. The streets, the bookstores, the film theaters, are shabby. Everywhere the crudest signs, images, language, assault one. Barkers shout out insults to those who pass. Even those who stand about reflect this atmosphere, as if they were drawn here by their own self-hatred. Every object the eye lights on seems to be ugly. But this ugliness should not be thought of as coincidental. It accompanies every district where pornography is sold. In this neighborhood, where an industry flourishes, one is surrounded by dilapidation and seediness. Entering such a neighborhood, one feels cast down, chastised, invaded by a dangerous hatred, a terrible cynicism, in which one's own tenderness cannot survive.

And let us understand that the ugliness of pornography cannot possibly stay bound up within the confines of a neighborhood. It is not in the nature of a being, a thought, or an image to be confined. Even images of confinement and death have a life; they have the structure of life itself. They radiate out from a center and make themselves felt. The pornographic image has a life like the life of a sound wave. Set in motion in one place in a city, it affects a man walking through this part of the city. He begins to resonate with its frequency. He carries the ugliness of pornography outside this neighborhood. Let us say an image of a man beating a woman makes him more ready to strike a woman he knows. Or if this is not the case, let us simply that *he carries this image of a man striking a woman* with him in his mind. Unless he repudiates this image, argues with it, decides definitely that it is not part of his nature, and rejects it, it becomes part of him. And inside his soul a man beats a woman. But this is not all. The images we carry in our minds make us into who we are. *If I look on a river I become like a river.* Thus, in some way, this man comes to be like the image of a man beating a woman. Perhaps he becomes more callous. Perhaps he becomes cruel to his own softness. And now we, who have not walked in the neighborhood where pornography lives, see this man, we sense his brutality, his violence. We do not recognize that he has been shaped after an image in his mind. We take him for a natural being, a being who is cruel and violent by nature. We assume he is real. Finally, pornography has succeeded in reaching us; it has even penetrated our notion of reality. We begin to believe that the world is pornographic in its nature. And through this belief, we, too, suffer from pornography's sadism.

Illusion and Delusion: Culture's Desire to Replace Reality

> The most striking difference between ancient and modern sophists is that the ancients were satisfied with a passing victory of argument at the expense of truth, whereas the moderns want a more lasting victory at the expense of reality.
>
> HANNAH ARENDT, *The Origins of Totalitarianism*

> It was necessary to make the difficult decision to make this people disappear from the face of the earth.
>
> HEINRICH HIMMLER, October 1943

Certain ideas have the power to transform our lives. "The nexus between idea and act," Lucy Dawidowicz writes (of the history of the Holocaust), "has seldom been as evident in human history with such consistency as in the history of anti-Semitism." Yet that anti-Semitism should have been the central idea for an effective political movement surprised us. Before Hitler's rise to power and his genocidal acts, we did not take the political and social consequences of anti-Semitic ideas seriously. (Thus, in the early twentieth century, one did not take the French writer Céline's call to "massacre all the Jews" seriously.) One does not think of the pornography of racism as "ideas." The central idea of anti-Semitism, for instance, that "the Jew" cunningly plots our destruction, has no weight for our minds once it is stripped of the delusionary state which supports it. We understand racism to be a brand of madness. And were pornography not a kind of mental addiction, an enthralled fantasy, who would seriously credit its "ideas"?

Underneath our conventional understanding of pornography, we somehow know that the man who *believes* pornography must be mad. We can see the shape of the insanity of this mind in Huysmans' portrait of Gilles de Rais;

> He sobs as he walks, haunted by ghosts that rise up unexpectedly before him, looks around and suddenly discovers the obscenity of age-old trees. It is as if nature transforms itself before him, as if it was his presence that spoils it. . . . He sees the tree as a living thing, but reversed, head down, buried in the hair of the roots. The legs of this being stick up in the air, spread themselves, divide once more into so many crotches that become smaller and smaller, the farther away they get from the trunk; there between those legs, a branch is buried in frozen debauchery.

We say to ourselves, "This is the thinking of a madman; his ideas cannot affect reality." And in this way, we dismiss the power of these ideas to affect history.

And yet it is precisely because of the madness of the anti-Semitic or pornographic idea, and precisely because it is a delusion, that it must assault reality and try to change it. A man "believes" in anti-Semitic propaganda, or the pornographic ideology, because the illness of his mind *requires* that he believe these ideas to be true. Yet illness is of its very nature resistant. Thus, when a madman is told that he does not see the world correctly, and when he is given evidence against his prejudices, he will refuse to see the truth, and he will even distort this evidence to support his own delusion. But most significantly, he will even change reality so it supports his mad idea of the world. This is what anti-Semitism and pornography require of their believers. *The deluded mind must try to remake the world after an illusion.*

When we understand that it is in the nature of the pornographic idea to attempt to replace reality with itself, the fact that many pornographic fictional works disguise themselves as scientific "documents" appears to us in a new light. A fictional work entitled *Teenage Sadism* is subtitled "A Documentary Casebook." It is published as part of the "Dr. Guenther Klow Library." The author, a "Dr. Dean Copeland," is described as "one of the foremost authorities on sexual deviancy among today's uninhibited young people." Despite a disclaiming paragraph inside the first page warning that any "similarity between real persons and these characters is coincidental," we are told in the introduction that the stories are "graphic true life accounts." A magazine filled with photographs of women chained and beating one another announces itself as a "Casebook in Lesbianism." Another fictional collection is called *The Multiple Climaxing Woman* and bears the subtitle "In-depth Case Histories." In a magazine we find a fictional "study" entitled "Rape: Agony or Ecstasy?" Here we read the fictional statistic that "nearly one-half of all women who are forcibly raped experience orgasm during the assault," and we encounter the fictional conclusion that "the emotional impact of forced intercourse . . . is an aid to orgasm." In this way pornographic fantasy masquerades as fact.

Perhaps it is the pornographer's desire to replace reality with fantasy which ultimately leads him to prefer the image and the symbol over what is real. We read from Gay Talese in *Thy Neighbor's Wife,* for instance, that Hugh Hefner spent much of his adolescence obsessed with photographs of women. In the 1940s, he decorated the walls of his bedroom with photographs cut from the pages of *Esquire* magazine. And reading his sexual history, we suspect that as a young man, he had a far more passionate life with images than with real women.

In Talese's detailed sexual history of this man, we learn that at eighteen his sexual experience "precluded masturbation" and he had "not experienced sexual intercourse" by the age of twenty-two. We might understand this slowness as a natural condition of the rebellion he was making from his fundamental Methodist background. And yet one cannot help but notice that throughout his life he was fascinated, and even obsessed, with the photographed, the documented, the filmed, the *observed* experience of reality. When Talese recalls for us Hefner's childhood, we do not hear a scene of masturbation or childish exploration described. Rather, the memory that he could recall "decades later," and the experience with which, as a child, he was "mesmerized," was essentially voyeuristic. Thus we learn that as a thirteen-year-old-boy, while attending a Boy Scout meeting, he saw a young girl getting undressed "through the half-raised shade of the window next door." And later we read that before his marriage he photographed his fiancée in the nude. And that when he had an affair outside this marriage, he filmed himself "making love to his girl-friend." And we learn that Hefner has kept cartons of photographs and films of himself, along with documents and mementos which record his entire personal life.

Telling us that the magazine Hefner created "had re-created him," Talese describes Hefner in the early days of *Playboy* as a man who "virtually lived within the glossy pages." We learn that he marveled over the photograph of one young woman because "her skin did not glisten with perspiration" (and of course, we discover that as a youth, Hefner "perspired freely"); that, in the words of Gay Talese, he seemed "to be getting as much pleasure from what he was seeing as from what he was feeling"; that he kept portfolios of all the women who ever modeled for his magazine; that he regarded these women, in some way, as his "possessions." All these attitudes speak to us of a certain architecture of the mind. Here is the essence of the voyeuristic experience. Above all, the voyeur must see and not feel. He keeps a safe distance. He does not perspire and his photographs do not glisten with sweat. He is not touched by reality. And yet in his mind, he can believe he possesses reality. For he has control over these images he makes and he shapes them to his will.

One finds the same architecture in the design of Hugh Hefner's house. For he has isolated himself completely from nature. His house has no windows. Nothing unpredictable or out of his control can happen to him there. Sunrise makes no difference to him. He rises and sleeps at odd hours. Seasons do not affect him. And he never has to leave this house. Food emanates from a kitchen supplied with a staff day and night. Inside the house he has a projection room, a swimming pool (with an underwater bar), a fully equipped office. Here he is never compelled by a need which cannot be immediately answered. And even within this house, as if one layer of protection from the world were not enough, his bedroom contains another self-sufficient and man-made world, with a desk, and food supplies, and a bed which is motorized so that it not only changes positions but also carries him about the room. Thus he never has to leave his bed. In this passive manner, he can have total control over nature.

Yet can the pornographer be satisfied with this degree of control? Within Hefner's bedroom and over this bed he has a camera which will photograph him as he experiences coitus. The pornographer must replace even his own experience with a cultural record of his experience. For otherwise, how can nature be completely controlled? The attempt to control her must be like the labor of Sisyphus, a task which promises despair and rage. For nature will always make herself felt. Even if we hide the sunrise from ourselves, or escape knowledge of rainfall, of hunger, of death, we cannot escape nature in ourselves. We feel. Here is the great and terrible irony of that soul which would escape itself. Like Gilles de Rais, running from himself into the woods, even as we escape ourselves we confront ourselves. When we turn away, all that we have denied rises up like a ghost to terrify us. We are trapped.

The philosopher of language Ludwig Wittgenstein writes that "Symbols appear to be of their nature unsatisfied." And yet it is not the nature of the symbol itself to deceive us, nor to act as the escape from reality in which, eventually, we are imprisoned. As Susan Sontag reminds us, we have been used to thinking (in the tradition of Plato and Feuerbach) that the problem lies with the nature of imagery itself; we complain that human beings have become dependent on images of reality rather than reality. And yet this way of thinking exists inside our collective amnesia. We have forgotten that an image can reflect and reverberate with reality. We forget that an image can enchant us precisely because it opens our souls to a greater knowledge of the real. We forget that the beauty of an opening rose can make our hearts "open." We forget that in the image we can find an embodiment of what we thought was unknown; that the image, instead of entrapping us, can open a door in our own minds, into our own nature and into the nature of nature. And we do not see that instead of an imagery filled with the power of reality, pornographic culture has chosen an imagery which tries to deny reality.

It is because of this denial that, finally, we must find the pornographic image dissatisfying. This dissatisfaction colors all of pornography with a kind of anger. For the pornographer imagines he has been betrayed. His promises have not been fulfilled. Henry Miller writes, for example: "Paris is like a whore. From a distance she seems ravishing, you can't wait to have her in your arms. And five minutes later, you feel empty, disgusted with yourself. You feel tricked." Thus he forgets that he himself created the illusion he calls "Paris," and that this emptiness is his own, that it was he who tricked himself.

Beyond this trick, reality waits like a shadow. For these words from Wilhelm Stekel, about the sadomasochistic ritual, speak to the experience of pornography:

> The actual scene is a disillusionment because it never corresponds to the unconscious desire; and in itself it is a fiction behind which a totally different scene is hiding.

The temporary illusion of realization which pornography gives to its audience must always turn into despair.

And whether the image has given us despair or given us hope, whether it has imprisoned us or opened a door for us, we do not stand still. Again Wittgenstein tells us: "The proposition seems to set over us as a judge and we feel answerable to it—it seems to demand that reality match the symbol of reality which has captured our minds."

If that symbol is a lie, our experience of reality will deny the truth of that symbol. The mind which is not deluded allows the symbol to be disproved by reality. But the pornographer is not sane. He has the madman's commitment to an illusion. Even his sense of *himself* is bound up with that illusion. He imagines he is invulnerable. In his pornographic fantasy he has placed himself above nature. He has placed himself above her as culture. In his mind he imagines he *is* culture. For in his mind he has replaced his actual, material self with a cultural image of himself that denies that materiality. Now if the reality of his delusion is destroyed, he imagines he himself will be destroyed. In a world of delusion made of images, his only conscious knowledge of himself is an image. Without culture, he imagines he does not exist at all. Therefore, he must defend his imaginary existence against reality. And thus it is logical that he should imagine reality has set out to destroy *him*.

For of course, in a metaphorical sense this is true. Reality will destroy delusion. Nature will bring the mind back to whatever is the real and painful experience from which it hides. And the part of the mind which believes in this delusion will die. The delusionary self will die. This reality which the pornographer fears is a formidable enemy.

She has invaded him. She lives in his body. Even as he breathes, she attacks him. Even as he touches, desires, aches, she assaults him. He must act out against her. He must silence her, imprison her, bind her, punish her, and if necessary, even annihilate her, if he is to defend his illusion.

Thus we see an ominous movement take place. Culture must turn into event. The pornographer imagines violence after he imagines object. Then he imagines his fantasy becomes an event. And finally, the fantasy *does* become an event. In a newspaper, for example, we read that a television drama in which a woman was set afire with gasoline was imitated by a man in Boston. There, a real woman's body was set afire with gasoline. We read that a television drama which depicted a group of girls raping another girl was imitated by two girls. Thus, in California, a nine-year-old girl was actually raped.

But the movement of the pornographic mind does not stop here. Culture has been made into event. And now event will be made into culture. Thus we read that in New Jersey, a wealthy man is tried for the rape of several women. And in the testimony we learn that he filmed himself and four other men while they raped, sodomized, and beat their victims. And we discover that when, in a California desert, the bones of women's bodies are found buried along with ropes, knives, and saws, the man who is arrested for these murders is said to have hired women to pose for him, to have tied them, to have tortured and murdered them, while photographing each stage of these events.*

But all this, and the attraction, also, that so many men have to the crime magazine which reports, in issue after issue, the details of a real murder of a real woman, becomes finally understandable to us when we see that the "final solution" for the pornographic mind is to annihilate nature and replace nature with culture. Thus the document which records the death of a real woman, a woman who represents nature, reality, and the part of the self that is denied, becomes the ultimate pornographic form. For this document, which is a piece of paper and therefore a cultural artifact, *proves* the death of nature, the destruction of a woman's body, the annihilation of the denied self. Now the mind can both have and not have this denied part of the self, and reality is replaced with culture.

But pornography gives us a lucid mirror of itself.† In the film *Peeping Tom*, for instance, the pornographer has provided us with a self-portrait. The hero of the film is a pornographic photographer. And it is from this film that we learn the pornographer's secret fantasy about his own art. For in this fantasy, the hero uses a camera that conceals a deadly spear. As he photographs a woman, his camera releases a spear which simultaneously murders her. Thus he is able to murder her as he makes her into an image, and to replace her body with a record of her death agony.

---

* Here an old pattern from history can be recognized. Even though the United States Army denied its record of atrocities against native Americans, in fact the best record of these atrocities was kept by the Army itself. In the same way, the Soviet Union, according to Nadezhda Mandelstam, has kept roomfuls of letters, records, and descriptions attesting to its persecutions against dissidents. The best records of the burnings of witches were kept by the witch-burners themselves; for the history of slavery, we read the accounts of slave traders and slavemasters. And the Third Reich, even while it was calling the accusation of genocide a "Jewish fiction," made meticulous records, photographs, and even moving pictures of countless numbers of imprisonments, tortures, and deaths. And we have learned that Hitler liked to watch these films of executions.

† On the back of *The Skin Flick Rapist* we find an imitation of a document, a tabloid newspaper, which records the mutilation and murder of women by a pornographic hero as if it were fact.

And pornography also records the ultimate despair of its own final solutions. For indeed, what the pornographer would really annihilate is a part of himself, that self which is feeling, which is vulnerable. But of course, when a woman dies in fantasy or reality, that self does not die. Thus even a murder is not satisfying. Both in actuality and in fantasy, a pornographic murder must be followed by another murder, and this by another murder, each more violent and devastating. In one novel after another, the hero murders one woman after another, and each time he is more cruel and more destructive. For after each murder, his feeling of powerlessness returns. And so, too, a frenzy grows, and a desperate realization, which the mind must want to quiet, that this vulnerable self will always return and cannot be destroyed. Thus the pornographer's rage grows with each murder, for with each murder he fails more miserably. At the end of one pornographic novel, after his last murder, the hero stands on a fire escape, trembling and paralyzed with fear. To the detective who had discovered him, he sobs, "Please help me . . . I'm afraid of heights."

Here pornography stands trembling before nature, afraid of falling, afraid of the power and knowledge of the body, pornography which in its fear of being ravaged has ravaged, which has attempted to reduce living beings to things, which has and must inevitably seek our death. Far from vitiating violence, culture writes a script for death, and produces and directs countless acts of violence against women, against children, even against men. And far from freeing the spirit from the idea of limitation, pornography slowly imprisons us in an illusion which replaces reality and leaves us devastated and despairing.

Freudian Despair

> . . . now suddenly, inspired by the absolute hopelessness of everything, I felt relieved, felt as though a great burden had been lifted from my shoulders. . . . If rape were the order of the day, then rape I would.
>
> HENRY MILLER, *Tropic of Cancer*

We wonder what these strange forms of human behavior tell us about ourselves. That Baudelaire "wanted to see his mistress, a beautiful woman, hanged by her hands so that he could kiss her feet." That a man pays a woman to have himself beaten with a whip and spoken to as if he were a naughty child. In studies by Stekel, Freud, Krafft-Ebing, we read of men who want to perform cunnilingus because they feel this to be a humiliation. A man asks his wife to have affairs, and demands that he be able to watch; he wants to be publicly degraded through her associations with other men. Another man takes the *nom de plume* of a woman. Calling himself "Elizabeth," he writes servile letters to a woman and offers himself to her as a slave. A young man explodes into violent rages with his family, blistering and terrifying his listeners with cruel language. A man goes to a prostitute and asks to have his penis cut off with a razor. Another man goes to a prostitute and, asking to be tied up and put in a diaper, defecates. After he has soiled himself, he asks to be chastised.

In all this actual behavior we see the mirror image of pornography; but we must also see something of ourselves reflected, if not in our actual acts, or even in our desires, surely in what we fear in our nightmares, or in the world we see about us. For the very horror and repulsion with which we wish to deny these images must mean that they represent a shadow side of our lives. And the very exaggeration of these images forces us to confront this shadow self.

Both Freud and Wilhelm Stekel, who began as his student, described this shadow side as an inevitable outcome of the conflict between nature and culture, and an outcome which in some form affects us all. In his study on sadomasochism, Stekel concludes that his patients have become ill because they have a stronger "atavistic" instinct than normal men and women. Thus the conflict between culture, or socialized life, and nature, or instinctual life, has become intensified to the point of breakdown in these beings. He writes: "In order that man shall become social, that a sense of community shall be developed, every individual must nail himself to the cross of culture, that is, have firm control of his instincts, express them in culturally permitted paths."

Sigmund Freud's idea of human nature, and hence inevitably his vision of our future, is just as bleak. Like Stekel, he finds the rift between culture and nature to be irreparable. "It is not possible for the claims of the sexual instinct to be reconciled with the demands of culture," he writes, and continues this thought with the prediction that human beings may indeed perish from the earth because civilization will destroy in them the desire to procreate. For those events where sexual feeling and creation come together he uses the word "sublimation"; he tells us that the work of genius, the painting, the poem, is a neurotic expression, the attempt of the repressed sexual feeling to live in a civilized distortion of itself.

Everywhere he felt the force of a wedge between civilized knowledge and instinctual desire. He found this force at work in a condition which he called "psychic impotence," and of which he wrote: "I shall . . . put forward that psychic impotence is far more widespread than is generally supposed and that some degree of this condition does in fact characterize the erotic life of civilized peoples." In this common state, what Freud thought of as civilized love, which includes tenderness and respect, has become divorced from sexuality. Thus a man suffering from "psychic impotence" cannot make love with a woman he loves. Instead, in order to satisfy the desires of his body, he must be in the presence of "a lower type of sexual object," by which Freud meant a prostitute, a mistress, or a woman somehow degraded by society.

Here, according to Freud's study, we find the most popular form of sadomasochism. For Stekel has defined this illness in its essence as the compulsive marriage between sexual feeling and humiliation.* But now our dark vision of the world is complete. For, from the man we have looked to as a healer of the mind, we find that we cannot be healed. We are all in some ways afflicted with sadomasochism; we are doomed, as Marcuse writes of the Freudian vision, to "hideous forms" of the manifestation of this illness, "so well known in the history of civilization . . . in the sadistic orgies of desperate masses of 'societies' elite,' of starved bands of mercenaries, of prison and concentration camp guards." Thus, we are told, the pornographic portrait of the underside of our minds is true; it is inevitable that we are violent, and that we will destroy ourselves.

But this pessimistic vision was not created by Freud. He inherited this vision from a long tradition in which the separation of body and mind and a bleak notion of an apocalyptic future have been mingled. Here is the cosmology and morality of Jehovah, delivering the ten

---

* To his category of psychic impotence Freud might have added the number of men or women who cannot feel sexually unless they themselves are humiliated. His rather rigid adherence to the Victorian idea of sexual roles blinded him to the prevalence of this social illness among many women, as well as men.

commandments in the wilderness; the Biblical proclamation that wildness is evilness, and the setting of law and order against the natural; and the apostles' prophecy of a terrible battle between body and mind, in which the whore of Babylon returns and is vanquished. We hear the echoes of this prophecy everywhere we turn. Our very idea of culture and of the body has become infused with the terror of such a future.

Now we are reminded of the paintings of Franz Marc. Of the death of Kate Chopin, and of her heroine Madame Pontellier, of the death of Madame Bovary. Poe's words that a woman's death is "poetical" ring in our ears. As do the words of an American medical adviser, writing in the nineteenth century: "only lust creates semen, pure love, never any." Or those of the editor of a German political journal of the nineteenth century (attacking Vienna's feminist movement), saying that women and culture are "irreconcilable." Everywhere we turn, we hear that hope is impossible. We become convinced that we cannot be whole, but we must choose between our bodies and our minds. As Strindberg writes, echoing the dilemma of a whole culture: "The same alternatives again—love or knowledge."*

We hear the voice of cynicism in the words of Edmund Behr, writing an introduction to Helmut Newton's sadomasochistic photographs, as he tells us: "There is a secret garden lurking in every one of us. We are all, on occasion, voyeurs, sadists, freaks—we treat women as objects . . . we seek to freeze them . . . we think unthinkable thoughts. . . ." It is the voice of complacency, which turns tragedy into a bland fashion. And it is also that voice of the pornographer, which, like the voice of the sadist himself, ridicules feeling, ridicules tenderness, and above all, ridicules hope. In *The Story of the Eye,* for example, we read: "To others, the universe seems decent because decent people have gelded eyes. That is why they fear lewdness." Implying that we ought to see lewdness in nature, he tells us: "They are never frightened by the crowing of a rooster or when strolling under a starry heaven. In general, people savor the pleasures of the flesh only on condition that they be insipid."

---

* Strindberg associated this choice with his wife's "cold and frigid" reaction to his success as a playwright. And metaphorically, taking up for himself the old religious battle against Babylon, he concluded: "I did not hesitate, I struck her down with a final letter of Farewell, and felt as pleased with myself as a murderer who has dealt his blow successfully."

Yet this is a familiar voice, this voice of cynicism; we ought to have recognized its tone, for it is also the voice of illness and resistance. Stekel points out to us that the sadomasochistic patient is one of those most highly resistant to cure.* And significantly, the arguments Stekel's patients use to defend their illness (even as they are asking to be cured), is that *their bodies have made them seek cruelty* and punishment; they claim that their illness is a property of the nervous system, or of physical inheritance. Like the philosophers of despair, they say they are *victims of nature.* And they claim, therefore, that they cannot be changed.

In this way the sadomasochist convinces himself that his psyche is in no way responsible for his behavior. In order to heal him, both Stekel and Freud tell us, the therapist must move past this belief in an inevitable and structural illness. He must discover a deeper meaning which the patient tries to hide from himself in the metaphor of his body. And yet, when the sadomasochism of a whole civilization is described, both Freud and Stekel offer us precisely the same explanation which the resistant patient has given to explain himself. For these healers tell us that the illness of civilization is structural and inevitable; they insist that the conflict between nature and culture is incurable.† Culture and nature are forever irreconcilable. And now one might ask, as Freud and Stekel asked of their resistant patients, what truth, what knowledge does *this* resistance hide?

The Myth of Oedipus.

In "A Child Is Being Beaten," Freud writes: "For in our opinion, the Oedipus complex‡ is the actual nucleus of neuroses, and the infan-

---

* Freud himself gives us the notion that an illness tries to resist cure, tries to reinstate itself, to survive at the expense of sanity.

† Toward the end of his career, Freud even decided that the movement toward death is an "instinct," fighting with the instinct to survive for possession of the body and mind.

‡ Freud named his theory after the myth of Oedipus Rex. In it, Oedipus receives the prophecy that he will murder his own father and marry his mother. In order to escape this prophecy, he travels away from the mother and father who raised him. He goes to the land of Thebes. But Thebes was his real birthplace. His father, King Laius, had left Oedipus to die as an infant because the king received a prophecy that his infant son would grow up to murder him. Now Oedipus does murder Laius, and after he successfully answers the riddle of the Sphinx, he marries his mother and becomes king of Thebes. When he discovers he has indeed fulfilled his destiny, he puts out his eyes. And Jocasta, his mother, kills herself.

tile sexuality which culminates in this complex is the true determinant of neuroses." Thus, Freud posits his theory that at the base of all human suffering is the Oedipal experience. The boy wishes to make love to his mother, Freud tells us. And this child wants, therefore, to kill his father—the rival for his mother's love. But because of these murderous wishes, the boy fears that his father will castrate him in revenge. Hence the boy puts away instinct. He represses his sexual feeling. This feeling returns to haunt him as neurosis.

Freud discovered what he called the Oedipus complex in his own dreams. He argued that this complex was universal, not only for his own culture, but to human nature. In Freud's thinking, rather than a social illness, the Oedipus complex was the cornerstone of all illness, which culture and society must express as they express a dilemma which is part of the fundamental condition of humanity. But in this perhaps he was only being a loyal son. We can see that he began as a rebel. For he introduced the instincts of the body, the life of the infant, sexual desire, into consciousness. He showed the great influence which the knowledge of the body has upon our consciousness. His revolutionary insights showed us that what we thought was *cultural* manifestation alone had indeed sprung from and been shaped by *nature*.

And yet Freud was a son of civilization. Like Franz Marc, he became alarmed; like Franz Marc, he inherited his culture's fear of the knowledge of the body. Now in his own mind, and in his dreams (from which the idea of the Oedipus complex sprang), a struggle must have seized him. He had moved dangerously against culture's greatest taboo. And finally this struggling mind came up with a solution through which he could remain in the good graces of the culture of his fathers. Thus, when he describes the Oedipus complex as universal and inevitable, he tells us that it is nature, who made us as we are, that must be at fault for our illnesses. Nature—who is in her perverseness as opaque as a woman's desires—made us beings who simultaneously wish for civilization and for naturalness, who simultaneously would wish to murder our fathers for our mothers' love, and would feel great guilt at even the faint suspicion that this might be so. In a word, reality herself created in us the tendency to lie and the will to destroy reality.

But Freud's view of human nature is not the only one imaginable. Of Freud's theory, Wilhelm Reich writes:

> The fear of evil instincts which dominates the whole world . . . se-
> verely blocked the work of psychoanalytical therapists. They had taken
> for granted *the absolute antithesis of nature* (instinct, sexuality) *and
> culture* (morality, work, duty) and had thus arrived at the thesis that
> the "living out of impulses" was contradictory to the cure.

In his own psychoanalytic work, Reich became convinced that the cause of illness lay with the *idea* that impulses are evil. He conceived that such impulses become evil only so long as "the discharge of energy by way of a natural love life is blocked." And he replaced Freud's bleak picture of humankind as incurable with another vision, one which held within its tragic dimensions the possibility of a universal healing. For he saw that culture had made a decision to repress the knowledge of the body, but that this decision was not inalterable.

This way of thinking suggests to our minds that the rift between the body and the mind is not natural but instead causes us pain and suffering precisely because it goes against nature. In this sense, the truth *is* erotic. And eros longs for meaning. Therefore, within the tragedy of human suffering a memory speaks to us, a memory of what we have lost, and thus a hope of finding ourselves again. But now we must remember that the myth of Oedipus Rex *is* a tragedy.

In this light perhaps we can see what Freud could not see in the story of Oedipus Rex. There is to begin with a curious matter about his interpretation of this myth. In all his other work, the greatness of his thought rests precisely with the fact that in a casual statement, a gesture, a myth, a dream, he finds a metaphor for psychological truth. But now, when he comes to sexuality and to the desire of the body in the myth of Oedipus, he ceases to see metaphorical meaning. Now he sees in the human experience of desire only a mechanical biological function.

The Oedipal complex has entered our language and our minds as a virtually irrefutable part of the understanding of human nature; but what is astonishing to see, especially given the significance of Freudian thought, is that Freud's understanding of the Oedipus myth is merely literal; he brings to the play little more clarity than a simple retelling of the events themselves.

Yet to say that nature and culture are not separate is to understand that every event in the body has a psychological meaning. In her *First and Last Notebooks*, Simone Weil writes of the "phenomena of psychological transferences":

> If people were told: what makes carnal desire imperious in you is not its carnal element. It is the fact that you put into it the essential part of yourselves—the need for Unity, the need for God.—They wouldn't believe it. To them it seems obvious that this quality of imperious need belongs to carnal desire as such. In the same way it seems obvious to the miser that the quality of desirability belongs to gold as such, and not to its exchange value.

It is of the nature of a myth, or any story which springs from culture, to be like a dream and thus precisely not literal but symbolic in every detail. (There do exist dreams which are very simple and literal presentations of wish fulfillment, but according to Freud's own insights into the psyche, it is surprising to find a myth which would lay forth the mind's deepest and most fundamental crisis in such a simple and naive manner.) The more profound is a myth, the more its seeming simplicity echoes with meaning upon meaning, until it begins to embody all the complexity of life itself.

An interpretation of a myth, just as it opens up new insights for us, can at the same time close the door upon other meanings. In his pessimism Freud had already closed a door for himself on the full range of meanings available to a mind willing to understand the effects of culture on behavior. When he encountered the Oedipus myth, he imagined he had found for himself a *sine qua non,* an ultimate knowledge in the simple material events of the story. Thus he closed the door of his mind.*

But let us open this door, and consider that the sexual passion played out in the tragedy of Oedipus Rex has a metaphorical meaning. Let us imagine, for instance, that Oedipus's passion for his mother and his murder of his father stand for more than these actual events, for more, even, than the hidden desire to commit them. Let us imagine that the story of Oedipus is a fable about knowledge.

The word "knowledge" has two meanings in our present culture.

---

* Whether or not the sexuality in the Oedipus myth had a symbolic meaning was the question that created a rift between Freud and Jung.

By one meaning we indicate the knowledge of the mind, and by another, the knowledge of the body, or in its more literal sense, knowledge of the sexual act. Let us suggest that in our culture we imagine our mothers give us the knowledge of the body, while we believe that our fathers give us the knowledge of culture. The knowledge of the body (which is the knowledge we have as infants) is a firsthand and physical knowledge, a basic sensual experience of the world. While our father's knowledge, the knowledge we receive from culture, is the knowledge of authority. What we know from him we know because of the word, because of the image, or idea. Culture gives us symbols of experience. The knowledge of his world is a knowledge of abstraction, always removed from direct experience and thus also from the self (and from the authority of self). Therefore the authority of this knowledge must be conferred by culture; it must be titled and decorated and plumed, decreed and bowed down to, precisely because it does not possess natural authority.

These two kinds of knowledge are at war within our culture. As Dorothy Dinnerstein writes:

> The process consists on the one hand . . . of a pushing out of awareness of our early delight in the vulnerable body's joys, and a compulsive concentration for attention and energy on that which can be predicted, controlled, manipulated, possessed and preserved, piled up and counted. And it consists on the other hand of the ashamed eruption of a dirty interest in this rejected body, an interest that is a deformed version of our original delight, dirtied and deformed by the crooked paths that a feeling must take to break through repression.

Because of our fear of nature we use abstract knowledge to deny and debase physical reality.

Now let us imagine that the young prince Oedipus has been born into a culture which is afraid of the knowledge of the body. Within the story of his life, this knowledge is called "fate," and it is supposed to create havoc. We learn in the beginning of the legend of Oedipus that in the form of "fate," a decree from the gods, Laius will suffer a death from the hands of his own son. But why has this fate been set upon him? He has abducted a young boy and by this he made the gods jealous.* Of course, one knows the gods are capricious, but their

---

* See C. Kerényi, *The Gods of the Greeks* (London, 1974).

caprices contain another level of meaning than the "ordinary." So let us assume that this jealousy has other than a literal meaning. For in coupling with a boy, Laius was escaping the knowledge of the body, both by escaping a woman's body and by choosing a lover he could kidnap, overpower, and control.

Thus it was for attempting to create the illusion that he is a god, and hence above both nature and mortality, that Laius is cursed by the gods with death. And he is cursed with a death which will come to him precisely through *carnal knowledge*. For it is through sexual union with a woman that his son will be born to him. In the myth of Oedipus, we learn indeed that Laius has tried to evade fate by remaining celibate with his wife. But Laius and his wife were *afflicted with madness*. Thus they made love and engendered a son.

And what is this *madness* with which they were afflicted? It is the same madness that the Eumenides and the Furies are famous for: it is sensual raving, a passionate state beyond reason, a state in which the knowledge of the body overpowers cultural knowledge.

But Laius believed he could still evade the *fate* of mortality. Thus he resolved to murder his son. (It is significant here to note that for this murder Laius took his son to Mount Cithaeron, a mountain according to one story named after a king who was bitten by the snaky locks of a Fury after he scorned her.) Now, in an act which reminds us of that place in Achilles' body which made him mortal, Laius pierced his son's heel. And then he tied him to a stake and left him to die.

But let us now remember that all the characters in a myth or a dream are really only one character. Thus this boy who belongs to Laius is also a part of himself. In killing his son, he has not only staved off death, he has killed that part of his soul, his infant self, which knows and fears mortality.

Yet the boy does not die. And is not this also true? We cannot murder this part of ourselves. Always, the knowledge of the body lives. Therefore Oedipus lives. He is tended by a compassionate shepherd and his wife. (For compassion *is* kind to this forgotten self.) And so the son of Laius wanders back to Thebes.

But why does he come back? The myth does not tell us. We only learn he is led there by fate. Yet what is fate? This is the knowledge of the body. So we must assume that Oedipus, despite his desire to escape fate, has let the knowledge of the body live in him. After all, he has grown up out of the shadow of his father, out of the shadow of culture. This knowledge has remained intact for him. This is the symbolic meaning of Oedipus's love for his mother. As he is drawn back to her, he is drawn back to Thebes, his original birthplace: the knowledge of his body brings him there. His flesh remembers. His body knows.

And it is this same knowledge which allows him to answer the riddle of the Sphinx. This dangerous creature asks him what crawls on four legs in the morning, two in midday and three at night. And he knows! This is not even a riddle to him. He knows himself. He has not denied the power of nature to himself. He remembers that he was a vulnerable infant. This infant still lives in him. And though he is a man, he does not deny that one day he will weaken, and perhaps walk with a third leg, with a cane. And he knows he must finally die. Thus his picture of himself, and of man, is identical to the Sphinx's knowledge of man. He recognizes himself.

Yet he did not recognize his father as belonging to him. He murdered his father as if he were an enemy. And so his father was. After all, his father had tried to murder him, as on another level, the authority of culture tries to murder carnal knowledge.

Thus Oedipus returns to his mother and he has knowledge of her. But now Tiresias, a blind seer, a "seer" who will not *see material reality,* brings him to recognize his father. He accepts culture's authority as his own authority. He feels "guilty." And he takes out his rage against bodily knowledge. For in the dream, we must remember, Jocasta is a part of himself. She is the source of his physical knowledge. When she learns that Oedipus murdered Laius, she kills herself. And at the same time, Oedipus destroys his ability to perceive the sensual world. He puts out his eyes. Now, like the "seer" who taught him to recognize culture, he is blind.*

But why was it that Oedipus asked Tiresias, even forced him, according to the tragedy, to speak? Because Thebes was plagued by disease. The kingdom of Oedipus had fallen under the fatal power of nature.

* We learn in another story that Tiresias lost his earthly sight when he was "hunting" and, like Actaeon, chanced to see the beautiful body of a goddess.

And it was at this significant moment that Oedipus became the loyal son of Laius. Thus he chose to retreat from the power of nature into the authority of culture.

Finally, Oedipus retreats to the grove of the Eumenides (those Furies who have been softened by compassion). And there, with a clap of thunder, he is welcomed into death. His body vanishes. Only in death is he reconciled with fate. For this is the tragedy of our culture: we can have knowledge of the body only in the destruction of the body.

Of Woman Born

> Somehow her relationship to him is connected with death.
> ADRIENNE RICH, *Of Woman Born*

Sigmund Freud tells us the story of how he learned about death from his mother. Bothered by the black and curled pieces of epidermis which appeared when he rubbed his hands together, Freud asked his mother what these were. She told him that this was earth, and that we are made of earth, and to the earth we must return. From this moment, Freud tells, he had the knowledge that, in his words, "Thou owest nature a death."

But let us imagine that this is only a screen memory, a substitute the adult mind uses to both hide and contain the meaning of another, more powerful memory. Let us suppose that the infant Freud associated the experience of death with his mother's body before he even knew there was a name for this. He, for instance, suffered hunger pains enough to make his body feel the panic any animal body will feel when it is endangered. Or, in the comings and goings of his mother, some separations perhaps long enough to be terrifying, he confronted the terrors of loss; his mind tasted of grief, despair, and above all, a terrible powerlessness when faced with circumstance.

Let us assume that the infant Freud was like all infants. Unable to speak or articulate movement. Vulnerable. Utterly dependent on his mother's body. He gropes toward a knowledge of the world, toward a sensual comprehension and enjoyment of all that surrounds him. His hand learns to move toward his mother's face while he suckles her breast. He, yes, learns to focus on her hands, her mouth, her eyes.

He studies her expression. Learns to read her moods. He studies her size and his size. He sees her come and go and learns he cannot yet follow her. But now, at a certain moment in his growth, he must feel an overwhelming frustration, and with this, rage. For with each new grasping of the nature of reality, he must also come to terms with the immense implications of his own powerlessness. And it is not only his ego, if he even has one, which is threatened by this. It is his very animal sense of being. For as he learns more and more about his relative smallness and weakness in the world, so does he become frightened, and thus, eagerly seeking independence, he becomes more dependent, in his mind, on his mother's body.

But this mother's body *is* the world to him. All sustenance comes from her. All bliss. All comfort. And also, all fear, all pain, all rage, all hunger and thirst, come to him from her. And above all, the knowledge of these things, the knowledge of the body, comes to the infant from his mother. How, in these moments of rage, he has to hate her and love her; wish to keep her forever and obliterate her.

And perhaps he would be torn apart by these feelings, were it not that his mind had certain defenses. Against the knowledge of death that his mother's absence brings him, he can imagine her presence. He can imagine that his mind, wanting her, will bring her to him. He can even imagine he has invented her. So this least powerful of all creatures is able to fantasize himself as the most powerful of beings, and this for a time soothes him.

This is how the mind of the infant denies fate. He will not accept the fact of separation. He projects himself and his desires onto the world. Space collapses at his command. He tyrannizes food with his will. And he replaces reality with the fantasized images in his mind. We might say that the infant has entered a perhaps quite natural period of adjustment for which he has had to relinquish reality.

Yet in this infant mind we can see the genesis of pornographic consciousness. We can see the beginnings of sadism and masochism. For the knowledge of the body, which he would slay, is like a several-headed dragon. And it is not easy to forget the real shape of our mother's body. The memory of her powerfulness haunts us; our bodies remember her. Even with the sleeping postures of our bodies, her presence comes home to us. We read in Proust:

Sometimes, too, just as Eve was created from a rib of Adam, so a woman would come into existence while I was sleeping, conceived from some strain in the position of my limbs. Formed by the appetite that I was on the point of gratifying, she it was, I imagined, that offered me that gratification. My body, conscious that its own warmth was permeating hers, would strive to become one with her, and I would awake.

This dragon cannot be slain. She is present even when all images of women have been erased. She comes back to us even when the mind would deny the existence of her power.

And so, in our desperation, in the despairing infant's mind, the body of the mother is subdued, mastered, controlled, tied up, and even whipped and tortured if necessary. And in the farthest corners of our minds, we imagine we murder this body.

Dorothy Dinnerstein gives us a similar account of this process. Of the infantile thought process, she tells us:

> The mixed feelings for the body that are now projected onto woman include more, and worse, than simple love for it and simple anger at it for sabotaging our projects and making us abjectly open to outside control. They include also burial and denial of this simple love, and its return in the form of a morbid ashamed obsession which then complicates the simple anger.

Certainly in this portrait we can see a likeness of the pornographer. But let us push this story of the development of Freud's mind, of the infant's mind, of our own minds, further. Let us imagine that this period of morbid obsession is one which an infant might pass through on his or her path to a larger knowledge of reality.

For here is where culture must enter to affect the formation of the psyche. We have assumed before, along with Freud, that the choice our culture makes, to repress the knowledge of the body, is a choice inevitable to all civilization. But let us imagine that other choices exist. A culture might, for instance, enter the child's life as a mediation, a larger wisdom containing reconciliation with fate, a deeper understanding that we *are* nature: culture might give us the knowledge that in our reconciliation with nature, we become whole beings, no longer divided against ourselves. This is a wisdom which might be taught to a young mind. Such understandings seem remote to us, almost beyond our reach. We have all been schooled in a culture of denial. And yet we know another way than our own exists. We have glimpsed it in the visions of certain mystics, in our own pastoral and utopian imaginings, in our projections of bliss onto the *infant sauvage*, our secret longings for something more, for eros.

But we live in a culture that has made a different choice. At the moment when culture might help us through and past our rage, we are instead given forms with which to express that rage. All our institutions, our language, the thought of the world, maintain our denial of the body.

For ours is a civilization which, instead of leading us to a profound understanding and love of the universe, sets us forever at odds with existence. As R. D. Laing tells us, "the Stone Age baby" entering our civilization "is subjected to these forces of violence called love" from the moment of her birth. When this child grows up, we are left with "a half-crazed being more or less adjusted to a mad world." But we accept this boy or this girl as normal, for in this child we see ourselves; and we ourselves, as our mothers and fathers, "and their parents, and their parents before them, have been" exposed to the same violence against our natures.

Perhaps now, and in this light, we can understand why the Freudian analyst Marie Bonaparte believed that nature had made woman a masochist and man a sadist. For everywhere culture has made us mimic its fantasy of omnipotence over nature. Culture has created a male mind which would exercise absolute power, both with kindness and with cruelty, over nature in the body of a woman. So deeply do we associate the knowledge of the body with woman, and culture with man, that we imagine nature to have divided these two sensibilities, giving one to each gender.

Thus Wilhelm Stekel, writing of the regression of the sadomasochist back to childhood, tells us that he or she "stands between man and woman and cannot decide which direction to take." But let us substitute for the words "man" and "woman" the words "masculine qualities" and "feminine qualities." And let us say that this decision we force the child to make is an impossible one, which requires us all to maim ourselves.

All that we know as "feminine"—grace, intuition, sensuality, carnality, softness, vulnerability, concrete knowledge, beauty, motion, passion—all these are human qualities, and belong also to men. And all that we associate with men—language, the capacity and desire to understand, to calculate, to create, the generation of ideas, imaginings, the desire to master, to craft, to know, the longing for meaning—all these, too, are human and belong to women. For our ideas of "man" and "woman" have nothing to do with reality, but are simply cultural manifestations of the choice to sacrifice and divide ourselves.

And yet, ironically, the sexual roles, a product of the mind's imaginings, like pornography itself, become reality. In loyalty to culture, we try to shape ourselves after the cultural images. We become what we imagine we are. We behave as "men" and "women" are said to behave. And our behavior affects the minds of our children. In this way, an image of being becomes an event. Just as sexual roles embody sadomasochism, so, too, they teach us to be sadomasochists, and we come to believe, as we see "men" and "women" around us, that this state of mind is inevitable. We are surrounded by cultural mirrors.

Thus the experience of a child raised in a culture which has decided to divide itself against its own nature becomes more complicated than the first story of the infant's mind we have described. For this child now faces not only the natural crisis of its own body and mind, but a culture which at every moment reinforces and institutionalizes this crisis.

Now the institutions of this culture even begin to deepen this crisis. Even the institution of motherhood becomes damaging to both mother and child. A woman who is a mother is divided from culture. And because of this she must be split in her own soul. Despite the propaganda of a culture which excludes women, women have a capacity for cultural expression which is as large as the human capacity. But culture has ordained that woman has no need of culture and culture no need of her. And so she is excluded from the life of her society. One of the means of this exclusivity is to make her a mother. Motherhood, as Adrienne Rich describes it so clearly and unforgettably in *Of Woman Born*, is made unnaturally separate, and unnaturally becomes that which keeps a woman away from all which might interest her mind or her soul except her infant.

Such deprivation as a woman with a child suffers includes the fact that she cannot attend a musical concert or a museum or a theatrical performance because she is sitting at home with children. But of this, the musical concert is only emblematic of a more complete spiritual and physical absence from society. And, ultimately, an absence from oneself. For the loss of a shared meaning makes a being less than she is, in one part of her soul. She is diminished, suffocated in her growth. Like a bonsai tree, she is deformed to resemble a cultural ideal. Now perhaps the tragic configuration in these events is becoming clear. Because it is this woman who *mothers*, and she knows that motherhood is associated with her diminishment and her imprisonment.

The problem of ambivalence in motherhood has been written of widely and to it have been ascribed many serious effects, including the schizophrenia of children. What is astonishing, considering the use of the institution of motherhood to injure women, is that women still are moved to tenderness by the vulnerability and innocence of our infants, that most women do not take out rage against our children. Hatred and mistreatment of children is not the common fact of society. But ambivalence is, the ambivalence of the mother who, despite her presence and her caring, has inside her a heart which longs for freedom, which cries out for language, which cannot bear this unnatural isolation from the life of the psyche shared by other beings. And the infant must know this and must take this fact in, which indelibly maims and instills a feeling of rejection and unworthiness in the child's heart.

Thus the social institution of motherhood protects the division of instinct from culture and makes it deeper. To the cultural message that women are degraded and lesser beings is added a powerful childhood memory of rejection, and here is born a desire for revenge which colors both male and female feeling toward women. For the revenge which culture offers to wounded children is, in fact, the exclusion of women from culture. The rejected can reject. Children can grow up to inflict a revenge which reflects their own suffering. Thus through countless images which the pornographic sensibility lends to culture, the powerless can degrade and humiliate the one who humiliated their love.

The feeling of rejection is almost universally connected with humiliation. In his autobiographical writings, Franz Kafka, in love with a woman he calls F., confesses that in the effort to win her he has "tried every sort of self-humiliation." He has offered to love her, despite the fact that he knows she will not be able to return this love. In one pornographic novel, a man murders a woman because he has seen her with other men and he imagines she would have rejected him. And in another story, before the hero rapes a woman, we are told: "he could hear those terrible words ringing in his ears. He could hear her telling him off. He could hear her tell him to get out of her apartment. . . . Now he was obtaining meaningful revenge." Indeed, we catch a glimpse of this revenge in all rape. (An old myth about rape argues that men rape because they have been denied their natural needs.) The idea that a woman might reject a man seems to exist at the heart of culture's rage against women, in both pornographic fantasy and actual event.

We read in the papers that an intelligent young man, a student at Yale, has murdered his former girlfriend because she rejected him. In a California high school, a senior murders the girl he has loved for the same reason. Over and over again, behind a male act of violence toward a woman we discover the theme of rejection. But we begin to suspect that in the pornographic drama of the mind, finally, the experience of rejection stands for more than loss. For when a woman rejects a man, he must face the reality that he does not control her. And that therefore he does not control nature, nor even his own nature. This is why a rejection implies a humiliation.

Thus culture expresses its power over nature by rejecting women. The child sees that his father, and the world of fathers, rejects his mother. This being who in the child's experience has been all-powerful is reduced to a state of powerlessness. She appears to *be* nothing, to be insignificant in the world of fathers. Her words have no power. Over and over she is portrayed in humiliating images, given humiliating names.

But now the child's great love for her, his dependence on her, his trust and even worship of her, must also be humiliated, as is the object of his love. The child has been tricked. He has been disappointed. The child has been misled into a dangerous alliance with his mother. For now it appears that the knowledge of the mother (which includes a knowledge of death) cannot protect the child.

And indeed, the child does need protection from some quarter. For in addition to death as a fact of nature, the child comes to understand that culture, too, is murderous toward flesh, and perhaps toward the child's own body. Let us not forget that the child's birth signifies mortality to his father, and that Laius murdered his son. Early in his childhood, Freud remembers, he overheard his father say to his mother, "That boy will never amount to anything." He tells us that this remark was formative, that it may have goaded him to cultural greatness. Yet let us listen to those words with the ears of a child. "He will never amount to anything." "He will never be anything." "He will not be." "He will not exist." In these words we hear the father's veiled wish that his son did not exist. The father has had a father and a mother who trained him in this civilization, and he does not accept the law of nature, "Thou owest a death."

Freud tells us his father's remark goaded him to greatness. And is this not the solution of a whole culture? We enter the world of the fathers. Here we become powerful, and over and over again slaughter the image of our mothers. For we must do this, and we must be cruel, even if she has not rejected us, because *we have rejected her*. We have rejected her, and yet we still want her. All that is "feminine" in us desires to live and breathe. For in our slaughter of her we kill part of ourselves. What a dilemma we face! For if we do not kill her, we face the murderous rage of our fathers, and the secret plan of a pornographic culture to destroy our reality.

In his personal life, Freud found a kind of solution to this cul-de-sac in which we find ourselves. He became a brilliant student. He began to work at all hours. The household of his family revolved about him. His dinner was served to him in a separate "cabinet," his living quarters were separate from the household, and its work of cooking and cleaning, and his own rooms were given over entirely to a life of the mind, to books and study. When his sister's piano music interfered with his train of thought, the piano was removed from the house.

And into this study, which we might have supposed was an arid space, he brought words for feelings, sexual ecstasy, the memory of the infant suckling at his mother's breast, the dreams of the body and the nightmares, defecation, pain, fear of loss, all the body's cravings, imaginings, desperations, bliss. He lived with the deeper level of himself; he dwelt in the place where mind and body meet.

Separated from the material world, Freud had taken possession of the feminine realm again with his mind. And now, in his mind, he transformed the power of nature to powerlessness. In his theoretical formulations, the world of culture, which is the realm of the father, "represents to his son the principles of denial, restraint, restriction, and authority." The realm of the mother, on the other hand, represents "the pleasure principle," sensuality, and the material world. But now Freud described his father's authority and denial as "the reality principle," in direct opposition to his mother's "pleasure principle." Thus he had named the experience of the feminine "unrealistic," and simultaneously he had given the mantle of reality to culture. Now he could both have nature and at the same time imagine that he had destroyed her power.

But there is another form of revenge which the world of the fathers takes on nature and which the child learns. Sexuality itself is turned into an instrument of rage. The child may see his father treat his mother with brutality. He may witness the legal rape which occurs in many a marriage. Or he may witness as his father humiliates his mother by taking a mistress, perhaps a younger woman. Or, if he grows up in a home where the love between his mother and father is not of this nature, still the child grows up into a culture filled with pornographic images of sexual congress in which all women are degraded and mastered.

Moreover, society gives the fathers and their sons still another form of revenge: this is social power itself. This power is most clearly expressed through money. Money, like the power of fathers, is an abstraction. In the child's world money is never real until he learns that it represents an entire social complex on which a mother's ability to feed her children depends. The father brings home money, and the mother, the once powerful being to whom the child trusted his being, has only a secondary power. She cannot create food; she cannot *buy* it. Thus the social power of the fathers has a double effect in the life of the child. First it is offered as a form in which to disguise, and yet still hold on to and eventuate, a rage against the mother. But secondly, it in itself gives birth to a rage against the mother. For she is now less than the infant first perceived her to be. The mother appears to be a sham, her power is secondary; and therefore the knowledge of her power—that bodily knowledge inseparable from one's own instinct or from one's own experience—also appears to be a sham.

In the wake of the authority of culture, a girl who felt pride in being like her mother must now either perceive herself to be a fallen being or secretly identify with the father. But the son has already received a wound, upon his discovery that he is a being different from his mother. For when he first learns he is a male, he learns that he is different from his mother, and will never take on the power which emanates from her body. He cannot give birth or sustain life. He may even imagine he cannot instill desire. He loses a sense of his own natural power. When he discovers he is not like his mother, he must fear he has lost a part of himself. Culture accentuates this difference, but to this loss culture brings a means to perceive the mother as the lesser one, to reject and humiliate her as the son has felt himself humiliated.

Yet still the son must bear, in his inner soul, the same conflict which his sister faces. Either he hates a lost self or he denies his true nature. For he is human, and he is not really other than his mother; he shares with her the power of instinct, the powers of bodily desire, a powerful bestial love of being. And he cannot ever be content to be without this shared nature, this lost self.

Only he has made this lost self into a phantom. For culture has irrevocably identified the human qualities of femininity, of instinct, of the knowledge of the body, with beings who are "other." And because the son cannot reclaim the power of this knowledge as his own, a part of himself which he does not recognize as himself comes back to haunt him. He is terrified of women. The bully is terrified of his "weak" victims. The mind is terrified by the body. What he has lost to himself exists for him only as nightmare, a continual and silent presence which is above all ominous.

This knowledge of the self which the son is taught to deny now lives in that region of the mind which Freud has called the "unconscious" (and later the "id"). In Freud's writing about this part of the mind, we can see the terror of a man who has disinherited a part of himself. Just as does culture, Freud associates the id with "the feminine." He writes that women are more easily influenced by this region of the mind, and less able to exert the power of the ego over it. He associates the "pleasure principle" with his mother. He likens the ego's relationship to the id as a relationship of mastery that might be compared with "that of a rider to his horse." The id, he tells us, is "dark" and "inaccessible." He says it is "a chaos, a cauldron full of seething excitations," without organization or logic. From his descriptions, we can practically see the blackness, feel the hot fires, the wild horror of hell.

In Freud's vision of the id, we find the same apocryphal flavor which exists in the image of the witch, the femme fatale, and the female vampire of the nineteenth century. The id is described as a "tyrannical master" of the ego. And Freud declares that the task of psychoanalysis is to lessen the unspoken power of the id, to "appropriate fresh portions" of the unconscious for the ego, so that, "Where id was, there ego shall be." We are reminded of culture's ambition to replace nature, when we read from Freud that this healing "is a work of culture—not unlike the draining of the Zuider Zee."

And like the witch-burner, Freud begins to see himself as imperiled by this dark and inaccessible world, this chaos, this region of the pleasure principle which honors no morals, no judgments, no ideas of good or evil. He writes that only too often, the rider merely guides the horse along a path which the horse has chosen. And toward the end of his work, he posits the existence of a "death instinct" which belongs to the pleasure principle (and thus to his mother, and the province of women), and this instinct, he writes, is the "most universal endeavor of all living substance—to return to the quiescence of the inorganic world."

For this fear that the self will return, and that nature is indeed really more powerful, always accompanies culture's sense of having mastered nature. Perhaps here is the clue to why daughters, who face the same human condition, and must have the same desire to master nature, move toward self-punishment and self-diminishment rather than to dominance and sadism. For the daughter is taught by culture to identify the "dark" and the "inaccessible" within herself. She herself is culture's lost self; she is the power that is both denied and feared; hers is the nature which must inevitably imperil not only those around her, but even herself. Just as culture teaches its sons to take revenge against nature in the body of a woman, so does culture give this same lesson to a woman, only it is her own body she must hate and fear.

But whether we are sons or daughters, inevitably it is ourselves we damage. For one born into this culture must make a tragic choice at an early and naive age. Just as we begin to move into the world and taste the ambivalent joy of separation, to realize that we are separate beings from our mothers, and that we might find other beings, and other spaces, or become voyagers into a world which might delight us and find us delightful, a world in which we might create as well as be created, we learn of the power of our fathers. We have known without a doubt that our mothers are the most powerful beings in our universe, but we are told by language, by culture, by custom, by human gesture and sign, that the world beyond our mother's power over us is ruled by fathers. This is not a firsthand sensual knowledge, but a knowledge we must take on authority. Yet now we must believe in the power of authority if we are ever to be allowed to enter the world of culture and society. Therefore we must choose to believe authority above the knowledge of our own bodies.

At the very moment when we would seek the world, when this choice is forced upon us and while our fathers hold out to us a promise of the joy of independence, our mothers must carry out the wages of culture's denial on our bodies. As Kim Chernin points out in her work* on the significance of food, it is at this moment that our mothers take us from the breast. They demand that we give up our feces, control our micturition, wash our hands, and in some cultures and classes, lower our voices, make of our bodily exuberance a hidden thing, cease to touch our bodies where they give us pleasure. But what is the gift our fathers give us in exchange for these treasures? Yes, he will let us see the world; he will educate us, discuss truth with us; but this truth is no longer our truth, no longer a deep knowledge, for all his gifts are wrapped in the mantle of authority. And if we would try to seek the closeness from him that now we must give up from the mother, he will not give this to us. He himself has lost the capacity for this, or does not wish to remember it, or remembers it only as an unforgiving rage, because he himself was once a child who had to face the same maiming choice which now we confront.

---

* Kim Chernin, *The Obsession: Reflections on the Tyranny of Slenderness* (Harper & Row, forthcoming).

We know, of course, that all fathers have not lost the capacity for intimacy, or for bodily knowledge. One speaks here of the general and shaping patterns for human behavior within our culture. Few actual beings, indeed, manage to conform precisely to culture's idea of how we ought to be. A father may be "feminine"; a woman may identify herself with authority more than experience. A mother may have refused the silence culture enforces on her. Moments of rebellion exist, and they must, for the patterns we live by are inhuman. But no one in our culture can have escaped the inhuman choice forced upon us. To grow up, to come to maturation, to become effective beings in society, we must sacrifice a part of ourselves.

Somewhere in the child's heart, she must know that she is a being whose nature demands both physical survival and pleasure, and the needs of the soul for truth. And so when she (or he) is asked by civilization to choose between culture and the needs of her own body, she must feel that a part of herself had to be torn violently away, a part for which she is left in violent mourning because this death and this loss is never acknowledged. And because, in reality, no creature can really ever give up an essential part of her nature.

This fact alone, the old fact of this choice, could account for sadism or masochism. And such a movement of the psyche back to a moment of terrible loss of self—which must have been a humiliation accompanied by terrible suffering and terrible rage—can also be seen as a movement in search of what is lost. What has been lost lies just beyond that moment of choice in our memories; the moment before the choice, when we were whole.

But we cannot go past that moment of choice, and thus we become trapped in our rage or our suffering, and why is this so? Because we cannot forgive. In this way our childhoods commit us to a self-mutilating blame. For we have taken our mothers and our fathers inside us as knowledge. And since in our culture the knowledge of the mother is silenced and denied by the knowledge of the father, these two kinds of knowledge are at war within us. We may blame our mothers, or blame our fathers. In either case, the rage we feel is ultimately a self-hatred, and when we take revenge, we take revenge on ourselves.

In the light of this story of all our damage, one begins to understand the scenes that the patients of Dr. Stekel describe. At first sight, the scenes are strange and repulsive. A grown man goes to a prostitute. He demands to be dressed in large diapers like an infant. He is left alone in the room. He defecates. Then he is able to experience an orgasm. Now, according to his instructions, a prostitute enters the room. She cleans away his feces and tells him in a stern voice how naughty he is. How badly he has behaved. And for all this he pays her.

But beyond our first shock at this event is a kind of awful reason. For by these acts this man has assuaged temporarily the bitter warfare inside his own soul between culture and instinct. He has allowed himself to feel an infant again, to be close and helpless, to be taken care of, to sit in the substance of his own body, indulge in the pleasure of his bodily self. And yet he is not really powerless. The woman who administers to him and who pretends to be his mother is a woman *he* has humiliated because he has paid her. Moreover, she is a prostitute; she has a denigrated and debased position in society. And finally, he himself cannot be said to have been disloyal to culture by desiring to rest in his own feces, because he has also paid this woman to upbraid him, to put him in line, to admonish him. Even so, he has avoided internalizing this voice, and he has avoided confronting his own guilt, for while the dicta of culture still come from the voice of another, he can be relieved from the burden of his own choice and from his own conflict.

Thus one of Stekel's patients seeks abasement from a woman to whom he has become attached. She publicly humiliates him and he apologizes to her. He writes her letters castigating himself, making himself her "servant." And he signs these letters with the name Elizabeth. Of this, Stekel writes that in taking the name of a woman, this man has stripped himself of all manhood and taken "the humiliating position of woman, servant, slave." (But he does not reflect on the fact that all three of these words as he has used them have been invented by our culture—a "woman," a "slave," and a "servant" are all ideas of culture and not essential, natural states of being.)

We can see the conflict of a whole culture play itself out in the life of a man, another patient of Stekel, who argues, "I cannot understand . . . how the socialistic theorists can wish to give woman equal rights with man . . . a woman is too much under the dominion of passions." And we see this conflict in this man's acts as well as his words. For he has told the analyst that when his wife is gone from his apartment, he dresses himself up in her underwear and beats himself. After this enactment he masturbates. And this is the only way he can have sexual pleasure. Divide himself as he will, everything he attempts to deny returns.

But how different is this man, who says that as a woman feels pain he feels a "secret joy," from the woman who chooses to have herself beaten by a man? Stekel has told us that the sadist and the masochist are one. That in the act of cruelty, the sadist projects his denied self onto the masochist and can be both the vulnerable sufferer and the punisher. So, too, the woman who is beaten can become in her mind the master and the controller. With each stroke of the whip, she controls, disciplines, punishes herself. Now, as she is beaten, she can also be her father and vanquish her mother in herself. And just as the man, in this act, rages and grieves against the loss of his feminine self, so does she rage and grieve against the loss of the power of this self, and at the same time, take on herself the power of culture.

In this light, does it any longer seem strange that often women who advocate the most "submissive" behavior for other women identify most strongly with men, and prefer sons to daughters?

Over and over again, throughout the history of sadomasochism, we find the same love and hatred of the female body, and of the feminine soul in the self. A man goes to a prostitute and asks to have his penis cut off with a razor. A man bites through the anus of a young boy and then strangles him. We learn he has had a horror of women, and that in his dreams he acted as a woman toward men. A man beats another man. And this act reverberates throughout our culture, in the literature of flagellation, in the myth of the hero and the warrior, in imagined and real combat, in warfare. Men beating men in prisons, in police rooms, in political vendettas, barroom brawls, athletic events. And it is always the most "masculine" of men who involve themselves in these beatings, in beating and being beaten by other men. Because here is the same conflict, the same raging desire for a lost part of the self, the same denial returned as violence. For would a man, in beating another man, be wishing to turn him into a woman?

When a man beats another man he turns him into a vulnerable and mastered being. He brings this other man to the verge of tears, to trembling, and he has, in this act, also brought himself to vulnerability, to trembling for as in any sadomasochistic act, the one who beats is also the beaten.

And in beating or being beaten, a man returns to his childhood. He can have his "feminine" nature back and punish it in this act, but he can have something else too. For in his mind, the man he beats may represent his father. And now, at the same time that he enacts revenge on his father for his father's mastery of him, he can also turn his father into a child, and see the feminine in his father. In his soul he must have known all along that somewhere behind his mask his father had this vulnerability. And beyond any thought of revenge, the son must have longed to see the wholeness of his father, to see his softness, his humanness, and longed for this to be expressed to him, longed for the man whom he loved, and whom he sought to become, to be all that he might be.

We see this same history in the most ordinary of acts. Children learning to grow up band together to insult the weakest and the shyest child. The young boy lifts up the skirt of the young girl in order to embarrass and humiliate her. The comedian tells jokes about his wife. A woman who cooks for a living is approached by her boss. Because she rejects him, he "grabs" her breasts in front of "a whole line of customers." Another woman who rejects her boss's approaches loses her job. A husband beats his wife, or his daughters, or his son. A man or a woman is known to have a "biting" tongue. A man destroys his body with alcohol. Another man destroys his mind with drugs. (A poet speaks of "deranging the senses.") Like the man who asks to be mutilated, or the woman who wants to be beaten, or the man who dresses in women's clothing, in these acts we witness the self divided.

But the self cannot be found in such acts. For it is not "wholeness" to find master and slave in one being, to discover the beaten and the one who beats together. These are acts which, instead of recovering what has been lost, annihilate even the dream of wholeness. For in these moments of pornographic ritual, sense is purchased for the price of insensibility. What is sensitive in ourselves is deadened. Far from reaching wholeness when we practice these ritual acts of cruelty, we fall even more deeply into the realm of obsession. So patient after patient whom Stekel treated sought a greater and greater punishment, and found in his acts of cruelty not release or catharsis, but only a greater addiction.

For after all, as the critic Kenneth Burke elucidates for us, the tragedy of Oedipus contains three moments, and these are *Poiema, Pathema,* and *Mathema*—Purpose, Passion, and Perception. In our blind seeking, we have purpose, and we suffer passion, but we never reach perception. And it is perception above all which will free us from tragedy. Not the perception of illusion, or of a fantasy that would deny the power of fate and nature. But perception wedded to matter itself, a knowledge that comes to us from the sense of the body, a wisdom born of wholeness of mind and body come together in the heart. The heart dies in us. This is the self we have lost, the self we daily sacrifice. The tragedy of Oedipus Rex is our tragedy, and we relive this again and again, in our own lives, and in history.

△

His Star of David rose higher and higher as our people's will for self-preserva-
tion vanished.

ADOLF HITLER, *Mein Kampf*

We read that a pink triangle pointing downward was sewn
on the uniforms of homosexual prisoners in the Nazi concentration
camps. (The downward-pointing triangle meaning the feminine, the
yoni, the shape of the vulva, mouth, that place of darkness, from which
we were, that place of birth, the dark memories, the dark side, the
abyss.) And we read that a brown triangle pointing downward was
worn by the Gypsy prisoner. And a red by the political prisoner. And
black by the shiftless. And green . . .

And of the triangle which points upward we learn that this means
the masculine, the sky, sunlight, logos, that this means spirit and the
flame of knowledge.

And of two triangles touching, we read this means death. And we
learn that two triangles, one pointing downward and one pointing
upward, placed on top of each other, were worn by the Jewish prisoners
of the concentration camp. (The Mogen David meaning *as above, so
below.*) The union of opposites. Described as male and female (the
hermaphrodite), as the spirit in the body (the cultured woman, the
female man). Each being the image of the other. Interpenetration
and knowing. Meaning nature who knows nature, who sees nature.
As in self-knowledge, and we say, *I am the star which goes with thee
and shines out of the depths.*

THE SACRIFICIAL LAMB

> Therefore, I saw my own task especially in extracting those nuclear ideas from the extensive and unshaped substance of a general world view and re-molding them into more or less dogmatic forms which in their clear delineation are adapted for holding solidly together those men who swear allegiance to them.
>
> ADOLF HITLER, *Mein Kampf*

There are two kinds of delusion which it is possible for the civilized mind to embrace. The first delusion is a private one. The mind possessed by such a delusion is often perceived as mad. Certainly as strange. For the private delusion sets the one who believes in it apart from the rest of humanity. But exactly the opposite is true of the second delusion. This is the mass delusion: it consists of a *shared* set of beliefs which are untrue and which distort reality. A whole nation, for example, decides to believe that "the Jew" is evil. This type of delusion brings the man or woman who believes in it into a common circle of humanity. And because the mass delusion is a shared delusion, the mind which shares it is perceived as normal, while the same society perceives as mad the mind which sees reality.

Pornography is a mass delusion and so is racism. In certain periods of history, both of these mass delusions have been accepted as sane views of the world, by whole societies or certain sectors of society. The pornographic ideology, for instance, is perceived as a reasonable world view by parts of American and European societies today. And various forms of racism have been the official ideologies of societies, political parties, and even governments. Most notably, we remember the official racism of the Third Reich.

But are we arguing that because of the prevalence of these delusional systems they are an inevitable outcome of civilization? This is indeed what the delusional mind would have us believe. And when we grow up inside a culture of denial, a culture which embodies and expresses delusion, we begin to think of this distortion as part of human nature.

We see a film in which a woman is murdered. Or a series of women are murdered, or beaten, or raped. The next day, we read in the newspaper that a woman has been shot to death by a stranger. We hear that the man next door has several times "broken down" and threatened the life of his wife, his son. An advertisement for a novel depicts a woman's throat cut open and bleeding. And in our minds all this is woven into a fabric which we imagine is inevitable.

We begin to look on the violence of men toward women as a kind of natural phenomenon. And slowly, our own behavior becomes a part of this delusion which we have called reality. If we are women, we grow up with a fear which we come to believe is as common as hunger, or thirst, or anger. This fear becomes so much a part of us that it forms a background to all our movements, and we begin to believe this fear is a part of ourselves, born at the same moment as our souls. If we are men, acts of violence toward women become part of a range of behavior which we think of as human.

And in this way, we cease to realize that culture has a profound influence on our minds and on human behavior. For in fact, it is not inevitable that the human mind choose delusion over reality. It is a choice which temporarily solves the human feeling of powerlessness before nature. Yet it is not the only choice which might solve that dilemma. For example, one can imagine that a child might, for a period of time, believe in the fantasy of mind over matter and culture over nature, and then grow beyond such a delusion, just as the child does in fact, in our society, come to understand that his infant body is separate from his mother's body, which in an earlier state of mind he did not perceive.

But in this society an event intervenes in the child's life and helps to determine what choice he or she will make. And this event is culture. Our culture offers to the mind of the child socially acceptable forms through which to hold on to delusion. These are the mass delusional forms which we know as racism and the pornographic sensibility.

Through these systems of thought, the mind learns to deny the natural part of its own being. It learns to project this denied part of its own being onto another, playing out against this other its own ambivalence toward the natural self. So a woman is hated and loved, ridiculed, sought after, possessed, raped. And so, also, the black or the Jew is captured and brought into slavery, or exiled; owned or dispossessed; humiliated, excluded, attacked, and murdered.

For the pornographic mind and the racist mind are really identical, both in the symbolic content and in the psychological purposes of the delusionary systems they express. And now, if we undertake to study this mind, we shall begin to see precisely how a cultural delusion gradually shapes itself into such devastating social events as the mass murder of European Jewry, which we have come to know as the Holocaust.

Finally one comes to recognize that the contents of the racist mind are fundamentally pornographic. And with this recognition, it can be seen how the pornographic images of racism provide social forms through which private disturbances may be expressed as public conflicts. In this way, the pornographic sensibility affects history even more deeply than one would have suspected. And when one examines the dynamic shape of racist propaganda, one can see that it, too, has the same shape as the movement of the pornographic mind. Indeed, here is a classic mental pattern by which images must accelerate in their violence until they become actual events, events which devastate countless human lives.

The Chauvinist Mind

> Among our secrecies, not to despise Jews (that is, ourselves) or our darknesses, our blacks, or in our sexuality where it takes us. . . .
>
> MURIEL RUKEYSER, "The Despisals"

On the leaflet are two familiar figures. A monstrous black man menaces a voluptuous white woman. Her dress is cut low, her skirt torn so that a thigh shows through; the sleeves of her dress fall off her shoulders. She looks over her shoulder in fear and runs. The man's body is huge and apelike. The expression on his face is the personification of bestiality, greed, and lust. Under the words "Conquer and Breed," and above a text which warns the reader against intermarriage, these two figures act out an age-old drama.

At the heart of the racist imagination we discover a pornographic fantasy: the specter of miscegenation. This image of a dark man raping a fair woman embodies all that the racist fears. This fantasy preoccupies his mind. A rational argument exists which argues that the racist simply uses pornographic images to manipulate the mind. But these images seem to belong to the racist. They are predictable in a way that suggests a more intrinsic part in the genesis of this ideology.

And when we turn to pornography, we discover that just as the racist is obsessed with a pornographic drama, the pornographer is obsessed with racism. In *Juvenal,* for example, we read about the "trusty Jewess" who will "tell you dreams of any kind you please for the minutest of coins." *Hustler* magazine displays a cartoon called *Chester the Molester* (part of a series depicting child molestation as humor), in which a man wearing a swastika on his arm hides behind a corner, holds a bat, and dangles a dollar bill on a wire to entice a little girl away from her parents. The child and her parents all wear yellow stars of David; each member of the family is drawn with the stereotypical hooked nose of anti-Semitic caricature. In another cartoon, a young black man dressed in a yellow polka-dot shirt and eating watermelon stands outside the bars of a cage in which a monkey dressed in the same yellow shirt eats watermelon and listens to a transistor radio. A film called *Slaves of Love* is advertised with a portrait of two black women, naked and in chains. A white man stands over them with a whip. Nazi memorabilia, helmets, SS uniforms, photographs of the atrocities of concentration camps, swords, knives, are sold as pornography along with books and films. Pornographic films bear the titles *Golden Boys of the SS, Ilse the She-Wolf of the SS, Leiben Camp.*

Writing of the twin traditions of anti-Semitism and obscenity, Lucy Dawidowicz tells us of a rock group called "The Dictators," who declare "we are the members of the master race," and she lists for us a mélange of articles found in the apartment of a Hell's Angel: devices of torture, a Nazi flag, a photograph of Hitler, Nazi propaganda, and of course, pornography. She writes: "Pornography and propaganda have reinforced each other over the decades."

Indeed, the association between pornographic thought and racist ideology is neither casual nor coincidental. As Hannah Arendt points out, both Gobineau and Houston Chamberlain (anti-Semitic ideologues who had a great influence on the philosophy of the Third Reich and on Hitler himself) were deeply influenced by the writing of the Marquis de Sade. Like de Sade, they "elevated cruelty to a major virtue."

We know that the sufferings women experience in a pornographic culture are different in kind and quality from the sufferings of black people in a racist society, or of Jewish people under anti-Semitism. (And we know that the hatred of homosexuality has again another effect on the lives of women and men outside of the traditional sexual roles.*) But if we look closely at the portrait which the racist draws of a man or a woman of color, or that the anti-Semite draws of the Jew, or that the pornographer draws of a woman, we begin to see that these fantasized figures resemble one another. For they are the creations of one mind. This is the chauvinist mind, a mind which projects all it fears in itself onto another: a mind which defines itself by what it hates.

The black man as stupid, as passive, as bestial; the woman as highly emotional, unthinking, a being closer to the earth. The Jews as a dark, avaricious race. The whore. The nymphomaniac. Carnal lust in a woman insatiable. The virgin. The docile slave. The effeminate Jew. The usurious Jew. The African, a "greedy eater," lecherous, addicted to uncleanness. The black woman as lust: "These sooty dames, well vers'd in Venus' school/Make love an art, and boast they kiss by rule." As easy. The Jew who practices sexual orgies, who practices cannibalism. The Jewish and the black man with enormous sexual endowment.

The famous materialism of the Jew, the black, the woman. The woman who spends her husband's paychecks on hats. The black who drives a Cadillac while his children starve. The Jewish moneylender who sells his daughter. "There is nothing more intolerable than a wealthy woman," we read in Juvenal. (And in an eighteenth-century pornographic work, the pornographer writes that his heroine had "a natty little bourgeois brain." And in a contemporary pornographic novel, the hero murders a woman because she prefers "guys who drives

---

* Homophobia is a clear mass delusional system. Yet to draw an analogy between this system and racism and pornography would require another chapter. Suffice it to mention here that the fear of homosexuals historically accompanies racism, sexism, fascism, and all forms of totalitarian or authoritarian rule.

Cadillacs.") The appetite which swallows. The black man who takes away the white man's job or the woman who takes a man's job.

Over and over again the chauvinist draws a portrait of the other which reminds us of that part of his own mind he would deny and which he has made dark to himself. The other has appetite and instinct. The other has a body. The other has an emotional life which is uncontrolled. And in the wake of this denied self, the chauvinist constructs a false self with which he himself identifies.

Wherever we find the racist idea of another being as evil and inferior, we also discover a racial *ideal*, a portrait of the self as superior, good, and righteous. Such was certainly the case with the white Southern slave owner. The Southern white man imagined himself as the heir to all the best traditions of civilization. He thought of himself as the final repository of culture. In his own mind, he was an aristocrat. Thus Southern life was filled with his pretensions, his decorum, his manners, and his ceremonies of social ascension.

Just as he conferred the black men and women he enslaved with inferior qualities, so also he blessed himself with superiorities. He was "knightly" and "magnanimous," filled with "honesty" which emanated from the "flame of his strong and steady eye." He was honorable, responsible and above all, noble.

And the anti-Semite frames himself in the same polarity. Against his portrait of the Jew, he poses himself as the ideal, the Aryan: fair, courageous, honest, physically and morally stronger.

But this is a polarity deeply familiar to us. We learn it almost at birth from our mothers and fathers. Early in our lives, the ideal of masculinity is opposed to the idea of femininity. We learn that a man is more intelligent, that he is stronger than a woman. And in pornography, the male hero possesses an intrinsic moral rightness which, like Hitler's Aryan, allows him to behave toward women in ways outside morality. For according to this ideology, he is the more valuable member of the species. As the Marquis de Sade tells us, "the flesh of women," like the "flesh of all female animals," is inferior.

It is because the chauvinist has used the idea that he is superior as a justification to enslave and exploit the other, whom he describes as inferior, that certain historians of culture have imagined the ideology of chauvinism exists only to justify exploitation. But this ideology has a raison d'être intrinsic to the mind itself. Exploring this mind, one discovers that the chauvinist values his delusion for its own sake, that above all, the chauvinist mind needs to believe in the delusion it has created. For this delusion has another purpose than social exploitation. Indeed, the delusions of the chauvinist mind are born from the same condition which gives birth to all delusion, and this condition is the mind's desire to escape truth. The chauvinist cannot face the truth that the other he despises is himself.

This is why one so often discovers in chauvinist thinking a kind of hysterical denial that the other could possibly be like the self. The chauvinist insists upon an ultimate and defining difference between himself and the other. This insistence is both the starting point and the essence of all his thinking. Thus, Hitler writes on the beginnings of his own anti-Semitism:

> One day, when passing through the Inner City, I suddenly came across an apparition in a long caftan and wearing black sidelocks. My first thought was: is this a Jew? . . . but the longer I gazed at this strange countenance and examined it section by section, the more the first question took another shape in my brain: is this a German? . . . For the first time in my life I bought myself some anti-Semitic pamphlets for a few coins.

In this way, by inventing a figure different from itself, the chauvinist mind constructs an allegory of self. Within this allegory, the chauvinist himself represents the soul, and the knowledge of culture. Whoever is the object of his hatred represents the denied self, the natural self, the self which contains the knowledge of the body. Therefore this other must have no soul.

From the chauvinist ideology we learn, for example, that a woman's soul is smaller than a man's. The misogynist and anti-Semite Otto Weininger tells us that a woman "can have no part in the higher, transcendental life." The church tells us that in order for a woman to get into heaven she must assume the shape of a man. Her body is incapable of spirituality. She is called the "devil's gateway." She brings evil into the world.

But "blackness" also comes to stand for evil in this mind. In seventeenth-century theology, we discover the explanation that the real origin of the dark races can be found in the scriptures. According to this legend, a man named Ham, who was born on Noah's Ark, knew his wife, against God's will.* Ham disobeyed. Thus in punishment a son was born to him, named Chus, and God willed that all the "posteritie after him should be so blake and loathsome that it might remain a spectacle of disobeidiance to all the worlde."

And Adolf Hitler tells us: "The symbol of all evil assumes the shape of a Jew."

And now, if the other invented by the chauvinist mind is a body without a spirit, this dark self is also nature without a capacity for culture. Therefore the other has a kind of passivity that the chauvinist mind supposes nature to have. A woman is docile. A black man is lazy. Neither has the ingenuity and virtue necessary to create culture. For example, Alfred Rosenberg, the official anti-Semitic ideologist of the Third Reich, tells us that the Jew went into trade because he did not want to work.

For the same reason, the chauvinist mind describes the despised other as lacking the intelligence for cultural achievement. A white anthropologist argues that instead of language, the black races have "a farrago of bestial sounds resembling the chitter of apes." A gynecologist argues that a woman's ovaries are damaged by serious intellectual study. Another doctor argues that menstruation moves a woman's blood away from her brain and into her pelvis.

Here one might assume that the anti-Semitic portrait of the Jew diverges from the racist's idea of the black, or the pornographic idea of a woman, over this question of intelligence. But such is not the case. The anti-Semitic idea of Jewish intelligence, on a closer examination, comes to resemble the racist idea of black intelligence or the pornographic idea of female intelligence. In the chauvinist mind, all three are described as possessing what may be called an animal cunning. All three, for instance, are called liars. Schopenhauer calls women the masters of deceit. Hitler calls the Jew a master of lies. And the racist invents the figure of the black trickster, the con artist who can never be believed.

Thus, when the chauvinist is confronted with the fact of Jewish cultural achievement, he decides that the Jew uses culture for material

---

* Another scriptural interpretation has it that Ham looked on "the nakedness of his father."

ends only. We read in the writing of Alfred Rosenberg, for example, that the "Jewish art dealer of today asks only for those works which could excite sensuality." And Rosenberg goes on to declare that the Jew is incapable of thinking metaphysically.*

Thus, as the anti-Semite tells us he hates the Jewish intellectual, he speaks of the "materialism" of his thought. But the idea of the materialistic Jewish spirit is very old. It has been part of the anti-Semite's repertoire at least since the Middle Ages. In an anti-Semitic legend from pre-Renaissance England, for example, a Jewish man converts to Christianity in order to protect his material possessions. Before this conversion, he leaves an image of Saint Nicholas to guard his shop and his possessions while he is away. When he returns, his belongings have been stolen, and in anger and retribution, he beats the image of the saint until "his sydes are all bloodie." But he is not impressed by this miraculous blood. However, when the same bleeding image of the saint appears to the thief, the thief is impressed enough to return to the shopkeeper what he has stolen. And it is only then, when the shopkeeper has his goods back, that he converts to Christianity. Thus we are given a portrait of the Jew as a brutal man, without Christian compassion, whose spirituality only serves mammon.†

Similarly, and in the same historical period, woman's intelligence was described as essentially devilish. Thus the *Malleus Maleficarum* tells us that when "a woman thinks alone she thinks evil." For during the period of the witch-burnings and the Inquisition, the chauvinist mind had constructed a portrait of both female and Jewish knowledge as an intelligence of sinfulness. Both were supposed to practice a *black* magic through which they learned the secrets of the earth and manipulated the powers of nature. In the chauvinist imagination, witches were capable of causing the plague, an earthquake, a drought, a pestilence; a witch could bring about impotence or sexual ravings. And the Jew, practicing his own black magic, also caused infanticide, plague, hurricanes, earthquakes.

---

* In this sense, that he would separate the material from the spiritual, the chauvinist is often an anti-intellectual. At the heart of a certain kind of intellect, we discover self-reflection. But the chauvinist deplores this. He calls it "effete." For in the act of genuine self-knowledge, we know ourselves as part of nature, and we encounter the knowledge of the body as inseparable from "culture."

† Many other such legends exist. For example, a Jew studying to be a monk is visited by the devil, who tells him that he will one day be a bishop. The Jew then steals a horse and a cloak so that he will be a more impressive candidate for this office.

Significantly, the chauvinist mind of this time imagined that the Jew or the witch gained power by desecrating the religious symbols of the dominant culture. The Jew was said to steal the consecrated host in order to defile it; the witch blasphemed the cross and anointed the devil. For of course, to a mind which protects itself with a culture that denies nature, *to destroy the symbols of that culture is to invoke the powers of nature.* (And now should we be surprised to learn that both Jews and witches were burned during this period of history?)

It is essential that within its own mythology, the chauvinist mind believe that culture is more powerful than nature. Thus, over and over again, this mind invents legends in which a cultural symbol vanquishes the evil forces of nature. We have the legend of a Jewish boy, for instance, thrown into the flames by his father for going to church. This boy is protected by an image of the holy virgin and passes through the flames unscathed. For as much as the chauvinist mind fears the power of nature, this mind must deny the reality of that power. It is for this same reason that the pornographer must humiliate women.

This denial reaches a fever pitch in the writings of Otto Weininger, who raves that "the absolute female has no . . . will, no sense of worth or love." He tell us, "The meaning of woman is to be meaningless." And within the allegory of the chauvinist mind this is quite literally true, for in this mind the knowledge of self which woman represents has been erased. The female is "little more than an animal," he declares, she is "nothing." Thus in one stroke he has told us that women and bestiality do not exist.

But the more the chauvinist mind denies the existence of the power of nature, the more he fears this power. The pornographer, the racist, the anti-Semite, begin to believe their own delusions. The chauvinist begins to believe he is endangered by the dark other he has invented.

And yet he cannot acknowledge his fear, because fear is another form of vulnerability. It is evidence of mortality. It is natural. It is bestial. It is part of what he wished to deny in himself from the beginning. Thus now the dark other must come also to represent another side of the chauvinist mind: the other must now symbolize the chauvinist's own fearfulness.

Therefore the chauvinist projects onto the other his own sense of inadequacy in the natural world. And therefore we understand a different meaning when we hear from the chauvinist that the black was supposed to be like a child "whom somebody had to look after . . . a grateful—a contented, glad, loving child." Or we hear that a woman is a "kind of middle-step between the child and the man."

A monstrous black man threatens a defenseless white woman. But now we can see the meaning of this drama. Here are two aspects of the self personified. In the black man, the force of desire, of appetite, of wanting, is played out, and in the white woman, an awareness of vulnerability, weakness, mortality, fear can be lived. Through the forms of these two imaginary figures the memories of infancy and the knowledge of the body return to haunt the mind which would erase them.

In this sense, the "purity" of the white woman is like the blank space in the chauvinist's mind, the vacuum with which he has replaced his own knowledge of himself. And the bestiality of the dark man is his own desire for that knowledge, a desire which always threatens to contaminate ignorance. Now, perhaps, we can understand the nature of Hitler's fear when he writes:

> With satanic joy in his face, the black-haired Jewish youth lurks in wait for the unsuspecting girl whom he defiles with his blood, thus stealing her from her people.

The symbol has a life of its own. A writer invents a character and suddenly the character begins to surprise that writer with her acts or his words. The chauvinist has invented the black or the Jew or the woman to contain a part of himself. And now, through these invented personae, that buried part of the self begins to speak and will not be controlled by its author. Secretly, the chauvinist longs to be overtaken by the dark self he has exiled. And he would have this dark self punish the idea of purity. Therefore he imagines that women want to be raped, because he himself does not want to remain pure.

And yet he is terrified. He does not want to *know*; he does not want to be contaminated with knowledge. He is a man split against himself. So he projects his secret desire to *know* the body onto a woman. He believes that she does not want to remain pure. He tells us, in the words of an anthropologist: "women eager for venerry prefer the embrace of Negroes to those of other men." But now he is like the hero of the pornographic novel who is enraged because his doll was unfaithful to him. He has come to believe his own fantasies. He calls the woman—whom he had venerated for purity—a "whore." He becomes terribly jealous of the prowess he has imagined the black man to have. His fantasies torture him.

His mind is filled with contradiction. He tells us the white woman is both licentious and vulnerable, eager and frightened, innocent and guilty. For in the coupling which he imagines between the defenseless white woman and the monstrous black man, the chauvinist can be both rapist and raped, seduced and seducer, punished and punisher, soiler and soiled.

He invents many ways to play out his ambivalence. He hates the other and so he forces this other away from himself. He excludes this other from places of power, and from social meeting places. And yet at the same time, through complex lines of social dependence, he ties this other to him. Fearing the actual life of the other, he makes a "doll" to stand for the other. In a bar which excludes women, he stirs his drink with sticks shaped like women's bodies. In a neighborhood which excludes black men and women, he adorns his lawn with a statue of a black "boy," and his kitchen with a plastic likeness of a "mammy." In a book written for children, the same mind which hates black people creates this fantasy of a black woman: "She is a nice, good, ole, fat, big, black Mammy."

Fear and want construct a dilemma in his mind. And like the pornographer, he can never solve this dilemma. For he is at war with himself, and every allegory he constructs becomes a terrible cul-de-sac in which he must face this self again. He would separate himself from himself and yet still have himself. He would forget and yet remember. He both longs for and fears the knowledge of the body. Nature is a part of him. He cannot divide what cannot be divided. His mind is in his body. His body thinks; his mind feels. From his body, nature renders meaning. He is trapped inside what he fears.

We are familiar with the effect of this mind on our lives. It is not the mind of a single man or woman, or even of a few. Rather, this is a structure of mind which is woven into the very language of our culture and into all its institutions, habits, visions. The delusion shaped by this mind is a mass delusion and touches us all. In the wake of this delusion, millions of men and women and children have been kidnapped into slavery; men have been lynched; children murdered; women raped and murdered, held prisoner, beaten; men, women, and children systematically tortured and annihilated; people denied the most basic human rights, denied the dignity of language or meaning, denied their own names.

Whether the chauvinist mind expresses itself through racist propaganda or through pornography, its delusions are not innocent. For the mind which believes in a delusion must ultimately face reality. And because the chauvinist desperately needs to believe in his delusion, when he is faced with the real nature of the world, he must act. He must force the world to resemble his delusion.

For because his body, or the reality of the other, or the force of nature, will eventually speak to him and tell him the truth that he has buried, he is driven to reshape the world to his madness and silence the voices he fears. Ultimately, the chauvinist must face a crisis in his delusion; ultimately he must be violent.

We have a record of such a crisis inside a mass delusion and of the terrible violence that followed it in the tragic events of the Third Reich. It is during this period of history that Nazi propaganda arose from a crisis in the chauvinist mind. And like pornography, the propaganda was soon translated into events.

A Crisis in Delusion: The Anti-Semite's Jew

> The wonderful thing about nature and providence is that no conflict between the sexes can occur as long as each party performs the function prescribed for it by nature.
>
> ADOLF HITLER

The Nazi did not think of himself as opposed to nature. Rather, he invoked nature, and claimed that his will to power was part of an inevitable natural movement. In *Mein Kampf*, Hitler tells us that: "Eternal Nature inexorably avenges the infringement of her commands." He claims for himself the privilege of understanding nature's secrets. He has "lifted a corner of nature's gigantic veil."

Just as the Marquis de Sade justified his philosophy of cruelty by describing nature as cruel, Hitler described his vision of violence against the Jew as natural. He began by claiming that the hatred and fear he felt for the Jew was part of his blood. Nature made the children of "inferior races" weak, he said, and the children of mixed marriages even weaker. At the same time, he argued, nature gave the "superior races" a stronger will to survive. And finally, Hitler asserted that the survival of the Aryan depended on the destruction of the Jew, for the Jew, he said, was bent on polluting the purity of Aryan blood as part of an attempt to master the world. In this way, Nazi ideology explained the murder of millions of human beings as a natural act.

A common defense of the mind wishing to control the power of nature is to claim a supernatural knowledge of that power. In this way the most unnatural acts are defended as acts of nature's will. (Euripides has recorded this in his portrait of Agamemnon, who defends his murder of his daughter as "fate" and "necessity.") In *The Origins of Totalitarianism*, Hannah Arendt writes that the totalitarian government "is quite prepared to sacrifice everybody's vital immediate interests to the execution of what it assumes to be the law of History or the law of Nature." But far from experiencing nature directly, or as part of himself, the fascist mystifies natural knowledge. In this way he imagines himself to have been conferred with a special dispensation by nature, which paradoxically places him above nature.

Thus the chauvinist confers upon himself the right to manipulate nature. He uses natural power to control his enemy. He transforms the natural experience of this other into an experience of helplessness, terror, and pain. He uses nature as an instrument of revenge against those men and women he has chosen as a symbol for his natural self. (We encounter an incipient form of this revenge in the little boy's attempt to frighten his mother with the sight of a frog or a spider.) In the pornographer's world, therefore, sexual coitus, a most natural act, becomes an act of aggression, rape, and violence. And it is no accident that for the prisoner of the Nazi concentration camp, every natural impulse—hunger, thirst, the need to defecate, even to swallow, or to sleep—became another form of suffering, the basis for ridicule, or a means of torture.

By manipulating nature in this way, the chauvinist can control his experience of nature. Because he projects a disowned self on the other, whom, vicariously, he tortures with nature, he can experience his own fear of nature. (And at the same time he can prove to himself the truth of his conviction that nature is terrible, that nature is sadistic.) Yet like the pornographer, who never admits his hatred and fear of eros, the Nazi ideologist does not experience himself as afraid of nature. For the chauvinist mind is a mind which escapes from self-knowledge. The traces of the chauvinist's feelings come to us, therefore, only by inference and allegory.

We know that the chauvinist would have and simultaneously push away the natural part of himself. Thus on the one hand, the Nazi tells us that nature directs him through his own blood and that he is moved by an instinct which demands purity of this blood. From this we might understand that he has made nature a part of himself, and that he knows and trusts nature. But such is not the case. Rather, he conceives of nature as different from himself. He conceives of nature as "feminine." He calls nature "she." He mystifies the nature of nature, and makes a real natural knowledge, that is, sensual knowledge, inaccessible to his rational mind. Now he justifies his own irrational thoughts and actions by calling nature irrational. He exalts this "irrational" quality that he has given to nature, placing it above logic, calling it "blood" or "lust." Just as he has projected a denied self onto woman, or the Jew, he projects his own delusional rage onto nature. And finally, drawing on culture's indelible association between woman and nature, he decides that woman is closer to nature, and that she more than man "deeply fathoms the nature of things." Thus he separates himself from himself once more, making certain he cannot account for his own actions, his own soul.

And now the Nazi mind constructs another allegory of self, based on the idea of the masculine and the feminine. The National Socialist movement is, Goebbels declares, "in its nature a masculine movement." In the Nazi idea of utopia, the bearer of culture, the commander, the soldier, the governor, the ideologist, the statesman—all those who have power—are male. And with a rigorous consistency, the female, that part of the self who is closer to nature, is separated from culture and from cultural power. A woman "who engages in parliamentary activity will be violated by that activity," Hitler announces. And the Nazi party begins a movement which encourages women to return to the kitchen and the nursery and to worship. For in the Nazi mind, the woman has come to stand for nature. She is, according to Fritz Von Unruh, "the womb of the Third Reich"; as such, she is required by the state to possess "a minimum of intellect and a maximum of physical aptitude." She is the body. And because he is masculine and not feminine, the Nazi has separated himself from the body, and made nature mysterious, other than himself.

Indeed, the very degree to which the Nazi insisted that masculinity and femininity were absolute qualities which forever and distinctly separate men and women measures the depth of the need he felt to separate himself from nature. He had transposed his own natural self onto woman. And the hysteria with which he insisted that she was essentially different from himself reveals to us that his mind was in a state of severe crisis.

In the period of history which preceded the Third Reich, the dominant culture appeared to be failing. The existing order of things was crumbling. We know and have studied the outward signs of this crisis. The absence of governmental control. Economic collapse. Devastating inflation. Terrible poverty. Unemployment. But as both a cause and an effect of these events, a crisis of the mind was also affecting Europe.

Here and there, like explosions, the old fragmentations began to give way. The soul crept back into the body. The spirit into matter. And the idea of eros began to shine like a forbidden but longed-for light in words and images. In the works of the Bauhaus school of architecture, in Einstein's theory of relativity, in the paintings of Paula Modersohn-Becker and the poems of Rilke, in the psychoanalytic theories of Wilhelm Reich and Otto Gross, an old wholeness was being sought. All these works, fraught with contradiction and resistance as they were, contained an incipient hope for a picture of humanity in which culture might finally express and embody rather than deny nature. The idea of female liberation was growing. Women participated in government, in culture. Germany witnessed the beginnings of a large feminist movement. The old separation between culture and nature was breaking down.

But the chauvinist mind must cling to the delusion that culture is separate from nature. In defense of his allegorical delusion, the chauvinist must separate women from culture. Therefore, the Nazi revolution was a revolution in favor of the traditional religious idea—which is also the pornographic ideal—of the male and the female.

And should it surprise us that the Nazi blamed the breakdown of traditional sexual roles on the Jew? Hitler tells us that "the emancipation of women" is a product of the "Jewish mind." He decries the "Semitic wire pullers" who do not appreciate the "majesty of young motherhood." History has long known an association between anti-Semitism and misogyny; in his account of anti-Semitism, Leon Poliakov tells us that an "obsession with women" and an "obsession with Jews" most often coincided in one personality. This was true, for instance, of Proudhon, Saint John Chrysostom, Fichte, Juvenal, Otto Weininger, Charles Manson. But the connection between racist ideas and the status of women in society is even more common than this. For almost everywhere that one finds a virulent form of racism, one also finds an idea of traditional roles oppressive to women. This was as demonstrably true in the American South as it was in the Third Reich, and as it always is in reactionary political movements.

But of course, these associations are predictable. For as we have seen, the racist mind and the misogynist mind are really only one mind, a mind trying to escape the dark, "feminine" self. And it is therefore that this mind presents us with an idea which at first we may describe as strange, but which after all is wholly predictable. For now the chauvinist conceives of the man from another race—the black or the Jew—as "feminine." During the first centuries when European explorers and anthropologists wrote of the characteristics of African society, for example, one quality which they frequently mentioned, with a mixture of ridicule and disgust, was the "femininity" of African men. There were dark men, they reported, who wore skirts. They followed orders given to them by their wives. Centuries later, the idea that black families suffered because black men were dominated by their wives became part of the American racist ideology. Moreover, an early anti-Semitic legend tells us that Jewish men as well as women menstruate. And the anti-Semite Weininger declares with derision that the Jewish man "has more than a touch of woman" in him.

For centuries, Jewishness has been associated in the anti-Semite's mind with the feminine: In medieval anti-Semitic iconography, the synagogue was represented by a statue of a woman who carried a broken sword. And the Nazi ideologist Alfred Rosenberg traces Jewish religious and racial history back to the non-Aryan gods of Asia Minor, who we discover were, according to Rosenberg, the more "feminine" gods.

Here, in the racist idea of the black man or the Jewish man as "feminine," the chauvinist could draw a picture of himself which he nevertheless would never recognize as himself. Even in a mind pathologically distorted by a need to lie, the truth forces its way to the surface. For it appears to be almost a need intrinsic to the structure of the mind to speak some truth about experience. Thus, when we interpret the racist's allegory and assign to the symbols of his imagination their true identity, and when we recognize these symbols as parts of the racist's self, we see that the "femininity" of the black man or the Jew is his own. Through the image of the dark female man the mind whispers to itself that the female, and hence nature, is not inseparable from the male. But this idea which might lead to wholeness proves intolerable to the chauvinist. He must insist that this feminine man is in no way like himself.

So does the symbol take on a life of its own. The very metaphor which the mind has created in order to deny the truth about itself begins to speak precisely that truth the mind fears. And the same ironic process occurs when the mind projects its symbolic content onto a living being. For that being has a real life, a life which is not controlled by the chauvinist's imagination, a life which is actual. There is such a thing as the anti-Semite's "Jew"—this "Jew" exists only in the mind of the anti-Semite. And there is also such a being as a real Jewish man or woman. And the real human being must constantly defy and contradict the symbolic portrait which the chauvinist mind has drawn. A woman learns to read. A black woman becomes a political orator. A Jewish man writes eloquent German. And all this terrifies the chauvinist, for it challenges his delusion.

Thus the Jew came to embody a severe crisis which the anti-Semite suffered in his own mind. In the early twentieth century, a series of psychological and cultural events began to create a crisis in the chauvinist delusion. The old political and intellectual order was giving way: women were behaving like men; culture began to reflect the natural. And at the same time, the Jew, whom the anti-Semite could count on as being so different, as speaking a different language, wearing different clothes, eating different food in a different part of the city, began to speak German and dress in German clothing and act like a German. For the Jew was being assimilated into German culture. But now we begin to see the shape of this crisis and the real meaning that the assimilation of the Jew had for the Nazi mind. For to the twentieth century anti-Semite, the Jew still stood for his own denied femininity. The Jew was a symbol for his delusionary belief that he himself was *not* feminine. And thus, if the Jew began to resemble the German anti-Semite, a crisis in that delusionary belief had to occur.

Now the old idea that the racist hates what is different from himself must be reversed. For it was not the fact that the Jewish people were different from European culture that alarmed the anti-Semite but rather the new fact of similarity. As Hannah Arendt has pointed out, the most virulent anti-Semitism appeared just as the Jew was assimilated into society. Now the anti-Semite might be forced to recognize this "feminine" man as himself.

When Hitler, in *Mein Kampf,* outlines an anti-Semitic history of the Jew, he records the assimilation of the Jew as a terrible historical moment. "Up until now," he writes, "they have been Jews; that is, they attach no importance to appearing to be something else." But now, he tells us, "all this was to change . . . Ridiculous, nay, insane, as it may seem at first," Hitler tells us, the Jew "has the effrontery to turn 'Germanic,' in this case a 'German.' " For of course the anti-Semite cannot bear that the Jew resembles him. And this resemblance becomes particularly intolerable when it occurs at a time in history when the traditional order is breaking down, the female converges on the male, and nature and culture threaten to come together.

For of course, the idea of the feminine contains the idea of the natural. The "feminine Jew" *is* that dark natural self the chauvinist would banish from his own mind, and from culture. He *is* the beast the chauvinist separates from himself. But now this feminine man began to speak German, to write in German, to make scientific discoveries, to compose music. Thus "the beast" became cultured. This, then, is the terrible taboo that the anti-Semite's Jew had broken in the early twentieth century. In the allegory of the anti-Semitic mind, the Jew had brought culture and nature together in one being!

It is therefore inevitable that the anti-Semite imagines the Jew steals culture. In the nineteenth century, the first man to use the term "the

Jew" used this phrase as part of a biting satire on Jewish "hunger for education," writing that this hunger was "upstart" and "philistine." And in the Vienna of Hitler's youth, the idea that the Jew was a threat to Aryan culture was a major polemic in anti-Semitic ideology. An anti-Semitic publication which the young Hitler habitually read during the formation of his political career published this headline:

ARE YOU BLONDE? THEN YOU ARE A CULTURE-CREATOR
AND A CULTURE-SUPPORTER!
ARE YOU BLONDE? IF SO, DANGER THREATENS YOU!

The chauvinist mind has always been terrified of cultural achievement in the despised other. For to serve his delusion, he must keep nature and culture separate. Thus he hates the idea of the educated black or the articulate woman. But neither women nor blacks had been so assimilated into the dominant culture as had the Jew.

Just as Goebbels had boasted of the masculinity of the National Socialist movement, so the Nazi also boasted of the power of his culture. The anti-Semite Chamberlain had written that the "Teutonic race" had "acquired a mass of perceptions and a command over nature never equaled by any other human race." And Hitler in *Mein Kampf,* after calling the Aryan the Prometheus of the human race, writes: "If we were to divide mankind into three groups, the founders of culture, the bearers of culture, the destroyers of culture, only the Aryan would be considered as representative of the first group."

This same mind that dreamed of itself as the bearer of culture conceived that its nemesis, the destroyer of culture, was the Jew. As a shadow to the fantasy of Aryan dominance, the anti-Semite invented an enemy of awesome proportions. In the fabricated document known as "The Protocols of the Elders of Zion," the anti-Semite imagined a congregation of Jews who meet in a cemetery to plan the death of Aryan culture. Of course, a pornographic image lies at the center of this imagined plan. Thus the imagined Jews in the imagined cemetery contrive a lurid plot to "demand marriage between Jews and Christians." Together they enjoy the idea of defiling Gentile women. And as the meeting adjourns, a huge and shapeless golden calf emerges from the tomb to symbolize the materiality of the Jew, just as the fear of matter and of mortality have emerged from the mind of the

PORNOGRAPHY AND SILENCE : *176*

anti-Semite in this fantasy of an evil power.

Finally, the Nazi anti-Semite convinces himself that the Jew is taking over the banks of Europe. But of course this feminine man who has dared to steal culture would now try to steal money. For what else is money but nature—goods, food, clothes, labor, time—in a symbolic and hence cultural form?

A coincidence of tragic proportions had occurred in history. Just as the chauvinist mind experienced a frantic need to separate masculinity from femininity, the soul from the body, and culture from nature, the Jewish people, who had come to stand for femininity and nature, had become remarkable for their cultural achievement. Now the anti-Semite's Jew was to become a sacrifice to a crisis in delusion.

But this was not simply a spontaneous psychological movement toward destruction. Rather, still another coincidence had to occur, and this is the coincidence between a psychological dilemma and the existence of a mass delusional system. A specific form of culture was popular in these times; now a personal crisis could be expressed by the mass delusion of anti-Semitism. Historically, this is the same coincidence which occurs between the crisis in a man's mind and the ideology of pornography, and which eventuates in rape; in this sense pornography teaches rape. For the violence of the mind's feelings must be shaped. The man terrified of himself must be given symbols through which he may continue to deny part of himself. In the midst of his private terror, culture must give him an enemy.

Hitler Becomes an Anti-Semite

When Adolf Hitler moved to Vienna as a young man, he entered, in the words of Lucy Dawidowicz, "an anti-Semitic milieu." Of the city in which Hitler shaped his political ideas, Dawidowicz writes: "anti-Semitic politics flourished, anti-Semitic organizations proliferated, anti-Semitic writing and propaganda poured forth in an unending stream." We know, for example, that Hitler followed the work of Georg Lanz von Liebenfels and read the magazine which Liebenfels published, *Ostara*. Hitler must have read Liebenfels' idea in the pages of this journal that the "problem of racial pollution" ought to be solved with "the castration knife." Certainly he must have been familiar with the notion which inspired all Liebenfels' writing: that Jews, Slavs, and Negroes, "the Dark Ones," were closer to apes than Aryans and constituted a dark force against the blond Aryan race. He must also have read Liebenfels' theory that in a happy marriage, men ought to be physically and psychologically brutal to their wives. We know that later he shared Liebenfels' obsession with syphilis. And we know that if he read *Ostara* at all, he read a magazine in which anti-Semitic propaganda was freely mixed with pornography. In the pages of *Ostara*, lurid illustrations abounded which pictured Aryan women as succumbing to the powers of hairy and apelike men from the "dark" races.

The juxtaposition of pornographic and anti-Semitic images was common in the publications available to Hitler during these years. The popular magazine *Der Stürmer*, for example, was also both racist and pornographic. And this was not a coincidental mixture. One must come to understand that just as the Third Reich did not simply exploit racism, but instead needed to believe in this ideology, the anti-Semite did not simply exploit pornographic images as a means to sell his racism. Rather, the pornographic ideology lies at the very heart of anti-Semitism.

If one explores the transformation of Adolf Hitler as he became one of many believers in the delusion of racism, one discovers that at the heart of the racist fantasy is a pornographic scene. And one also sees how perfectly this racist pornographic imagery served as an expression for the private conflicts and the private delusions of this young man who was to become a leader of a virulent anti-Semitic movement.

One can only speculate about the private genesis of trouble in Adolf Hitler's mind. We know that he was often severely beaten by his father. Some sources claim that as an adult Hitler practiced sadomasochistic rituals, that in his years in Vienna he went regularly to prostitutes, whom he paid to tie him up and beat him. Another source claims that Hitler demanded that his lovers humiliate him by urinating on his body. But whether or not these reports are true, everything in the configuration of Hitler's personality suggests that he was a sado-masochist. As Robert Waite writes in his psychoanalytic study of Hitler, "he displayed other behavior patterns thoroughly consistent with this kind of perversion." (Moreover, we learn that "he had a taste for pornography.")

What is the essence of a mind in this condition? It is a mind in conflict with itself. A mind which both desires feeling, desires knowledge of the body, and would annihilate feeling and destroy this knowledge which is a part of itself. It would have sexuality and punish feeling. This is a mind which feels humiliated by the power of nature. In revenge, it would humiliate and ridicule the natural. But this mind projects the knowledge of the body and the natural self upon another being. It plays out its hatred and fear of a denied self upon another. Thus the mind of the sadomasochist feels endangered by feeling, and endangered by the material. And projecting feeling and the material onto the body of another, the mind defends itself and takes revenge against its enemy by humiliating, punishing, and destroying this other.

Now, supposing that Adolf Hitler suffered from this condition of the mind, one can see how perfectly the anti-Semitic ideas which Hitler encountered in Vienna and which he made his own serve to express this condition. Let us begin with a scene which is played out in the minds of all racists and especially in the minds of the anti-Semites of this period. This is the pornographic drama in which an Aryan woman is raped or seduced by a Jewish man, a scene with which the anti-Semitic mind is obsessed and to which it reacts in rage.

Adolf Hitler tells us that he began to realize he was an anti-Semite in Vienna. Vienna itself, he tells us, was filled with "a conglomeration of races." Of this "racial mixture" he writes: "To me the big city appeared as the personification of incest!" Here, in this metaphor, he reveals to us another meaning in anti-Semitism. He tells us that this image of the "mongrel races" really stands for *incest*. He tells us this directly, but from this we can decipher an even deeper meaning. For here is the Oedipal scene again: a child gathers carnal knowledge from the body of his mother. And if we understand that a whole culture associates this mother's body with the knowledge of the body, we discover that at the root of Hitler's fear of miscegenation is the pornographer's fear of self.

This is no casual metaphor Hitler has used. We discover the same primal scene to exist within Hitler's racist idea about the purity of the blood. He believes, he tells us, that the Jew attempts to pollute and corrupt the purity of Aryan blood. And significantly, he describes this corruption to us precisely as "the original sin." Thus here again, in Hitler's own words, we discover a fear of the knowledge of the body, for partaking of this forbidden knowledge was the original sin.

Moreover, Hitler's words on the subject of pure blood serve to express another characteristic belief of the sadomasochistic mind. He tells us that in impurity he has found the source of all social problems. For all "really significant symptoms of decay," he says, "can be reduced to racial causes." From his jail cell he writes: "The lost purity of the blood alone destroys inner happiness forever, plunges man into the abyss for all time, and the consequences can never more be eliminated from body and spirit." And in these words—"destroys . . . forever" and "abyss for all time"—we hear the familiar cynicism of the sadomasochist and his despair as he tells us that the real cause of his unhappiness is an irrevocable nervous disorder, a physical condition, or indeed, *nature.*

But Hitler's anti-Semitic repertoire reflects the condition of sadomasochism in every way. For Hitler is also obsessed with the idea that he has been humiliated by the Jews. He tells us, in fact, that the Jews make fun of Aryan culture. The Jew ridicules religion, he says, and the Jew scoffs at German history, and the Jewish intellectual has mocked even himself. Thus his plan to annihilate the Jew is a pledge to stop this Jewish laughter. Moreover, he implies that the national humiliation which Germany suffered in the First World War and from the Treaty of Versailles was ultimately the result of a Jewish plot to degrade and defeat an otherwise invincible Germany.

We see, among other things, that this national cultural and military humiliation mirrors Adolf Hitler's own sense of humiliation as a young man in Vienna. For he was unrecognized as an artist. He was even denied entrance to art school, and his paintings did not sell. In addition, he was impoverished, lived under the most humble conditions, and even wore secondhand clothes. Thus his personal rise to power apotheosizes Germany's rise to power. In both events, which occur simultaneously and are inseparable, a former degradation is vindicated.

It is common for a young man or woman of later consequence to have been impoverished and obscure. Yet we know that Hitler's obsession with humiliation persisted way beyond his youth, into a time when a whole nation pledged absolute allegiance to him. For a sense of having been humiliated is of course that same feeling which the sado-masochist experiences. And it has its origins not so much in the real events of an adult's life as in the mind's humiliation before the power of nature. For the mind wishes to believe that it is invincible against nature's power.

In the light of this feeling of humiliation, it is significant here to know that in one psychoanalytic study of Hitler, he is described as being afraid of women. We learn that in 1924, because a woman suddenly kissed him at a party, a look "of astonishment and horror came over Hitler's face," which one witness never forgot. The same writer tells us that Hitler's mother could persuade him to rise from bed by threatening to kiss him.

Thus the sadomasochist is humiliated by his own fear. And this is why he asks to be beaten: so that he can simultaneously punish the body and control what he fears. But what he is afraid of *ultimately* is not a woman or a Jew. For these are only symbols for something inside himself. It is the feelings in his own body, which will vanquish him and make him lose control; his *body* is invaded by these feelings.

Therefore, as another part of the anti-Semitic doctrine which Hitler learned in Vienna, we discover the metaphor of the Jew as a disease. For as a disease, an invisible microbe, the Jew can invade the body and become part of the body. Over and over again, as he dramatizes the danger the Jew poses to the Aryan, Hitler uses the metaphor of contagion, plague, pestilence, poisoning; he speaks of microbes and tubercles and spirochetes. In 1942 he was to boast: "The discovery of the Jewish virus is one of the greatest revolutions that has ever taken place." He compares himself to Pasteur and Koch, and finally concludes: "How many diseases have their origin in the Jewish virus! . . . We shall only retain our own health when we eliminate the Jew."

It is significant here, as we consider the pornographic scenario inside the mass delusion of racism, that the most common disease which Hitler named as a "Jewish" threat was syphilis.* As Bleul writes, Hitler spoke of syphilis as a "typical Jewish attribute," a "quasi asset" of the

---

* Even the name "syphilis" derives from the mind's conflict with nature. The shepherd Syphilus, believing the gods to have been too cruel when they inflicted a drought on the land, changed his allegiance to a mortal king, and for this he was punished with the disease that later bore his name.

Jew. And finally, his political accusation that the Weimar Republic caused Germany's humiliation in World War I takes on a pornographic imagery when he declares that syphilis caused Germany's defeat, that the Weimar Republic surrendered Germany to a "syphilization" by Jews and Negroes.

But one recognizes the metaphor of disease from another story. For the existence of the plague is a significant event in the story of Oedipus. It is the plague which placed Thebes in danger, and which frightened Oedipus into forcing Tiresias to admit the identity of Oedipus's father. Because of the plague, Oedipus decided to choose the knowledge of culture over the knowledge of the body. Because of the plague, he destroyed the knowledge of the body in himself. Jocasta died. And Oedipus became culture's loyal son. Fearing the power of nature, Oedipus decided to use culture as a revenge against this power.

And the anti-Semitism of Vienna offered Hitler precisely the same choice. For in this doctrine, the Aryan was described as the "bearer of human cultural development," as a "culture creator." And indeed, it was culture that had saved Hitler from the conflicts of his soul, by offering to his mind the mass delusion of racism. As Hitler entered the life of Vienna, we can imagine that the ideas of anti-Semitism almost reached out to him. For they gave to him an almost perfect expression for his private conflicts, and at the same time, a way to escape from knowledge of himself. The sexual imagery of anti-Semitism, the idea that the Jew corrupted Aryan blood, the metaphor of the Jew as a disease, the notion that Jews spread syphilis—all these ideas came from the Viennese anti-Semitic movement. Through believing in these ideas, Hitler became an acceptable member of society. If he was an outcast, he was also valued as a member of a society of outcasts, who told themselves that they owned the future. Through his delusion he was to become effective in the world. Now Hitler was to unify the various ideas of anti-Semitism and make them into a powerful political doctrine.

It is significant in this light that the moment at which Hitler himself said that he decided he had been born to lead a movement which would restore Germany to racial purity and pride was a cultural moment. He had attended the theater, for he loved Wagnerian opera. And after a certain performance, moved to tears and near ecstasy at the sight of Teutonic warriors in all their glory, he resolved to himself that he would devote his life to regaining this glory. Thus culture at one and the same time told him who he was and what he must do.

Finally, the anti-Semitic movement gave to him a means of fighting "the Jew." Like Oedipus, he chose culture to vanquish "the plague." It was by culture that he had been convinced. And it was through culture that he would convince others. Thus, like the pornographer, who takes out revenge against "woman" with his images, Hitler used culture to take out his revenge against the Jew.

In *Mein Kampf,* Hitler writes that after his entrance into the German Workers Party, he "at once took over the management of propaganda." In shaping the Nazi party, he tells us he regarded the department of propaganda as "by far the most important." But of course this is so. For this is the scenario of the pornographic mind. And in order to exert power over nature, pornography must produce a set of illusions; it must change perception by distorting reality; it must replace the real with delusion. As Hitler himself tells us, propaganda "tries to force a doctrine on a whole people," because before the real event of a political movement can take place, propaganda "will have to first spread the idea of the movement."

And this is precisely what Adolf Hitler was to do. For among pornographers, he was a master.

Pornography and Nazi Propaganda

Propaganda is politically effective. From one historian, for example, we learn that "the ground for the final solution was prepared by a cultural revolution . . . in which the idea of German racial superiority was inculcated into everything." The idea that Nazi propaganda created an atmosphere in which the extermination of a whole people could take place is commonplace. But what has perhaps not yet been understood is that like pornography, Nazi propaganda provided its own raison d'être, existed for its own sake, and in itself fulfilled a need.

It is therefore a mistake to think that the Nazi propaganda against the Jews existed only to justify the eventual murder of the Jews. On a certain conscious level of the mind this is true. But on a deeper level, the truth is that the Nazi murdered the Jew in order to justify his propaganda. For racist propaganda constitutes a delusionary system. Like the pornographer, the racist desperately needs to believe in his delusion.

"We shall see that all sadomasochists are daydreamers and are never able to reconcile themselves with reality," writes Wilhelm Stekel in 1929. So pornography has the clear shape of a daydream, a fantasy which aims not so much at embodying an inner truth as creating a world of images which mirror obsession. And in this, pornography resembles nothing in modern times so much as it resembles that brilliant scheme of lies, images, and constructed rituals which we know as Nazi propaganda.

Through Nazi propaganda, the Third Reich offered a mass fantasy to the German people. The power of propaganda in the Third Reich went beyond the simple meaning of the mere propagation of an idea. In the Third Reich, culture and act became one; symbolic event and real act became indistinguishable. Looking back on this period of history, we are constantly fascinated to see the public displays of fascist power, as if a terrifying fairy tale had come true. For the mass Nazi gatherings which took place in the elaborate and dramatic settings designed by Albert Speer were performances. The uniforms, the SS order of the death's head, Hitler's black cape, the exaggerated kicking of the "goose step"—all these were like costumes or theatrical gestures. In this way, Hitler offered to the German masses an opportunity to live inside a cultural fantasy. Just as, in pornography, culture secretly wishes to become and does become event, here escape became reality.

Above all, Hitler possessed the qualities of a great theatrical producer. In addition to manufacturing an "enemy," he was able to produce convincing images of that enemy, and of himself, and of the German people as conquerors. Long an admirer of Wagner, Hitler freely used the "techniques" of Wagnerian "showmanship": torchlight parades, "mob choruses," "the grand gestures of Nordic heroes, the recitations of leitmotivs and ever rising climaxes." Whole events were staged by the Nazi party entirely for their theatrical and their propagandistic effects. Even the 1934 party convention was shaped partly "by the decision to produce the film *Triumph of the Will*," creating, as Susan Sontag writes, "an already achieved and radical transformation of reality: history become theatre."* Moreover, Hitler was an actor as well as a producer, "an orator of genius." According to Peter Viereck (who witnessed Hitler addressing the Nazi Party Congress of 1936), Hitler's speeches had the quality of "sweeping along impressionable listeners . . . making listeners feel heroic and uplifted." And we read that Hitler himself never felt so fulfilled or happy as when he was delivering his orations.

And it is significant that from the history of the Third Reich we learn the moments of greatest excitement for the German people—during which men and women fainted in ecstasy, and imagined "transcendence" and "transformation"—did not occur at any real events, but rather were experienced during these speeches by the Führer. For, as the philosopher J. P. Stern writes of Hitler's speeches, "Here at last myth and reality are one." Now the Führer's word *is* an event. While his speech "claims for the moment a greater national cohesion" than has ever existed before in Germany, the German people wish to believe this is true, and the power of Hitler's enacted belief in his words creates this cohesion. As Stern writes, "through its very act of affirmation, the claim is made good." In this sense, then, the purpose of the speech is not communication but an illustration of "strength, conspiratorial solidarity and nation-wide assent," and thus Stern tells us that instead of being informed, the audience is made into a mass of performers and "its performance makes history."

Here, as with the pornographic sensibility, one can no longer speak of culture as opposed to behavior, for now culture has become behavior and it is event. The German people fantasize that they are united behind one strong man; they enact this fantasy and indeed become united. And just at the moment when they prove this unity to themselves, they simultaneously prove every other idea in the panoply of fascist concepts. Thus the idea of fascist power and right is proved. The idea of masculine dominance is proved. And above all, the form itself, the power of culture to dictate event, the power of the utterance over natural conditions, is proved.

---

* In another essay (in the same volume), called "Syberberg's Hitler," Sontag writes on the film on Hitler directed by Syberberg: "One of the film's conceits is that Hitler, who never visited the front and watched the war every night through newsreels, was a kind of moviemaker. Germany, a film by Hitler." That is also one of the contentions of this book. See *Under the Sign of Saturn* (New York, 1980).

But the Nazi propagandist has constructed another way through which utterance replaces reality and establishes the power of delusion. The Nazi propagandist lies. Like the pornographer, he reverses the order of the truth.* And to the phenomena of reality he gives false names. We remember that the pornographer calls himself rebellious when he is actually a loyal son. In the name of pleasure, he gives us violence. Thus Hitler, who carefully constructs a delusionary world, calls "the Jew" the "master of lies." He claims that the Jew believes "man's role is to overcome nature." And completing this reversal, he tells us that Nazi propaganda expresses nature's will, that as an heir to nature's secrets, he is a "lord over other creatures who lack this knowledge."

Now we see how delusion serves the mind. For Hitler has given to culture the ultimate power which he fears in nature. (We shall see later that Nazi ideology consistently decides to sacrifice nature and the material world for an "ideal" world.) And because the masses believe that he possesses this natural power, he does in fact gain a terrible power over historical events.

But in every way, Nazi ideology reflects the reversals of the sado-masochistic mind. Like the man who protests that he beats himself in order that he may feel, or the pornographer who tries to convince us that pornography exists to give pleasure to the body, Hitler claims that his ideas derive from "pure emotion." Yet we know Hitler's emotions to be anything but "pure." For his hatred of the Jew is an emotion clouded by a delusionary *idea*. And this idea exists precisely so that he can hide from the experience of pure emotion.

This pattern of reversal in which the Nazi mind denies reality is perhaps more obvious to us when Hitler tries to convince us that he is a pacifist. He tells us that one of the German ideas which depend for their survival on Aryan blood is pacifism. Therefore, he argues, in order to save pacifism, those who believe in this idea must wage a war to preserve the German race.

We can see that this judgment is absurd, and at the same time, we think of it as Machiavellian or as clever, for Hitler has succeeded in using pacifist sentiments to justify war. But the real effect of such a lie and its real purpose reside even deeper in the psyche. Reversal

---

* For a thorough discussion of "reversals," see Mary Daly, *Gyn/ecology* (Boston, 1978).

is a part of the very structure of pornography and propaganda. When we hear that "war" is made for "peace" or that "pain" is sought for "pleasure" or that "brutality" helps one "feel," in our minds, language ceases to describe reality. Words lose their direct relationship with actuality. And thus language and culture begin to exist entirely independently of nature. It appears to us, therefore, that culture has successfully destroyed the power of nature. This is the real effectiveness of the lie.

Hannah Arendt has observed precisely this pattern in Nazi propaganda. She tells us that the announcements of the Third Reich consistently contradicted themselves. Even within the same statement, contradictory assertions were to be found. Moreover, continually, with almost no attempt to conceal the divergence between fact and statement, the pronouncements of the Third Reich contradicted what the German people could see with their own eyes. But here we are at the heart of both the experience and the raison d'être of Nazi propaganda. Like pornography, the medium of propaganda itself speaks, gives us a message, and this message is that the knowledge of culture and of authority is to be trusted over direct sensual knowledge. "The effectiveness of this kind of propaganda demonstrates one of the chief characteristics of modern masses," Hannah Arendt writes; the masses "do not believe in anything visible, in the reality of their own experience, they do not trust their own eyes and ears but only their imaginations."

Thus the German people participated in Hitler's imagination. Along with Hitler, they chose to abandon reality. And they entered the world of imagined symbols. But this is where the horror of this period of history begins; it is the point at which we who are still in the sensual world say, "These atrocities were *unimaginable.*" For what is unimaginable to the sensual self is entirely possible to the mind which believes only in a symbolic world. Language, Wittgenstein tells us, has no natural limitation but the limitation of grammar, and thus can conceive of what it will. In language, for instance, we can imagine an endless line of trees, when, in fact, no endless line of trees exists on earth.

In this world which Hitler creates, propaganda would have to be the most significant of political acts, for here the idea is synonymous with existence. In *Mein Kampf,* he tells us that an idea cannot exist without a man. And now, if we reverse this statement, we hear him to say that a man cannot exist without an idea. But of course, the man who has abandoned his own sensual knowledge of the world does not exist without an idea. He has become entirely dependent on delusion.

And this dependence on a false idea is precisely the reason why the propagandist must finally destroy reality. For the mass rally ends. The feeling of satisfaction, elation, and power which the Führer, and his masses, experienced during the height of his oration come to an end. And what exists afterward? Doubt exists; a question, in the form of sensual knowledge, creeps back into the mind. The body is persistent, reality is persistent, and despite all his stage sets, his costumes, his repeating rituals, Hitler and the German masses cannot escape the continual evidence of the power of nature. The Nazi had predicated his own existence on fantasy. And now he felt that reality was about to annihilate him, about to destroy him. "The Jews, the Jews," he cried. He felt hounded. And he moved once and forever to solve this problem.

The Holocaust: Culture's Final Solution

The chauvinist mind is more loyal to its own mythology than to reality. Thus this mind begins by establishing delusion through cultural events which assert the power of those delusions over nature. But these events must be dissatisfying. After he has ritually whipped a woman, the pornographer returns to himself and his own natural feelings. After he has pronounced his power invincible, the Nazi must return to the vulnerability of his own body. Therefore, the mind captured by such a delusion must accelerate the effectiveness of delusion. Real incidents must occur. Real human beings must be ridiculed, raped, punished, or murdered. And finally, real lives must be replaced with the documents of their destruction.

Thus the events of the Holocaust seem to accelerate from within themselves. Both from the Nazis, and from the German masses, a certain movement begins to take place which seems to be "inexorable." After Nazi rallies, anti-Jewish riots begin to take place. Jewish people are attacked in the streets. Shopwindows are broken. Men and women are beaten. To satisfy this anti-Semitic clamor, certain laws are passed which forbid marriage with a Jew.

But these laws fail to satisfy the anti-Semite. For we know that it is not the Jew he fears but his delusion of "the Jew," and that this delusion stands for a part of himself. Therefore, forbidding marriage with a Jew cannot possibly quiet his fear that his blood might be corrupted by a Jew. For his denied self will always return to his consciousness. Moreover, each time this self returns, it seems to be more and more powerful. Because it has returned against such odds and in spite of a virulent denial, it appears to be all the more frightening. And because of the virulence of the mind's denial of this self, this self seems also to be more foreign, more alienated, more truly an "enemy." Therefore, the new threats he makes and the acts the anti-Semite commits against the Jew must be more severe.

After they have stripped the Jews of all their property, denied them any public office, denied them the vote, forbidden them access to public transportation, the Nazis must decide to banish the Jew. The Jew must be made more foreign. Must be physically separated, divided off, and sent away. And all the while, the racist mind, in the words of Adolf Hitler, screams, "The Jews are not part of us. The Jews are not Germans. The Jews do not belong to us."

But now we come upon a great irony of history. The policy to export the Jews failed. The Nazi was not able to separate himself from the Jew. (And of course, on a symbolic level, we know this must be true, because how can one separate from oneself?) For just as the Third Reich accomplished the exile of the Jews from itself, it invaded and annexed Austria and then Sudetenland and then Czechoslovakia; and in doing this, it took in 300,000 Jews, 300,000 of the "enemy" back into itself. And when Germany invaded and conquered Poland, another 300,000 Jews became a part of the German empire. And finally, with all its acquisitions, Germany acquired ten million Jews. The racist mind had claimed for itself all those territories to which it had banished this enemy.

But there is a method in this madness. We see that although he fears nature, Hitler is not able to abandon her. For it is a part of his subjective experience, and the experience of the German nation, that he does not feel whole. He feels he has lost a part of himself. The loss of territory which Germany suffered in the First World War was more than geographic. It represented, in the national imagination, some mutilation, or in Rosenberg's words, an "inner collapse."

And do we not recognize here a scenario which we have confronted in the pornographic imagination? For the pornographer would both have and not have that part of himself he projects onto "woman." Thus he pursues a woman only to bind her up or torture her. Without her, he feels a terrible loss, even an agony. He feels a rejection. Thus he takes her in rage, to dominate and master her. And this is exactly what the Nazi did with the Jew. He took him back; but he took him back as a slave, shackled, imprisoned. And if one looks at the shape of the persecution of Jews inside the Nazi concentration camps, one can see that just as rape and prostitution are enactments of the pornographic delusion, so also the concentration camp is a three-dimensional theater in which the imagination of the racist mind is played out.

Here is a movement of the mind which we have observed in pornography. The Jew, who is at first deprived of his status as a citizen and dehumanized in the Nazi mind, and who like the pornographic woman is made into an object, must now be submitted to an ordeal. Therefore, the concentration camp exists for the punishment of the Jew. The Jew is starved. He is exposed to cold and deprived of sleep. Men and women are purposefully terrified. Hundreds of people are packed into cattle cars, where they are nearly suffocated.

In every detail, the concentration camp resembled an enacted pornographic fantasy. Even the hardware of sadomasochism was present. Men and women were chained and shackled; and the SS officer, who wore high leather boots, carried a whip. And just as in a pornographic fantasy, the Jew was beaten. He was "disciplined." A man who attempted to escape, for example, was "beaten to a pulp." And then he was made to stand for hours in this beaten state under a hot sun or in rain before being lashed again or "thrown into a dungeon for further torture, or hanged before the assembled camp."

The Jewish prisoner was disciplined for the "most trifling offenses." A woman put her hands in her pockets because it was cold. A button was found missing on clothing that was already in rags. Shoes worn knee deep in mud were found to be "unshined." Another pair of shoes was "too shiny." We read that on one occasion "a newcomer was assigned the serial number" of a prisoner who had just been released and who earlier had been reported for some offense. This new man was given twenty-five lashes. For like the Nazi delusion of anti-Semitism, this punishment existed for its own sake.

But still, this punishment had a meaning. It was a symbolic act, carried out in the service of a delusion. We learn, for example, that the Nazi SS officers were more prone to punishing the weak. Thus did the pornographer, in his punishment of another, punish his own weakness.

The "scientific experiments" which the Nazis carried out on the Jewish inmates of the camps contained the most obvious pornographic symbolism. In one experiment men were immersed in ice water and then placed between the bodies of naked women. Gypsy children were sterilized without anesthetic. Chemical irritants which would burn through tissue were introduced into women's wombs. Men were castrated surgically and with radiation.

Through these sterilizations and these castrations the Nazi could express and act upon his horror of nature's power to generate life. Speaking from one side of his mouth, the Nazi propagandist exults woman as the womb of Germany, while from the other side of his mouth, as from a disowned fear, he speaks out against procreation; he carries out his campaign against birth and the cycle of life and death by sterilizing Jewish men and women (and by murdering Jewish children).

(It is significant, moreover, that these tortures were carried out in the name of "science." Here again, we encounter a symbolic meaning in this enactment of an ideological delusion. For it is through "science" that culture tries to control nature.)

But these camps had still another reason which dictated their design. And this was not a practical purpose. We know from the men and women who survived these places of nightmare that the camps did not have an organization based on a rational motive for "detainment." All the efficiency, all the logic of these places revolved rather around a purposeful madness: the Nazis' desire to humiliate the Jew. Thus we read:

> And I understood. I understood that it was not a matter of disorder
> or lack of organization, but that on the contrary it was a mature

and conscious principle that had presided over the installation of the camp. We had been condemned to perish in our own dirt, to drown ourselves in mud, in our own excrement; the point was to abase us, to humiliate our human dignity; to drag us down to the level of beasts, to fill us with horror and contempt for ourselves and our fellow sufferers. That was the purpose—that was the idea of the camp.

And another survivor tells us: "The Germans sought by every possible means to degrade us."

For even imprisoned and tortured, even reduced to a shadow of himself, starved, emaciated, beaten down, looking like a "living dead man," the Jew terrified the Nazi. Even as he prepared to murder the Jew, therefore, the Nazi felt compelled to humiliate him. For the Jew was a *presence*. The Jew symbolized to him the presence of his own nature. This living dead man whom he had annihilated through language still haunted him. For the living Jew threatened to awaken the Nazi from his dream of power over nature. As one historian tells us, the murder of the Jews "derived from a cult of illusion." For in his mind now the Nazi believed that the death of the Jew would be the final solution to his dilemma.

But we have discovered exactly this scenario in pornographic fantasy. The pornographic hero decides to murder a woman. But even as he murders her, he feels called upon to humiliate and degrade her. He tells her how strong he is, and how she deserves this death. He calls her a bitch and a cunt. In one novel, he recalls to us precisely those "scientific experiments" of the concentration camps as he forces an enema on his victim; in another, as he cuts apart a woman's breasts and systematically tortures her sexual body in an atmosphere of humiliation.

Like the pornographic hero, the Nazi imagined that his acts against the Jews were brave. Thus, near the end of the war, Himmler declared to a select group of military men: "Most of you know what it means to see a hundred corpses lie side by side, or five hundred, or a thousand. . . . In our history, this is an unwritten and never-to-be-written page of glory." Because indeed, not only was the Nazi mind, as was the pornographic mind, actually afraid of its victim, but the Nazi was willing to risk his own life and even his power so that he could annihilate the Jew. Thus was the Jewish Question predominant at all moments in the history of the Third Reich. In 1943, Himmler announced that "the deportation of the Jews is of the first importance." And during battles on the Russian front, German troop trains and supply cars were deployed at the expense of Hitler's own armies in order to transport men and women to their deaths at Auschwitz.

Finally, the chauvinist mind must choose victory over an imagined "enemy" before actual military survival. The delusionary war which the Nazi waged with the Jew was more real to him than any actual battlefield. He was even prepared to sacrifice his own life in order to murder this imaginary enemy, for like the pornographer, his physical existence had come to mean less to him than the cultural image he had of himself. He had come to live through and for this image.

And like the pornographer, the propagandist cannot be satisfied when culture turns into event. Just as, in the snuff film, a pornographer replaces a woman with a record of her death, now the Nazi propagandist must destroy the Jew and replace him with a document which proves that the Jew has been destroyed.

But this gives us a key to why the Nazis so carefully documented every aspect of their atrocity. In fact, the Final Solution was kept a secret. (Even though the vast majority of German people had ample evidence of what occurred, the official policy was to keep the annihilation of millions of Jewish men and women hidden.) For despite their belief that this act was initiated as "a moral fight for the purity and health of God-created humanity," the Nazi leadership knew that the murder of millions of men and women would be met with massive resistance and perhaps even with retaliation. (Hitler conceived of himself as part of an elite which could envision necessary acts and which was uniquely brave enough to carry them out.) From the very beginning, an elaborate secrecy surrounding the Final Solution was maintained.

And yet, despite this policy of secrecy, every act of pillage against the Jewish community, each exile, each imprisonment, each official humiliation and torture, every murder of every man, woman, and child, was carefully, painstakingly documented. And this documentation went far beyond what one would expect from a simple motive of pride which the men of the Third Reich had in this "heroic" program. Countless still photographs of bodies in graves were made. Eyewitness

accounts were taken. Every event was accompanied by detailed bu-
reaucratic reports. Even parts of the victims' bodies used by Nazis
to make objects were listed. Moving pictures were made of men and
women being tortured. (And we learn that Hitler watched such films,
in his private rooms.)

But here the inexorable motion has come full circle. Now event
has been turned to image. And the Jew, who was terrifying in his
physical existence, has been turned into a photograph, a written documentation, of his destruction. For this is the only way the racist mind
can finally have and not have that part of himself he calls "the Jew."
He creates for himself a cultural image of his enemy's death.

Now he can possess that which he has denied was a part of himself.
Out of the real Jew he has succeeded in making a pornographic fantasy.
Now he possesses the Jew in a form which cannot speak to the senses
and does not speak of any other reality outside fantasy. Like the racist
who owns an Aunt Jemima doll, or the pornographer who possesses
pinups of "women," the Nazi now owns "the Jew."

And in this same sense, the creation of a lampshade from a human
body, which in our minds is so horrible, was to the Nazi mind a comfort.
For in one and the same object he could possess what he feared: he
humiliated it, and dominated it, denied it as a part of himself, and
was constantly reminded that he had conquered it. Now whenever
this lost part of himself seemed to emerge from his own body and
say to him, "I am alive," in his fear and despair he could turn to this
object made from another's existence, he could turn to the film, the
photograph, the report of this death, and he could say to himself and
to his own trembling, "I have demolished 'the Jew.' "

The Annihilation of the Self

> Human wickedness, if accepted by society, is changed from an act of will
> into an inherent psychological quality which man cannot choose or reject
> but which is imposed on him from without and which rules him compulsively.
>
> Hannah Arendt, *The Origins of Totalitarianism*

Through the extreme and horrifying images and events of the Holocaust, perhaps we come to recognize that the pornographic mind is

identical both in form and in ultimate content to the Nazi mind. Thus we must also see, finally, that what pornography calls "love" is not that at all, but fear and hatred. Yet if we say the pornographer hates women, we cannot end our understanding here. For we know that in the pornographer's mind a woman symbolizes a part of himself. Therefore, we must come to see that on a fundamental level, pornography is an expression of self-hatred.

One sees the implications of this self-hatred in the political events of the Third Reich. The German masses wanted to abandon and deny the self. Therefore, part of Hitler's appeal was that he told lies. We know the German masses went to great lengths to believe in Hitler's lies.* Hitler claimed military victories even as bombs were being dropped on German cities. And the German people were not displeased to discover that they had been given falsehoods. Instead, they appreciated Hitler's power to make them believe in delusion. Most essentially, if Hitler could manipulate language so that *they could not believe their ears,* they would cease to trust their own sensual knowledge and therefore their own ability to distinguish truth from lie. In this way they could abandon the self which has knowledge of the body. But this is the self that is responsible for its own behavior and for the events which take place on this earth. This self wills. This self acts. This self, which the German masses abandoned, constitutes its own authority.

And now perhaps we can understand why German propagandists flooded Poland with pornography before the German army invaded that nation. For in the ideology of pornography they had to recognize the same hatred and abandonment of the self. Men or women immersed in the pornographic ideology would more easily surrender themselves to authority.

In this light, we hear a new dimension of meaning in the old protest of the Nazi war criminal on trial: "I just followed orders." When he complains that he should not be tried for his own acts, this man is

---

* Speaking of the concurrent gullibility and cynicism of the masses, Hannah Arendt writes: ". . . under such conditions one could make people believe the most fantastic statements one day and trust that if the next day they were given irrefutable proof of their falsehood, they would take refuge in cynicism." And later she tells us: ". . . instead of deserting the leaders who had lied to them, they would protest that they had known all along that the statement was a lie and would admire the leaders for their superior tactical cleverness." (*The Origins of Totalitarianism,* p. 382.)

denying that he had responsibility for himself. Implicitly, he tells his judges that he is not him*self*. He *is* only an empty shell of a man, a receptacle for the orders given him by the Nazi party, and by Hitler. He cannot be held accountable for what he has done, for he acted only as a puppet. He has sacrificed himself to this New Order. He has surrendered him*self*.

But this is exactly what Hitler envisioned the masses as doing. He says that the "great thing" about this Nazi "movement of sixty thousand men" is that they "have outwardly become almost a unit, that actually these members are uniform not only in ideas, but that even the facial expression is the same." He tells us that the men in the Nazi movement have "become a single type." Here we see reflected the recurrent pornographic image of female twins, or the racist stereotype of identical black people, "the gold dust twins," the mass-produced "doll" who exists only to serve, who does not talk back, who has no character, no *self*.

And yet where is the self? Clearly the mind still exists in these men who testify that they only followed orders; they stand in the courtroom with separate bodies; they utter their own words. One wonders what part of themselves, then, has vanished so that they themselves argue they should not be on trial for their acts. But this must be that part of the self which belongs to eros, that "mysterious," "secret" part of the soul which springs into being when mind and body come together, that knowledge of the body which gave Oedipus power, and which he destroyed in himself.

One might, in this sense, say that the masses gave up that part of themselves which culture calls "feminine." And yet this word must be used carefully. For example, Hitler saw the masses as being "feminine." And Hitler's idea of the "feminine" is a pornographic idea: the "feminine" nature he speaks of is weak, in need of control, crying out for fatherly authority. He writes in *Mein Kampf*:

> The psyche of the great masses is not receptive to anything that is half-hearted and weak. Like the woman whose psychic state is determined less by ground of abstract reason than by indefinable, emotional longing for a force which will complement her nature, and who consequently would rather bow to a strong man than dominate a weakling, likewise the masses love a commander.

Thus Hitler (like the author of *The Story of O*) decides that the feminine character does not want freedom.

And because of the quality of emotional catharsis displayed by the German mass "audience," certain critiques of Hitler have also described the masses as "feminine." Thus a witness of a mass rally writes: "Hitler's triumph was that of emotion and instinct over reason, a great upsurge of the subconscious in the German people." And Dr. Hans Frank, the former Nazi lawyer, now critical of the Third Reich, tells us that "the people are really feminine . . . so emotional . . . so fickle . . ." and thus attributes their "obedience," their willingness to give up a *self*, to this feminine quality of "surrender." "It was a madness," he writes, "a drunkenness."

But these are all pornographic definitions of the feminine. In this sense, "femininity" is defined as subjugated. Women, who according to the Nazi had the ability to "fathom the nature of things," were not allowed to hold public office. Like the Jew before the acceleration of anti-Semitic policy, the woman was only partially a citizen, only partially human. For the "feminine" in the fascist mind exists in the same relationship to leadership as does the masochist to the sadist. This is the part of human nature he must master and silence.*

Moreover, Nazi ideology had the same relationship to the "pleasure principle" as does the pornographic ideology. In both doctrines, the dominant aesthetic is not sensual but rather an ugliness verging on brutality. One sees this in every facet of the fascist persona. In the masculine, spartan dress of its leaders. In the physical ideal of "toughness" and "strength." In an abusive language filled with obscenity and threat (recalling the language of a Nazi commissar, Peter F. Drucker writes, "it was nothing but 'shit' and 'fuck' and 'screw yourself' "). Even in the notion that "joy" exists primarily to give "strength."

Just as pornography ultimately punishes sexuality, instead of seeing it as a celebration of pleasure, sacrifice was both the promise and the demand of the Third Reich. It is a hatred of instinctual pleasure one

---

* From Otto Fenichel, we read that anti-Semitism is "the condensation of the most contradictory tendencies: the instinctual rebellion, directed against authorities, and the cruel suppression and punishment of this instinctual rebellion against oneself." And in the acts and propaganda of the Third Reich, not only against the Jews, but against the "feminine" German mass, we discover an instinctual rebellion accompanied by an authoritarian punishment of instinct. See "Psychoanalysis of Anti-Semitism," a lecture read at Prague, April 1937. In *American Imago*, Vol. I, issue 2 (1940), pp. 24–39.

hears in Hitler's acid descriptions of a "Jewish mammonization" of German cultural, sexual, and political life, and in the words of Alois Rosenwink, the first organizer of SS headquarters, as he explains the symbolism of the SS uniform: "We carry the death head on our black cap as a warning to our enemies and an indication to our Führer that we will sacrifice our lives for his concept." Now the sensual world of nature is to be given up for authority. "National Socialism," Hitler declares, "is not a doctrine of inertia but a doctrine of conflict. Not a doctrine of happiness or good luck, but a doctrine of work and a doctrine of struggle and thus also a doctrine of sacrifice."

Yet Hitler claims this sacrifice be made in the name of natural law. "Destruction is nature's method of progress," de Sade writes, "and she prompts the murderer to destruction so that his action shall be the same plague or famine." And this is what Hitler tells us. Like the man who asserts "he was only following orders," Hitler declares that he himself follows the orders he receives from nature: he tells us his rise to power was fateful.

But there is another shade of meaning to this assertion from Hitler that he is led by nature. For indeed, one suspects he did feel overpowered by the natural self, that he was afraid of this self, much the way the German masses were afraid and in awe of him. One can see this fear depicted in the images of Hitler's favorite painter, the Viennese artist von Stuck. In these paintings, some of which hung in his room, beautiful women with menacing eyes stare out from the canvases. In a painting called *Sensuality*, an enormous snake coils itself around the neck and body of a naked woman. In a painting called *Pursuit*, a man who is half animal chases a woman who is half beast. In another painting, called *Sin*, a woman and a snake are coupled. Here is the obsessive idea of a man seduced and endangered by a woman. And here are the old ideas of a woman's sensuality as depraved and sinful, of the bestial man who pursues a bestial woman, and of the judge of carnality, the savior, the avenging angel, who witnesses bestial acts and names them. Through these images this mind, in its lightning movements from lover to woman, from feminine to masculine, from leader to puppet, in "conflict" and in "struggle" (to use Hitler's words about sacrifice), can inhabit all the regions of its own imagination.

In his book on the history of anti-Semitism, Vamberto Morais records

Hitler's repeated mention of "Jews in caftans" and the "filth" and "stench" of those caftan-wearers. He tells us "this becomes all the more ironical when one learns" that according to companions of Hitler who knew him when he was a younger man, and an artist, he himself "wore a long, shabby overcoat very much like a caftan, which had been given him by a Hungarian Jewish dealer in old clothes." And from Hitler's fellow artist Ganisch we learn that he "had a dirty, unkempt aspect."

But of course, we have known all along who "the Jew" really was. We have known all along that this "Jew" was Hitler himself. And that it was an aspect of himself he wished to punish. A self he would torture and confine and eventually destroy.

But that self which Hitler would destroy does not die so easily. The sadist is never satisfied with his latest drama. He must inflict greater and greater punishments. The circle of his violence must grow wider and wider, as wide as is reality, as is the capacity of his body to know the world, of his mind to imagine. For his violence will not stop until it reaches that self which he fears and hates.

Therefore, it should not surprise us that Hitler's destruction reached beyond the Jew. We know he also destroyed political opponents. He murdered physically disabled or mentally retarded men, women, and children. He tortured, imprisoned, and destroyed homosexuals. And had he survived his own apocalypse for any longer period of time, he would have begun the extermination of the Slavs and the Czechs and all those "mongrel races" of Vienna who reminded him of incest.

Even members of the Nazi party in good standing, and the party's own leadership, were in danger of destruction. At the height of Hitler's power, we read, "Nothing was genuine except fear, fear in all hues and shades, an atmosphere of servility, nervousness, and lying which made people physically sick." Even Himmler, Göring, and Goebbels felt themselves to be in danger from their Führer.

Late in the war, during his famous Table Talks, Hitler was recorded as saying, "All in all, it is surely best for someone who has no heir for his house to be burned with all its contents as though on a magnificent funeral pyre." And this apocalyptic vision was soon to be realized. For the hated self still existed. Like King Laius, the father of Oedipus, Hitler wanted no heir. He wished to destroy nature and nature's power over life and death. But natural feeling, fear and hunger, desire, invaded his own body. Over and over, he would have to destroy different symbols of this denied self, this knowledge of the body. Thus the vision of an apocalypse* rose from his delusions. And he was to perish in the flames of this vision. For the nature he feared was his own nature. He was the enemy he despised. He *was* his own heir.

---

* As Frye writes in *Fearful Symmetry*, "The real apocalypse comes, not with the vision of a city or a kingdom, which would be external, but with the identification of the city and the kingdom with one's own body." See Norman O. Brown, *Love's Body* (New York, 1966), p. 126.

O

The circle the mouth makes. O. The body speaks, the cry at the center of, voice; my feeling goes out to go; kiss, I take you into me. (And the elephants stand in a circle, they say, to protect their young.) And I take your left hand with my right hand and your right hand with my left hand, the circular structure of waves of sound: resonance. From the one to the other to the one again. *Let the circle be unbroken* the circuitous path to the center *I look at you* the coincidence *I see the long trail of your coming*. The spiral of DNA. The calculus of variations. (Round being the most natural of shapes, they say, the egg, they mention, the womb, we know the round belly, we remember, the stomach, the round grave.) Fate. *Capable of being the mother of the world*—the flower of possibility. Everything its own vortex. May it be beautiful above me. May it be beautiful behind me. Before me. The energy of the leaf, below me, into the air, around me, into the water, into the earth again to the root to the leaf. Ceaseless change and becoming. (The circular tree trunk telling time, the diameter of star light, telling time.) As in "How long has this star been shining?" or Where does this light travel? we ask, or What space is *in* this circle? The circle from which I came. And the law of gravitation. Why I am here and not there. The circle which means all bodies in the universe attract one another. And *the pilgrim circles the heart of the universe which is her own heart*. And the circle whose center is everywhere but whose circumference is nowhere. As in Zero. As in the terrifying void. As in emptiness. Closing. Opening. And all circled around her, the continual continuity, and responded to her, the infinite finitude. As in shell, cell, cervix, as in star, snowflake, crystal, as in atom, as in flower. The infinite *As a whirlwind* as opposed to the bound *shakes my heart* and the sound which speaks our names.

SILENCE

. . . it is no longer such a lonely thing to open one's eyes.
ADRIENNE RICH, *On Lies, Secrets, and Silence*

Our silence. The silence and the silencing of women. The creation of authority in the image of the male. Of god in the image of the male. Rape. The burning of witches. Wife-beating. Laws against women speaking in public places. Against women preaching. The imprisonment of suffragists. Force-feeding. Harassment on the public streets. Scorn for the woman who dares to *act like a man*. A woman's love for another woman, unspoken, hidden. Our invisibility in history. The manuscripts of Sappho burned, the writing of women never published, lives of genius spent obscurely, or in domestic labor and child-rearing; the life of the mother, of the housekeeper, unimagined and unrecognized. Woman's word pronounced full of guile. A woman's testimony held suspect in court.

These several centuries of the silencing of women are a palpable presence in our lives—the silence we have inherited has become part of us. It covers the space in which we live; it is a blank screen, and onto this screen a fantasy which does not belong to women is projected: the silence of women the very surface on which pornography is played. We become other than ourselves.

And the story does not end with this forced silencing. Just as silence leaves off, the lie begins. This lie is not only the lie the pornographer tells, but the lie a woman begins to believe about herself, or even if she does not believe it, the lie a woman tries to mimic. For since all the structures of power in her life, and all the voices of authority—the church, the state, society, most likely even her own mother and father—reflect pornography's fantasy, if she feels in herself a being who contradicts this fantasy, she begins to believe she herself is wrong. Wordlessly, even as a small girl, she begins to try to mold herself to fit society's image of what a woman ought to be. And that part of her which contradicts this pornographic image of womanhood is cast back into silence.

Over and over, pornography depicts acts of terrible violence to women's bodies. Yet even as part of these images of women beaten and dying and always as a ghost image behind these sufferings, a more silent and invisible death takes place. For pornography is violent to a woman's <u>soul</u>. In the wake of pornographic images, a woman ceases to know herself. Her experience is destroyed. As R. D. Laing writes, if "our experience is destroyed, we have lost our own selves." This is the cost of deception.

When we speak of deception, we must speak of a self destroyed. For the deceiver has two selves. One is a false self, manufactured for appearance' sake and set before an audience. This self is allowed to speak, to act, to express, to live. But the other self, who is the real self, is consigned to silence. She is hidden, denied, eventually forgotten, and even, in some cases, unnamed. Thus the deceiver is in danger of never remembering that she has a real self. The real self continues to experience, to feel, to move through life. But in our minds, we destroy her experience, and thus we lose ourselves.

And who is this false self? She is the pornographic idea of the female. We have learned to impersonate her. Like the men and women living in the institution of slavery, we have become talented at seeming to be what we are not.

Within the institution of slavery, and even outliving this institution, the racist mind of the slave owner required that the men and women he enslaved resemble the image which he had of them. Because he imagined that blacks were stupid and slow, he required of his slaves that they appear to be stupid and slow. And because they wished to survive, men and women of quick intelligence learned to mime a slow and stupid manner. That this racist mind had a frantic need to believe its own invention of black character we can see in the slave owner's injunction against the slave's learning to read. (Many slaves indeed did learn to read, but in secret, maintaining, under the eyes of their masters, a semblance of ignorance about the written word.) One might ask, why would a law against learning to read be necessary for a people supposedly too dull to perform this skill? But of course, the answer is that the people were not too dull, and that their masters, furthermore, had to be fooled, had to be deceived, *even against their own knowledge* of black intelligence, into a belief in black stupidity.

Black men and women in slavery learned to mimic emotional states of being. Because their masters needed to believe them happy, they mimed happiness. Thus we have a whole panoply of "black" characters, who like Aunt Jemima and Uncle Tom, were created by a white racist mind, and in turn were only acted out by black slaves. Here is a series of characters who are at once long-suffering, obsequious, careless and foolish, banjo strumming and delightful, but without any deep stirring of the soul for liberation, no wonder at the hierarchy of existence, no quixotic movements to freedom.

History gives us a record not only of the black slave who both pretended to be what his master wished him to be and, in other moments, rebelled and plotted rebellion, but also of another black slave, who appeared never to be any different from the racist idea of the slave he impersonated. In his *The Mind of the South*, W. J. Cash writes of "the remarkable talents as a mime" which allowed the slave to portray a part "so convincingly that his masters were insulated against all question as to their reality."

And yet what Cash does not write is that this "remarkable talent" does not belong to any particular race or class, but to a situation. Survival forces a people to learn to perform. But just as this ability to deceive was destructive of a people, so, too, was a fracture wedged between the real self and the false self of whole generations. There were those who became so deeply skilled at impersonating the white man's idea of a black slave that they began to convince themselves, as does any good actor, of this fiction. Thus an irreparable damage was done to their souls. (And ironically, that self is perhaps most lost who does not know that she is lost.)

Women, too, possess this "remarkable talent." For the same situation which created and is still creating the black actor also makes a woman into an actor. Just as the slave master required the slaves to imitate the image he had of them, so women, who live in a relatively powerless position, politically and economically, feel obliged by a kind of implicit force to live up to culture's image of what is female. That women impersonate a stereotype of the female is not so immediately apparent. Women do not have a readily available history to point to, nor another country to name, in which we were liberated and therefore different human beings. Where we have rebelled, or where there exists a history of a movement for liberation, this history and these rebellions have been silenced, or obscured. And where it is apparent that we are impersonating "the female" and thus being deceptive, another characteristic is simply added to the pornographic idea of the female and we are called, in our very being, artificial.

Nowhere is the idea of artificiality as a natural part of character so clear as in the woman whom culture has chosen to be a symbol for female sexuality. Just as the black comedian Bert Williams wore blackface so that he could more easily resemble the stereotyped Negro, the female "sex symbol" never appears simply as herself. Such women even have artificial bodies. We know, for instance, that Jean Harlow dyed her hair. We know that Carol Doda had her breasts enlarged with silicone. That Marilyn Monroe had her nose shortened. Often we are told directly that the female star is not real but is a creation of the pornographic mind. Chuck Traynor tells us that he "created" Linda Lovelace. We know that Judy Garland was packaged, trained, "made" into a star. We even disbelieve the life stories of these women, knowing that in place of history, a kind of mythology has been created for them.*

But this artificiality and this illusory history were not created by these performers. Rather, these women were impersonating the pornographic idea of a female, and of female sexuality. Marilyn Monroe actually created a character, whom she called "Marilyn," and who she knew was not her*self*. The actress Simone Signoret tells us that in Monroe's private life she rarely dressed anything like the self we know as "Marilyn." Signoret refers to the costume required to create Monroe's illusory self as her "Marilyn getup." She spent hours applying

---

* When Norman Mailer writes of the life of Marilyn Monroe, he refers to these manufactured illusions as "factoids."

makeup, teasing a lock of hair to drop "casually" over her forehead, choosing the proper tight and exposing dress. We learn from Signoret that in the actress's private life she wore loose and comfortable clothing. Moreover, the personality which she presented to the public was not hers. Signoret tells us that Monroe would suddenly assume a "simpering and sighing" attitude when she became "Marilyn" for the public.

From another actress who was a friend of Monroe, we discover that Monroe even referred to this other personality as "her." Susan Strasberg writes that this famous "M. M." was "someone else . . . she became by shifting into another gear. It was deliberate." She tells us that once when she and Monroe walked with a friend through the streets of New York, Monroe turned to Strasberg and her friend and said, "Do you want me to be *her?*"Suddenly, she took on the "Marilyn" personality, and just as suddenly, strangers on the street began to recognize her.

Pornographic culture does not entirely ignore the fact of this false persona. Norman Mailer writes of Marilyn Monroe that: "She is a mirror of the pleasure of those who stare at her." Yet, knowing that her symbolic existence was a mask, he refuses to look behind this mask. All he hypothesizes about a self behind this mask is that this first self must have felt a need to create a false self. Beyond that, he records no being, no will, no intelligence, no *self.* And in this we sense the attitude of a whole culture toward the "sex symbol." Beneath the extravagant worship of the sex goddess we can hear the echo of Otto Weininger's words: "Woman is nothing."

And yet, had another self not existed, a self to be lost and a self to be violated, the life of this actress would not have been a tragedy. In an interview before her death, she said: "I used to get the feeling, and sometimes I still get it, that sometimes I was fooling somebody, I don't know who or what—maybe myself." But this *is* the *experience* of loss. When one has lost one's *self,* one does not say, I am one way but I behave another. Rather, one has forgotten that the lost self ever existed. Only a feeling of falsity remains. One may feel empty inside. Or one may have a continual feeling of loneliness. And perhaps there is a kind of grief. A grief which seems inappropriate, for there has been no visible death; a grief which merely confirms emptiness. And which might lead one to believe that the assessment of culture is correct, that behind the mask there is nothing.

Yet this grief should be taken as evidence for a self which cries to be recognized.

If we are to understand the tragedy of this tale in which this woman who was the goddess of sex became nothing, turned a murderous glance at herself, destroyed herself, we must go back to a point before the male psyche began to speak to us. We must recognize that in our own experience of emptiness, that even though one feels "empty," one must *have* a self in order to feel this emptiness; a loss cannot be felt unless what is missed is really a lost part of the self. Unwholeness is a feeling which belongs only to a being born whole and somehow tragically denied access to this whole self. A being born "unwhole" would be whole in that partiality, happy with that cavernous state, and feel no emptiness, miss nothing, feel at home in a vacuum of identity. It is precisely because we have selves that we mourn, that we become depressed, take drugs, even, sometimes, die.

Our madness, the terror of a white room without sound or image. The fear of annihilation. The child's nightmare of being kidnapped. Here the soul attempts to play out for us our own knowledge of loss.

But this protest over a lost self turns its rage upon the false self. The real self would perhaps destroy this false self. She rises up from years of suffocated rage to take revenge. She imagines the false self has destroyed her. And because pornographic culture attaches this false self to her body, she confuses this false self with her own body. It is thus that a woman angry with pornography's false image of herself tries to destroy her own body. This is how a being in pain from an imposed silence comes finally to strike out against herself.

But in this, the extraordinary film star is not so different from an ordinary woman. Rather, she is emblematic of culture's expectations of us. Ordinary women wear makeup. Ordinary women attempt to change our bodies to resemble a pornographic ideal. Ordinary women construct a false self and come to hate this self. And yet the film star who represents to culture the perfection of a false image of women can represent a danger and a threat to an ordinary woman's life. For the image of the film star is held up to her both as what she must imitate and to show her how she has failed to live up to the porno-graphic ideal. Moreover, the ordinary woman can choose to project her hatred of her own false self upon the "sex symbol." It is always easier for a woman within pornographic culture to take out her rage over her silence and her powerlessness on another woman than on that culture itself. Therefore, certain ordinary women come to hate the women who are culture's sex symbols.

And yet, when we do this, we participate ultimately in a cruelty to ourselves. We become instruments of pornography's sadism against women.

Let us imagine that we are suspended in space, a space where no pornographic image of women exists. Therefore, we have never seen an image of ourselves. From the pure knowledge of our bodies, a kind of joy wells to the surface of our minds. We anticipate one day knowing more of this being we feel to be ourselves. Now, in the distance, a creature comes closer to us. And we see the outlines of her shape, we recognize her to be like us. She shall be our mirror. Finally, this knowledge we had been hoping for, not even knowing a name for it, shall be ours. But as she comes closer we are horrified. Her face is a mask. Perhaps the makeup is somewhat grotesque. Or perhaps it is the falsity of her expression, the very fakeness of her smile, that repels us. Or perhaps she opens her body up in the way pornographic models display themselves for the camera, and we mistake this posture for our own posture. Perhaps she is wearing lingerie that resembles a horse's bridle, but in black lace, an image which in its mixture of delicacy and sadism is inherently ugly. Because she wears a mask, we cannot feel compassion for her. If her face admits some trace of vulnerability, it is the vulnerability of one who agrees to be a victim, and in our animal bodies, this strikes us as a monstrosity.

Thus we cast her away, we become almost violent in our effort to remove her and all memory of her from our sight. We tell ourselves we despise her. We deny that this image of her has anything to do with ourselves. And yet this image has entered us. And now we are no longer free. For in another layer of our minds, we are convinced that we are like this woman, indeed identical to her. Thus, just as we have lost her, the possibility of knowing her, of resonating with her being, we have lost ourselves.

But let us suppose that instead we disbelieve the mask she wears. Let us say that being in space for so long has made us so certain of who we are that falsity has little effect on us. We see through delusion. Thus we proceed to peel away the mask she wears. We ignore her clothing. We respond only to the body, and know it has capacity for a quite different posture. Now, as we move to know this being, we are taking back an aspect of ourselves which has been stolen. We refuse to hate another woman. We refuse to enter this drama as pornography has asked us to act.

If we enter the life of Marilyn Monroe, we find that behind a facade of glamour is a life we can recognize. Let us begin with a simple recital of facts (some of which seem ordinary and others extraordinary). When she is a baby, her mother is abandoned by her father. And soon her mother abandons her to the care of a foster mother, who lives across the street from the child's grandmother. This foster mother is a traditional woman, who gives all her life to the care of children and a husband and who is, moreover, a Christian fundamentalist.

This child begins as a kind of tomboy, physically strong and tough. She is often admonished for overpowering her half-brother. Her mother will not allow her to be adopted by her foster mother. But her "brother" is adopted. In her early years in school she is described as a bright student, but after a few years, her efforts as a student suffer a sudden decline.

Now her mother, who works in the film industry, takes her child to live with her. But soon after, she breaks down and is incarcerated in a mental institution. Thus the child is sent to foster homes and to an orphanage. In one foster home, she tells us, she is molested by her foster father. In the orphanage she is given special attention by a teacher who tells her she is pretty and allows her to wear makeup. As she is growing up, she is happy to receive attention from boys and men who admire her body.

She marries conventionally, and very early, partly so that she will be able to leave her foster home. But this marriage fails. Then she begins work as a model. She comes to the attention of the film industry when she models for a pornographic photograph. She changes her name to Marilyn Monroe. Later she becomes one of the most famous actresses of her time or any other time. She is, in Mailer's words, society's "sex goddess." At the pinnacle of her career, she takes her own life.

Now we know that the circumstances of Marilyn Monroe's childhood were extreme. And yet her suffering is not wholly unfamiliar to the ordinary woman with an ordinary childhood. For there is a sense in which all women are motherless. The classic social idea of what it is to be "a mother" is that one is in effect a nonbeing. The mother's name has been erased and substituted with a man's name. She exists to please her husband and her children. She serves; she organizes herself about other needs. Therefore, her decisions have no meaning to herself. Her intelligence has no independent life. Of course, she must have a great intelligence to perform the work that she does. But this is never a perceived intelligence and she never speaks for her*self*. Or if she does speak for herself, she is perceived as being a bad mother or a bad wife, for the essence of a good wife and mother is to be selfless. Moreover, her sexuality is buried beneath the madonna-like image of her motherhood.

We know many women who have raised children who have indeed continued to express a self. But the idea of female selflessness has worked a terrible damage on many other women who raised children. Thus many women have had mothers who were not present as *beings*.

Perhaps one's mother has been without an identity. She conceals this, trying as much as possible to impersonate the most normal of mothers. But always there is something unreal, uncannily unreal, about her. Knowing she has fulfilled her role perfectly, the mind casts back, the heart longs, for something more. But always finds only a flat, perfect image reflected back, a deathlike and still mask of being. Inside, then, this supposedly perfectly mothered woman feels the same papier-mâché self. Polite. Correct. Normal. Empty. Or perhaps one's mother suffered her lack of identity in another way. Perhaps she searched for a self among men. She might have been what men called a "whore." Or she went mad. Or suffered terrible depressions. Took drugs of an acceptable nature, Miltown, Valium. Perhaps she was in her character rather vague, or silly, and hence insubstantial: the type of female impersonation for which Gracie Allen became famous. Or perhaps—and this is the subtlest of all the permutations upon the nonbeing of mother—one's mother, lacking a sense of self, hastily constructed an identity which was more armor than expression, containing "meaning" only as a protection, a kind of dogma of selfhood, this self a rigid mask. The pretense might indeed be felt as a presence in the world. This mother might act effectively, do significant work, garner to herself the esteem of a culture rarely conferred on women. And yet, when her daughter reaches to find a more intimate self behind this "presence," she finds only a frantic refusal on the part of her mother to be anything other than her public persona. Finally, the child alone comes to realize that this very present woman suffers from nonbeingness, from an inner silence of her real self. And the child, in her daily life, lives out the terror of her mother's loss, suffers a fear that *she* has no identity.

To look back into childhood, in the place occupied by one's mother, and find nothing, this is a desolation. Every moment of adult fear is colored by this backward glance into invisibility. No image for courage exists, none of the mind's way of creating courage. But it is precisely great courage which a woman needs if she is to step out of her pornographic role and to cease impersonating the female.

And to this absence of a female model of courage we must add the cultural idea of female destructiveness. We find this idea manifest in the childhood of Marilyn Monroe and in the lives of ordinary women. Here is the bright and tough little girl who slowly transforms herself into a simpering and sighing creature. Statistics have recorded that at a certain age, a girl's performance in school declines. The little girl decides not to be a "tomboy." But why? Let us make a conjecture about Marilyn Monroe's decision to become "feminine," for this decision may be emblematic of every female decision to give up the self in favor of a pornographic self.

First, we must recall that children are given to feeling guilty about events over which they really have no control. Indeed, guilt is one way in which they might pretend to themselves they can control an overpowering world. And in this light, let us suppose that Marilyn Monroe felt guilty about the fact that her father abandoned her mother. Thus, from guilt, she would look at her own character to find what might have caused this abandonment. And this is why she becomes extremely sensitive to those criticisms which are made of her, and which society makes of women. She learns that it is wrong for her to be stronger than her brother, Lester. She learns that men like pliable, submissive, quiet, and not too intelligent women. She imagines that her strength, her intelligence, the very power of her beingness, drove her father away, and therefore she becomes afraid of the destructiveness of her authentic self. *Her own erotic energy is set against her need to be loved.*

But this is not so far from an ordinary woman's experience. Even if she is not abandoned by her father, over and over again culture tells her that men abandon women who speak too loudly, or who are too *present*. And her very survival in the world depends on her being able to find a man to marry. Therefore, she gives up being a tomboy and learns "femininity."

Another incident in Marilyn Monroe's early childhood which appears to be extraordinary is in fact more ordinary than we might have supposed. She tells us that she was molested as a child. But now one begins to discover that the number of female children who are molested by a father or a foster father or an uncle or a neighbor is alarming. And we learn, too, that a typical response to this early rape or molestation is to become "seductive." For in this way, the child both reflects her feelings of guilt and of having been "soiled," and she also attempts to exert some control over the danger of rape.

But let us, from an "ordinary" woman's knowledge of female sexuality, reconstruct still another explanation for why Monroe became the seductive "sex goddess." To begin with, let us take note of the rather extraordinary suggestion made by Norman Mailer, which he tells us was based on "private," "reliable" male sources, that Monroe was almost "frigid." (She herself tells us that she did not understand what it was that made young men so "urgent.")

We do not know if Mailer's observation is truthful. But let us conjecture that there is some truth in it. And let us try to discover the meaning of that by translating a male word for female experience into female language. For a woman never experiences herself as being *frigid*. Rather, she feels *numb*.

Now inside numbness, or behind numbness, is the capacity for feeling. Numbness does not signify an absence of feeling, but rather an arrest. And certainly in the early life of the child who was to become Marilyn Monroe we can find much cause for an arrest of feeling. Yet, too, in this early life we discover a bright and energetic child, a child of much power, who must also have been very feeling. One can still sense this strong feeling even through the pornographic mask of the adult Marilyn Monroe.

Here is the classic condition of the female self: the experience of numbness and the burial of feeling. Yet this lost and feeling self, in Marilyn Monroe, must have been crying to be known. We imagine that she must have mourned this "erotic" self, this lost self. Indeed, she is not content at all with numbness or nonbeingness. She refuses to submit to this female condition. She would have nothing less than her own capacity to feel returned to her, her own eros returned to her.

But she is numb.* To be well again, she needs to find a way back to her original self. And that way is blocked to her. Therefore, in order to find herself, she turns to culture for some model of female sexuality to imitate.

We know what her culture gives her. We also know that, in fact, her mother was wedded to culture's image of female glamour. She was a film technician, who was enamored of Hollywood's world of fantasy. She kept a portrait of Clark Gable by her bed. Thus we can so clearly see the child, still wanting her mother's love, out of a colossal deprivation move colossally, not to imitate her mother, but to imitate that mother's ideal of love. (And let us acknowledge here the heroic effort toward wellness. She might have chosen to imitate her mother's madness instead of her mother's dream.)

But an ideal is so much more elusive, so much harder to follow than a real human being. To follow such a dream takes very large acting talents. Monroe must learn to impersonate not only a "woman," but she must impersonate culture's *ideal* of a "sexual" woman. And if she is numb to her own feeling, she must imitate culture's dream of female sexuality. For in this case, the knowledge of her own body is lost to her.

We have ample evidence that whatever else she was, she was a

---

*In his biography of Marilyn Monroe, Mailer quotes Natasha Lytess as saying of Monroe, "I often felt she was a somnambulist walking around." And later he quotes Nunnally Johnson's description of Monroe as "ten feet underwater . . . a wall of thick cotton . . . You stick her with a pin and 8 days later she says 'Ouch.' " Norman Mailer, *Marilyn* (New York, 1973), p. 27.

rebel against society's sexual double standard. She would not wear bras and girdles. She refused to be ashamed of having posed in the nude.

Yet, in this rebellion, what images did she have to follow?* She undoubtedly had never heard of Emma Goldman or of Isadora Duncan. In the years of her childhood, her culture had become silent regarding the lives of these two women. What she was offered as an image of female sexuality was much the same as the image she projected.

We read that Laurence Olivier described her as "being able to suggest one moment that she is the naughtiest little thing and the next that she's perfectly innocent . . ." But this is pornographic culture's idea of female sexuality. The virgin and the whore. Justine and Juliette. Complete innocence, or a destructive depravity. Moreover, this is an imagery which when combined expresses Monroe's dilemma perfectly. The quality she has of "lostness" and of grief becomes "virginal." That she is afraid of her own power, that her guilt causes her to repress her own intelligence, all this contributes to the sense of her "innocence." In her uncertainty over who she is, she whispers. (Like the black slave, she must appear to be incapable of learning.) Therefore, she exhibits carnal knowledge, but she does not dare to have carnal knowledge.

And again, nowhere can she find any feminine protest against this pornographic imagery. For any attempt which a woman makes to protest this falsity is described by the pornographic culture as prudery. Finally, those women who would protest this imagery even take up the language of prudery, because for them no other language exists. They worry that their daughters will be exploited and made into things. But they can only express this worry by asserting that certain behavior is not "proper." For they have no way to say that such behavior is dangerous to a woman's body and soul.

Thus Marilyn Monroe can find only one kind of image that expresses the female eros she wants to reclaim for herself. Now we might ask

---

*As an illustration of the power of images and models over our behavior, Frances Jaffer has told me of the following newspaper story: A little girl who was kidnapped and put in the trunk of a car managed to pick the lock from the inside of the trunk and free herself after her assailant drove into a gas station. When she was asked how she managed this brave and mechanically very difficult escape, she responded that she asked herself what Nancy Drew might have done in the same situation.

why this child was not strong enough to invent her own image of sexuality. But we must remember that *she was numb*. The truth her body might have given her was cut off from her. And we must add to that the understanding that very few human beings can shape their behavior without reference to images of human behavior. It is an inherent part of human psychology that one makes oneself after an image of what one wants to be. (Jean-Paul Sartre tells us he became a writer by pretending to be a writer.)

We know that indeed one of the shapes of eros is to bear knowledge of how to be in the world.* We imitate what we love. We even discover who we are by entering, in mimicry, the being of one we love. All our lives we enlarge our beings by encounters with beings and images of beings and natural symbols whose essence, on meditation, enter us. The sociologist Kenneth E. Boulding tells us people are what their images make them; he tells us we even have a tendency to remake ourselves after the images that others have of us.

Here one must make a distinction between two kinds of images. For there is a kind of image fatal to the soul and another which brings the soul to life. A culture can attempt to deny reality or to reflect the real. Culture which denies the real replaces reality with image. And a culture of denial is narcissistic.

Marilyn Monroe's "narcissism" was not of her own making. It was fabricated in another set of minds, in the pornographic imagination. Even the studio where she worked told her that they had created her. "Marilyn" did not belong to her. Indeed, the narcissist in this dramatic scene composed of film star and audience turns out to be not the star at all, but clearly the audience, for when they see her, they see a part of themselves. Like all pornographic heroines, the image which Marilyn Monroe impersonated was a projection of the male psyche.

Here is the essential tragedy of Marilyn Monroe. We sense that because she wished to reclaim her own eros, she was moved to impersonate a pornographic image of female sexuality. But if she was trying to escape emptiness, she unwittingly took upon herself an image of emptiness. For hidden beneath every pornographic image of female glamour is the conviction that a woman does not really exist.

*See Audre Lorde, *Uses of the Erotic: The Erotic as Power* New York, 1978).

Think of the ironic progress of her life. Increasingly, as she felt empty, she must have decided that if only she could improve her impersonation of a sex symbol, she might finally find her real *self*. All her life, she had been led to believe that it was herself and not the pornographic ideal who was deficient. That she felt herself to be a fraud, that is, to be in reality unlike the image she copied, only made her try harder and harder to perfect her impersonation. Finally, she became the sex goddess of her age. Now she was the very image she had hoped so desperately to imitate. Yet, even *being* this image, she still *felt* empty. Inside this perfection was the same nothingness and the same numbness she feared.

But the ordinary woman suffers a similar dilemma. All her life she tries to be the star, or to be like her. And all her life she fails. Or she decides that she is so deficient she cannot even try to become this ideal. (Or if she sees through this ideal and rejects it, all her life she senses that society measures her against an alien idea of what it is to be a woman.) Thus an ordinary woman has the same sense of inner failure as does the "star." And if this "ordinary" woman achieves some degree of extraordinariness, if she is perceived as very attractive, if she is sought after by men, if she is "loved," she will eventually discover this adulation, and the role she plays, to be empty too.

But, like Monroe, she has escaped into an image of glamour so that she will not share the fate of the ordinary woman. For everywhere in society we see that the "ordinary" woman is subjected to a subtle derision. At the same time that a woman is encouraged to be a wife and a mother, a woman who takes on this role says of herself, "I'm just a housewife." And we come to accept as common knowledge that a man will be more attracted to an extraordinary woman than to his wife. Everything that is exciting about the sex goddess speaks of a corresponding dullness in the wife and mother. For in the pornographic idea of sexuality, passion is opposed to the material necessities of daily life.

Therefore, like Marilyn Monroe, all women within this culture find ourselves caught between the Scylla and Charibdis of ordinariness and extraordinariness. We are afraid of "becoming our mothers." One hears the ordinary in Marilyn Monroe subjected to the most vicious language. When Norman Mailer describes Monroe's normal American girlhood, he tells us that she had "ice cream on her tongue, and the Church visible in her bland expression." He confesses to us that this description is "cruel." But we hear the same man speak of this same woman in her extraordinary aspect as "the sweet angel of sex."

Yet here lies another complexity in this relationship between true and false self and between a human being and an image of humanity. For this extraordinary woman made of celluloid and male fantasies and dreams is not entirely devoid of any real female experience. If a woman like Marilyn Monroe is in rebellion against culture's image of female ordinariness, her dream of a larger female capacity and creativity, her sense of her own power, begin to express themselves through the only image available to her which opposes itself to female ordinariness: the pornographic image of sex goddess.

Therefore, at the same time that she imitates the pornographer's idea of "the sweet angel of sex," she also lends to this role her own real energy and her own real power. Over and over again, in descriptions of Marilyn Monroe, we hear that when she became "Marilyn," a different kind of energy shone from her, a "charisma."

But now we are at the heart of a female tragedy within pornographic culture. For within this culture, when a woman expresses her real power, this power can only be expressed through images which transform female power into an image of submissiveness. Marilyn Monroe's "charisma"—a word used often about her (which means a "gift of grace")—was clothed in an image of "simpering and sighing."

And yet pornographic rage against female power does not stop with this diminishment and degradation. For pornographic culture has the same relationship of ambivalence with and ultimate hatred for its "sex goddesses" as does the pornographic hero for the pornographic heroine. Therefore, Monroe was aware of a continual current of hostility against her. She tells us that people see her as a commodity. She complains that she is "always running into people's unconscious." And finally, knowing from her own experience that the sexual object becomes the object of violence, she tells us, ". . . everybody is always tugging at you. They'd all like . . . a chunk of you. They kind of take pieces out of you."

But the ritual sacrifice of the female sex goddess is not new to us. We are accustomed to thinking of her as dying young. We are not shocked to learn she lives an unhappy life. Our image of her includes self-destructive behavior. We expect that she takes drugs and drinks too much and attempts suicide. For we know that the women who take the pornographic image of female sexuality upon themselves live out the tragedy of the female condition within pornographic culture. This is the culture which Mailer accurately describes as "drawing a rifle sight on an open vagina," a culture that even within its worship of the female sex goddess hates female sexuality.

And ironically, just as she becomes more extraordinary, as she is made into a supernatural being, a goddess, the pornographic star ceases to be a creature for whom one has compassion. She exists in the imagination, outside human identity and identification. Culture can imagine destroying her body as easily as in the 1950s Hungarian protesters destroyed a statue of the head of Stalin. For she becomes a pornographic symbol in pornographic culture and is no longer real.

Indeed, Marilyn Monroe's death has actually become a pornographic fantasy. In an "exposé" of her death in *Hustler* magazine, one reads that she was "murdered." And the prose of this exposé reminds one of the classic pornographic account of the murder of the pornographic heroine. Here is the same cold cruelty of language. Of her autopsy, for example, one reads that with "practised precision Dr. Noguchi eased a razor sharp scalpel in Marilyn's lower abdomen, slicing open the skin as he moved the blade up toward her sternum." Now the culture relishes the destruction of this body which it has said it worships.

In both image and event, fact and fantasy, pornographic culture annihilates the female sex. Thus pornography begins by annihilating the real female self and replacing this self with a false self. But this false self is finally only a projection which belongs to the pornographic hero. Therefore, the false self, too, must be annihilated. Thus along with the feeling of emptiness, a woman inherits from culture a continual experience of fear. For the image of a woman's body must be replaced with an image of her absence.

The Story of O

The image of woman as a void is a dominant theme of pornographic culture. A woman is less. She is less strong, less intelligent, less creative, less spiritual. She does not exist for herself. Rather, she is a shadow, whose existence depends on the real existence of men. She exists for men and is not, in Freud's words, "an end in herself."*

Therefore the pornographic mind conceives of female sexuality as a kind of bottomless pit, an empty space which craves male presence, and which cannot exist without the male. In the early pornographic work of Poggio, we read the familiar tale of a woman whose illness, which is a kind of madness, is cured by copulation. Later, the Earl of Rochester's *Sodom* gives us the same picture of female affliction and depravity when deprived of male sexual presence. We even hear an echo of this fantasy in the words of Wilhelm Reich as he describes "the sharp-tongued spinster" as an example of the relationship between sexual deprivation and cruelty. And in his own work, Freud implies that the feminists who were his contemporaries were maddened by a desire to have a penis for their own.

But the same ideology affects contemporary social science. In this decade, for example, we read from scientists who have created a new discipline called "sociobiology" that the female orgasm was not itself an adaptation to circumstances made by women but rather a "by-product of selection for male orgasm."

And in a final coup de grace, Mailer imagines that the "libido" of Marilyn Monroe came from her "stud father."

It is hardly coincidental that pornography's expression of female nothingness should erase the identity and presence of a female body and replace this with a male identity and a male presence. For finally we discover that pornography's adulation of the sex goddess and porno-graphic culture's denial of the female *self* are essentially expressions of sadomasochism. Through the ordinary or the extraordinary woman, a denied self is humiliated and punished. Nowhere is this relationship between sadomasochism and female nonbeing made so clear as in *The Story of O.* For here, the destruction of the character, will, and

---

*In a letter regarding his mother-in-law, Freud describes for us his notion of female nonbeing: "Because her charm and vitality have lasted so long, she still demands in return her full share of life—not the share of old age—and expects to be the center, the ruler, an end in herself. Every *man* who has grown old honorably wants the same, only in a woman one is not used to it. As a mother she ought to be content and know that her three children are fairly happy, and she ought to sacrifice her wishes to their needs." *The Letters of Sigmund Freud.* Cited by Mary Ellmann, *Thinking about Women* (New York, 1968), p. 132.

spirit of a female heroine takes place through and because of a systematic torture of her body. As O is reduced to nothingness, she learns to be deaf and dumb to the feelings and cries of her flesh.

The Story of O can be read as the account of a slow schooling in which the heroine gradually unlearns all the knowledge of her body. In the very beginning, she is told that her screams will have no effect on the severity of her beatings. (One sees in this a kind of reversal of those moments when the infant learns that crying out will bring a response from her mother. Here the groundwork, in the pornographic mind, for *autism* is laid.) No one will hear or respond to these cries. Next, O is told that she is never to touch her own breasts in the presence of her masters. Now the idea that one can give oneself pleasure, which is the infant's first power over herself, is eradicated. And eventually, O is told that she may never use her hands at all, until finally she begins to feel that her hands do not belong to her. When she is beaten, she is forbidden the natural response, for she cannot raise her hands in defense. She is carefully schooled out of every bodily impulse. She is made too hot, she is bound into uncomfortable positions, she is subjected to cold; during fellatio, her master deliberately tries to make her gag; she is awakened in the middle of sleep; she is whipped until welts rise on her skin, pulled by the hair, chained into painful positions. She is punished for resisting and for showing desire, for "wantonness." Finally, the very shape of her body is invaded and changed. So that she can be penetrated more easily from behind, her anus is gradually enlarged with bigger and bigger tubes. Her waist is made smaller and smaller with tighter and tighter corsets. And finally, a hole is bored through her vaginal lips so that a chain can be inserted, and she is branded with the initials of her master on her ass. Thus the destruction of O begins with and is carried out through the destruction of her body.

Will in the form of bodily response is carefully schooled out of her, so that she is no longer connected to her own feelings. The text tells us: "She was no longer mistress of her breasts, her hands, the nape of her neck . . ." It is made clear to us that she is ordered to say yes "in advance to everything she most assuredly wanted to say yes to but to which her body said no." And yet one form of will remains. O has agreed to be put through these ordeals out of love for her lover,

René. She has decided to do what she does and be what she is because she loves. Thus now this part of her existence is also systematically reduced to image alone: the physical existence of her love for René is gradually diminished. First she is asked to accept other lovers, masters, and punishments as extensions of René's being. She must in this sense enjoy him in the abstract. (Like Hitler, René cannot bear to cause her physical pain, yet he loves to see others cause her this pain.) Their love affair begins to take place on an other than physical plane. He touches her only "symbolically," through others. He punishes her through others.

Finally, René's physical relationship with O is all but effaced when he turns her over to another man, his "half" brother and his mentor, Sir Stephen. (And can it be a coincidence that his initials, S. S., call up for us all the horrors of the Holocaust?) If loving René was O's raison d'être, this reason is destroyed. René is replaced with Sir Stephen and slowly O is schooled to believe that her love for one man can easily be transferred to another. Now she has not even chosen the man whom she loves. He has been chosen for her. Even her emotional passion has become other than herself.

The book tells us that René instills in her *his* love of Sir Stephen. Thus, like Marilyn Monroe's libido in the imagination of Norman Mailer, her love is not even her own love, but is a man's love. And her being is ritualistically eradicated further as she repeats precisely the words which Sir Stephen gives her, "like a lesson of grammar," even taking on his identity, his vocabulary, as she promises to be his slave, simply transposing his words "in the first person." What she does, the book tells us, "even what she had to be," we hear in this matter-of-fact voice, "was decided without her." Thus we are not surprised to hear of O that at one moment she feels as if "she existed . . . in another life or perhaps not at all."

What remains in her annihilation as a being is that paradoxically she must learn that she does not exist. She becomes only an image to herself. Put through the excruciating ordeal of being branded and chained—terrified before, fainting from pain afterward—rather than regret her experience, she substitutes for the feelings of her body a feeling of pride in the initials branded into her flesh, and the chain hanging from her vulva. And this pride is the only remnant of her beingness, for this love of an image of herself remains after her ability to feel love in body and soul have been destroyed. It is a pride in *being* loved. Now her existence is predicated on Sir Stephen's love. The hope for and evidence of his love for her calls up her love and obedience to him. The weight of the chains with which he has bonded O signify to her his love for her. In this grotesque account we can see a ghastly reflection of the life of Marilyn Monroe, a being who, according to Norman Mailer, was supposed to exist for the sole reason of being adored.

And just as O's physical effacement led to her spiritual effacement, her spiritual humiliation leads to her physical destruction. In the first pages of the book, the whole of O's story is foreshadowed. We are told: "she lost herself in a delirious absence from herself which restored her to love, and perhaps, brought her to the edge of death." Now she will meet a more thorough annihilation. Like René, Sir Stephen begins to give her to other men. Thus he both punishes and takes her at a remove from his own physical being, again making his love a symbolic act. And finally, even this symbolic act dissolves into nothing. We read: "There exists a second ending to the story of O, according to which O, seeing that Sir Stephen was about to leave her, said she would prefer to die. Sir Stephen gave her his consent." Thus, because her reason for being has been to be loved, when she is no longer loved she ceases to exist. Even the choice to die is not her own. She is nothing.

Before her transformation into nothingness, O comes to us as an extraordinary woman, a woman who transcends the traditional social roles for women. She is a fashion photographer. Because of her work, she enjoys a different status than most women; moreover, because she is a photographer, in the battle between nature and culture she is placed on the side of culture. Behind the camera, she is the aggressor, the one who captures, the one who turns the real into the image and replaces nature with culture. This profession is not a casual detail in the fantasy; it is rather a solid part of her character and a necessary part of the allegory in which she is a symbol. As the fashion photographer, she takes the same sexual attitude toward women, and in particular the women who fall under the lens of her camera, that men have taken toward her.

In one passage of the book, we learn that before she met René, *she* "took" women unfeelingly, and only for the experience of sexual mastery. The text reads: "What she asked of women (and never returned, or ever so little) she was happy and found it quite natural that men should be eager and impatient to ask of her." She took a sadistic pleasure in causing feeling in another woman, while she herself remained in control. But as René enslaves her, although her desire to master women increases, and grows more sadistic, her identity with culture fades. Like the model under her lens, more and more she becomes a symbol of nature.

Her transformation into a symbol of nature is foreshadowed in a scene during which O, tortured and frightened, cannot "hold back the water which escapes from her body." Immediately the narrator's eye moves from O to the window and the scene outside, where "it was storming, a tempest of cold rain and wind." Continually she is associated with natural symbols. Later we read that O was "frozen like a butterfly impaled upon a pin"; and just as the pin she used to impale her models was, in effect, a camera, now this pin that impales her is "composed of words and looks." She has become nature. (She no longer works as a fashion photographer.) Over and over, we hear she is "spread-eagled" on a bed, a platform. As the book moves to a close, O is turned into a "bird of prey," when she is instructed to bring another woman into the same slavery. René presents her to Sir Stephen like an animal trainer who is showing off his work. And much later, Sir Stephen caresses her "timidly," as if she were a wild animal "one wants to tame." Symbolically, she moves further and further into wildness. In the last scene of the book, she appears at a party in an owl mask, her face covered with feathers, her humanness unrecognizable. The others at the party do not speak to her. They form a silent circle around her, poking her, staring, treating her like a real bird, "deaf to human language, dumb." She has become nature entirely separated from cultural power.

Yet we must look closer at this animalization of O and at the brilliance of its conception. For in this supposed wildness we, the readers, have been led to our final despair. We stand confronted with the vision of this fantasy, in which no alternative to O's vision of life seems to exist. Inside the world of O, every image mirrors slavery. For one might have supposed, in some inner reasoning place, that a being returned to wildness would begin to rebel against a pornographic culture. It is in the promise of wildness that our only hope from this bleak vision of slavery resides. We reason the animal would not seek to be beaten, not kiss the hand which causes its misery, not ask to be degraded, not give love for punishment. We feel the animal, who is after all the natural being in us all, the body, would move toward survival through widening circles of rage and recognition, and dignity. And that O becomes an animal and more and more wild has a double symbolic purpose. Now culture conquers nature and thus, inside fantasy, the possibility of a natural freedom is repudiated. Nature has become a mirror for culture.

The Story of O is filled with mirrors. In one of the first scenes, O is forced to see her body naked and opened in a mirror. But the most devastating mirror which O (and the female reader) is given in this vision is the image of other women. To begin with, if we wished to believe that O had a female nature free of the imprisoning syndrome of sadomasochism before she fell in love with René, the novel destroys this hope. Indeed, what draws O to René is that he masters her. Moreover, when she is not mastered, she plays the master, with both men and women.

Yet the book contains a dramatic transformation. Change does take place in O's character. She begins as one person and ends as another. Despite her proclivity to sadomasochism, when she is asked to bring her model, with whom she is in love, into her own condition of slavery, she rebels. She tells herself that she will not "go this far." She does not admit to herself any feeling of regret over her own state of denigration. And yet she expresses regret, and also a shred of knowledge that perhaps another female self does exist, when she recoils at the idea of thus "spoiling" Jacqueline. She comforts herself with the thought that Jacqueline will refuse to go to Roissy, the place at which she herself was enslaved.

But she is told by Sir Stephen that he will send her through an experience which will make her a different being, who, among other things, will think differently about Jacqueline's fate. Now she is to become more thoroughly a slave so that every shred of hesitancy, any idea that she might be different, any notion of freedom, will leave her being. And significantly, this final destruction of her soul is achieved through the hands of other women.

She is sent to a place called Samois, directed by a woman who claims to love women, who acts the part of a lesbian (but who in fact commits all her acts only to please men). Here the torture is worse, the cruelty more horrifying, the pain unbearable. Here O's body is permanently defaced, and the chain which is attached to her marks her in such a way as to forever circumscribe her freedom. And it is a woman who puts a ring through her vulva.

But can we escape the symbolic value of this chapter? Let us look at what lesbianism might mean outside the pornographic mind. A lesbian is a woman who loves another woman: a woman who loves, cherishes, touches, soothes, brings pleasure and ecstasy to the body of another woman. This is the capacity of the female self, of a female self, to love the female self, in *oneself or in another*. Thus here, in *The Story of O*, we discover pornography's secret message in its image of lesbianism. For in all pornography, lesbians are shown as existing and performing fundamentally for the pleasure of men. Moreover, most often, as in *The Story of O*, one lesbian is portrayed as acting cruelly toward another, pictured as torturing and punishing another woman's body. In the pornographic image of the lesbian, the female self is mirrored back not only as forever bonded to male pleasure, to self-sacrifice and to self-punishment, but also as being incapable of self-love.

When O returns from Samois, the embarrassment she had felt over her welts, and her desire to hide her marks from Jacqueline, cease. On a deeper level, we understand that the shame she projected on Jacqueline was in fact her own. Thus the remaining shadow of a thought that she might one day be free disappears.

Here in this allegory of the mind, we discover that the ability for a woman to be free is connected with her ability to love another woman. One of the first rules which O learns at Roissy is that she is not to speak to or with other women. Soon this rule is followed by another: she is not to speak at all. When O contemplates pursuing Jacqueline, she decides that she will await an order from Sir Stephen. She will not act of her own accord, for she "loathes her freedom." Thus a chain of associations develops between the death of O's love for other women, the death of her own self-love, and the loss of her liberty to speak or act. Of her silence, we are told: "nothing had been such a comfort to her as the silence, unless it was the chains. The chains and the silence, which should have bound her deep within herself, which should have smothered, strangled her, on the contrary freed her from herself." And later in the book, O compares "the peaceful reassuring hand of a master" to the bars in a cloister, which keep the convent girls "from each other and from escaping."

O's fear of freedom is precisely her fear of her self and of her self embodied. And her love of other women represents to her an approach to that self, to a self capable of feeling.

O's abandonment of her own freedom reminds one of the German masses' allegiance to Hitler. (But we must remember here that O is not an actual woman. Rather, she is an allegorical figure, named female, who represents one impulse in the human psyche.) And in this light, we can see another significance in her desire to have her body first enchained and then punished. A pathway to freedom exists in the body: the body itself desires freedom of movement, and cannot stand constriction. And the knowledge of the body, as Wilhelm Reich (and many others after him) has shown us, is a pathway to psychic liberation also. Thus when O punishes her body she defends her own madness. As she submits to pain, O attempts to erase from her body all memory of her own wholeness, and her responsibility for the knowledge of that wholeness.

After her transformation at Samois, during which O is even more deeply alienated from her body, from her love of other women, and therefore from herself, O shows Jacqueline her marks and bonds with pride. When Jacqueline responds with horror and contempt, O laughs. Now she ridicules the horror which she herself once felt. (One remembers here that ridicule is part of the sadistic trade, that it is a form of humiliation.) And she is eager to make Jacqueline a slave. She wishes to punish Jacqueline.

But now this book, which like the work of de Sade has its moments of stunning psychological insight, gives us a comprehensive glimpse into the pornographic mind. After the narrator has announced to us that O "is pleased to think she will deliver Jacqueline by an act of betrayal," we are led into O's mind. She looks out a window and we are told: "She blamed the sea, for washing up nothing more than an occasional piece of seaweed . . . she blamed it for being too blue . . . for always lapping at the same bit of shore." Just as she blames Jacqueline, now she is angry at the sea. She is angry at *nature*. And in a sentence which takes us to the core of meaning, she says, "The sea doesn't smell like the sea."

This desperate alienation from the female self and from nature which is at the center of *The Story of O* is mirrored by the very form of the book. To begin with, though we do not know who the author is, the book is signed with a female name. Thus we are led to believe that this fantasy is a female fantasy. Whoever the real author is, moreover, this is a being without any real identity in the world. And the nonbeing of the author of *The Story of O* is mirrored back by every character in the novel. René has no identity, no character to speak of, except as O's master. Sir Stephen is also unexplained. We only know them in relation to their mastery. Sir Stephen is the harder, surer master. René, loath to punish directly, is more O's equal. That is all we know of either man. (We do not even know their professions, though we know O's.) But of course, behind this mastery we know there is another zero. For the controlled rage with which they control another must only be a rage at the void inside themselves. Possessed of an impotent character, they destroy the character of another. That we know nothing about the author of this work is entirely fitting.

But the book itself, even without any author, comprises another mirror. For this work, as Susan Sontag has argued in her article on pornography, is a work of art. It has all the characteristics of art: beautiful language, symbolism, repetition of themes. Moreover, it has the allegorical shape of the quest for meaning, which is the form of what we regard as the highest art. And yet here again we find ourselves in a cul-de-sac of despair. For the book leaves us in a vacuum. At the end, the heroine, the character through whom we experience the narrative, has become like "stone or wax"; she dies. *The Story of O* leads us to an increasing absence of consciousness. The very theme of the novel is a negation of the self. And once that self is destroyed, the reader is left with a blank page, with silence. Thus this book which was supposed to lead us on a quest gives us only the shell of a quest.

Like the form of an animal that is not an animal, or the shape of a female body that is only a doll,* the shape of this "quest" only resembles what we seek. Inside this quest we discover only emptiness. And if we read *The Story of O* to find ourselves, we find nothing. *The Story of O* has led us to despair. Therefore, to experience the story of O is to experience the sadomasochist's despair about life. And because this novel comes to us in an artful form, we are led to believe that art, as well as sexuality, has disappointed us. Now the despair of the sadomasochist tries to convince us that even poetry, even graceful language in the distilled rendering of art and beauty, proves that life has no meaning. Using an artful form, and the form of the quest, the pornographic mind tells us that to search for meaning is hopeless. For in *The Story of O,* art only serves to speak of meaninglessness.

But we know meaning heals. Using the body of a woman as a stage, pornography plays out a drama to convince the mind that the language of the body and the language of the soul are at opposite poles. As we watch this tragedy, we are asked to accept that to speak one language is to become deaf to the other. To exist fully as a body is to cease to exist as a soul. This *is* the meaning that Susan Sontag finds in the meaninglessness of *The Story of O.* She writes that "O progresses simultaneously toward her own extinction as a human being and her fulfillment as a sexual being." Confessing that it is difficult to imagine whether in actuality such a split exists in nature or human consciousness, Sontag writes that such a split has "always haunted man."† And though Sontag places the extremity of this split outside the Freudian tradition, we know that above all, Freud, in his pessimism, both preserved this split and called it the source of illness. Yet, from another side of his being, Freud healed this split. In his own work, he used meaning to heal ailments, ailments of the mind which manifested themselves in the body. Women fainted, or were paralyzed. A girl was unable to swallow. These conditions of the body were healed with the restoration of consciousness. Paradoxically, Sontag defends *The*

---

* The word *doll* itself reflects the negation of a spiritual guest, since it is a debased derivative of the word *idol.*
† But of course. When Sir Stephen brings his whips to the apartment of O, in order to arrange them for her as a kind of artwork on her walls, she is recalled to Christian imagery—to "the wheel and spikes in the paintings of St. Catherine the Martyr," to the nail and hammer, the crown of thorns, and the spear of the cruxifixion.

Story of O not only as art but as an extension of *consciousness*. Yet consciousness in *The Story of O* extends ultimately only into its own annihilation.

It is pornographic culture's goal to separate *itself* from nature. But this is a separation which requires a kind of mental acrobatics. For such a separation is a delusion. Consciousness and meaning are part of nature. All our metaphors, our very language, emanate from and imitate the physical. The very capacity for symbolic thought is a structure of the mind. And in fact, the physical world holds a dimension of loss for us without knowledge and consciousness of knowledge. When bodily knowledge and language are separated, we ourselves experience a terrible separation which ranges all the way from grief to despair to madness. The depth of the loss of consciousness reaches us when we imagine what it would be like, for instance, to be both blind and deaf, and therefore outside the sphere of language. And we come to know something of what wholeness in our nature means when we read this passage from the life of Helen Keller, as she describes her entrance into language:

> Someone was drawing water and my teacher placed my hand under the spout. As the cold stream gushed over my hand she spelled into the other hand the word *water*, first slowly, then rapidly. I stood still, my whole attention fixed on the motion of her fingers. Suddenly I felt a misty consciousness as of something forgotten—a thrill of returning thought; and somehow the mystery of language was revealed to me. I knew then that w-a-t-e-r meant the wonderful cool something that was flowing over my hand. That living word awakened my soul, gave it light, hope, joy, set it free!

Now that everything had a name, she goes on to tell us, a "strange, new sight," a transforming inner vision of the world, had come to her.

For the mind which tries to separate culture and nature or consciousness and the body moves against actual experience. Susan Sontag tells us that *The Story of O* investigates a possibility. But this misses the point of the fantasy. What *The Story of O* indeed does is to investigate an *impossibility*. For it is impossible for a human being to abandon beingness. One who is cannot cease to be. The only way that culture can experience something as nothing and imagine a split between, therefore, the body and meaning is to imagine this split in the image of another being. For the experience of such a split as natural does not exist. Therefore, this experience must be invented, and a kind of paradoxical being who is a nonbeing must be invented to experience this experience. (Now, if we read the parable of Adam and Eve in this sense, we find it is accurate. For the mind of a patriarch invented from himself this idea of a woman as nothing.)

In this sense it is significant that *The Story of O* is not written in the first person. For how could it be? The voice which would be the voice of the novel is slowly destroyed. No one exists to experience O's experience. Thus, too, Mailer, in his writing, can never get inside the mind of a woman whose life he tries to recreate. In the end, she is an enigma to him, just as women remain an enigma for the pornographic mind. (And Sontag, herself a woman, never writes, in this connection, of her own experience.) For how can the experience of the pornographic idea of a woman *be* experienced? By definition, this woman has no experience. She *is* nothing, in her essential being. The book merely follows the "natural" line of her becoming completely "herself," which is nothingness.

This nonbeing is a fiction which exists only in male experience. The self itself cannot experience nonbeing.* As she moves into selflessness, O is described as having an extraordinary grace and a serenity. But the experience of the loss of self is anything but serene. In its common forms, selflessness is a definition, a name for the painful psychological condition of women within a pornographic culture. In its extreme form, the experience of the loss of self is insanity.

In the outward appearance of manifestations of the mind, *The Story of O* is identical in its shape to the illness (which we know as schizophrenia) described in the pages of *I Never Promised You a Rose Garden* and *Autobiography of a Schizophrenic Girl.* In all three narratives, the heroines become alienated from their bodies, lose dignity, a sense of self, and a desire for freedom, and experience greater and greater degrees of "unreality." And yet Deborah in *I Never Promised You a Rose Garden* and Renée in *Autobiography of a Schizophrenic Girl* are based on real women. And thus an inside to their experience of

---

* Absence is not at the core, for instance, of the Buddhist experience of the loss of ego. Rather, one's identity with the All, the Universe, is what is sought.

self-abnegation exists, and it is an agony. For beingness desires to live and will torture the soul who tries to die with *presence*. Unlike the meaningless suffering of the fictional O, this pain enters the consciousness of each real heroine and moves her toward beingness.

Therefore, the story of Deborah's recovery reads like a reversal of O's enslavement. Just as O is tortured and schooled away from the knowledge of her body, Deborah, who has tortured herself, and who begins in a state of physical numbness, returns to her body. As her mind heals, we read that: "She ate supper and found herself capable of suffering that she had to do it messily with fingers and a wooden spoon. The food tasted. It was substantial under her teeth and afterward she remembered having eaten it." As she becomes well again, dignity and sensation return to her and she can feel physical pain, and thus she ceases to torture herself.

In this narrative of healing, each moment of O's self-abnegation is echoed by a return to self. O has been schooled not to look into the faces of her masters. Deborah, as she begins to get well, "began to look into the faces of people, to talk to them and hear them." In her unwellness, Deborah lives in a fantasy world. She has abandoned reality for the severe masters of her imagination. Yet this is exactly the state of mind O chooses, for the book tells us again and again that she can leave her masters anytime she wishes. Moreover, the more she loses herself to these masters, the more she experiences, the narrator tells us, a sense of "unreality." (We see this same descent in *Autobiography of a Schizophrenic Girl*. The story of her madness begins with a chapter entitled "Appearance of the First Feelings of Unreality," and continues to a chapter called "I Sink into Unreality." But as this girl begins to get well, we read a chapter entitled "I Learn to Know My Body.")

Like the masters of O, the masters in the schizophrenic mind are cruel to the body. Deborah's masters order her to "punish" herself when she violates their rules. And just as in *The Story of O* the heroine is forbidden to take pleasure and, above all, to ask for pleasure in her body, illness in the mind of the schizophrenic girl, Renée, forbids her to ask for what she wants. (In a heartbreaking account, we learn that the girl can only allow herself the pleasure of being bathed when she does not ask for it. When her therapist tells her she will be bathed when she wants to be bathed, she is enraged. "To declare openly that it was I, Renée, who wanted this pleasure of a bath!" She cannot bear "the blame attached to this." Thus, to escape the possibility of desire, in her mind "abruptly wonderful reality disappeared, to be replaced by the old cinematographic scenes.")

From these accounts, one sees that the escape into unreality is clearly an escape from will, and that will, in turn, a will of the body, expressed by the mind, is an evidence of beingness. Here again, O and the schizo-phrenic woman mirror one another. And just as, in O, the escape from self expressed itself as a loathing of freedom, in the schizophrenic mind the fear of the self expresses itself as a fear of freedom from madness. For the very desire to remain within the safety of illness expresses itself in the mind of the patient as a resistance to wellness. In the voice of her masters, Deborah's mind warns her of the dangers of the world. For both the pornographic heroine and the schizophrenic mind choose to be enslaved in the same motion with which they choose unreality.

But this unreality, a shadow world constructed to look real, is not simply another way of being, either in the world of the schizophrenic or in the pornographic fantasy. For to choose to follow out the separa-tion of consciousness from sexuality, of culture from nature, or of self from self, is quite simply to choose death. Here the culture's veiled desire to annihilate reality plays itself out in the bodies of women as suicide. O dies. Deborah decides to live. And we are told: "Because she was going to live, because she had begun to live already, the new colors, dimensions and knowledge became suffused with a kind of pas-sionate urgency."

Finally, can we separate this "passionate urgency" to live from the recognition that the world has meaning? We learn from Viktor Frankl that those who survived the terrors of concentration camps with the wholeness of their minds lived in the camps with a sense of purpose. They believed their own existence held meaning to the world. Now we begin to see that the separation of meaning from the world which takes place in *The Story of O* is part of culture's revenge against the power of nature. But in culture's attempt to wrest meaning away from the world, existence is destroyed. For our very experience of existence depends upon its meaningfulness. Nowhere can we hear this more eloquently spoken than in the argument of the schizophrenic girl who had, until this moment, in her madness rejected the meaning of the material world:

> She tried to think of a truth to tell the doctor as a present. Perhaps it might be the one about seeing—that even when seeing every line and plane and color of a thing, if there was no meaning, the sight was irrelevant and one was just as well blind; that perhaps even the famous third dimension is only a meaning, the gift which translates a bunch of planes into a box or a madonna or a [doctor] . . . with antiseptic bottles.

But now we come to the most disturbing meaning of *The Story of O*. This book exists in our minds as an emblem of pornographic culture. It forms for us an image of women. And because images have real power over the mind, it becomes a fact in our lives. In this image of ourselves, we are portrayed as having only two dimensions, for the third dimension, the dimension of meaning, is absent from O. Even if we have not read *The Story of O*, our minds have been shaped by the same culture which shaped this tale. We have inherited an identity of nothingness from the pornographic culture. Not only is our silence the perfect complement to pornographic fantasy, the screen on which the image of ourselves as nothing can be projected; our silence is also a part of the annihilation which pornography wishes for us. For as our meaninglessness increases, so do we, like the prisoner in a concentration camp, or the schizophrenic girl, lose the desire to live. Like O, as we impersonate the pornographic idea of women, we betray ourselves, and someone within us, who is condemned to silence, begins to die.

The Models

They are stillness in the midst of chaos. Behind them a mosaic of faces: the wealthy buyers, reporters, men carrying trays, men with flash cameras, women with notebooks, women laughing, holding glasses of wine, opening a mouth in wonder, staring intently, a man straining to raise a camera over his head, a man with a cigarette hanging from his mouth, his hand pointing resolutely to the model's foot; all around them a mosaic of activity, of being, of animated expression, character, and vitality. And such is the contrast between the stark stillness of these two women, the rigidity, therefore, of their bodies, the posed carriage of their spines, the composed smoothness of their almost expressionless (one might say *serene*) faces, and this sea of human variation and unpredictability behind them and around them that they themselves appear to be two-dimensional cutouts placed against a three-dimensional background.

And so it is then, staring at a photograph, taken by Richard Avedon of two models surrounded by the press and onlookers, that I begin to recognize the postures of models. For they always have the feeling about them of Egyptian paintings, heads arched in peculiar ways forward and backward, and of course, finally, I understand their strange resemblance in this odd flatness, for Egyptian paintings were two-dimensional.

But this two-dimensionality goes beyond mere posture and enters into the absence of meaning. The look of disinterest on these faces is notable. Here, certainly, along with serenity, is zero, coldness, a void where sexual feeling would lie. In the face, for instance, of Marella Agnelli, photographed by Avedon in 1953, we might actually be confronting a stone resemblance of a woman, or a waxen likeness. Here the idea of composure becomes literal. The perfection of the line of her shoulders, her long neck, her precisely drawn eyebrows, suggests above all that rather than a subjective soul we find here a *made object*, a *construct*. Yes, the expression of the face is impermeable, but something about her pose tells us that behind this impermeable mask would be nothing, and thus any curiosity regarding the unique identity of this being would be wasted. One looks then at her gown.

This is a gown which exists to be envied. It will be copied by other women. And this woman in her nothingness is also to be envied. For this is one of the meanings of the word "model": a model is something we emulate. And like any model, this woman presents to us a whole set of rules for our behavior. And these rules come to us more powerfully exactly because they are not spoken but rather communicated implicitly through this flesh-and-blood symbol of propriety. *This is how you ought to be*, we hear. *Imitate me.*

But now the act of modeling becomes more complex. Indeed, the wealthy woman does appear to be like the model. And in turn, the

model, perhaps born not so wealthy, but coming up from poorer circumstances, decided to imitate the model which wealthy women present for the rest of female society. We all know their names. Guess at
their private lives. Are given freely the details of their outward appear-
ances. The clothes they wear to social occasions. What they do and
do not do.

And what is it that is held up to us in this image of the privileged
woman and this image of the model to imitate? What besides this
long, silky, exposing, expensive gown must be drawn over ourselves?
But again, we find the image of nothingness. Everything about this
polite, upper-class image suggests not an actuality, but only the absence
of human qualities. We learn from her: reserve, quietness, a hauteur
suggesting a limit to desire and wanting. Her calm would suggest to
us that she never intends, never goes out into the world hunting, but
that every request which begins to form in her mind has been met
by a hand different from hers and superior to hers. She is above all
idle. Idle in her thoughts, her emotions, her acts. Her every step must
indicate ease. She never strains. She does not endeavor. Like the
woman of another century and culture with a bound foot, her very
existence is the epitome of dependence. She becomes a symbol of
her husband's or her father's power to support her. Thus her magnificent style signifies his magnificence of strength. Not only does she
not do anything, but her very existence does not even mirror herself.
She does not stand for herself but for a man. As with O, in this model
we find essentially nothing.

Should we then be surprised to find out that when O is sent to
Samois, the training school run by women, between sessions during
which she is mutilated and tortured she is subjected to a kind of forced
idleness? Or that the narrator tells us Samois is steeped in and defined
by female idleness?

And would it be too farfetched to conceive that under certain circumstances, idleness, too, might be a form of torture? Let us consider,
first of all, what other women, those of us who cannot afford such
idleness, but instead work very long hours, feel about these idle women.
We are, of course, turned against them. Some of us, perhaps tired
from years of both earning money and raising children, not enough
sleep or leisure, feel a kind of rage, which we direct against these
"models." If they complain of frustration or boredom, we ridicule them.

We say we hunger after such "boredom." We say, What does she have to worry about? When Patty Hearst is kidnapped, terrorized, raped, we take her bad luck with a kind of exultance. Finally, we say, she has gotten hers. For yes, she has become the symbol of her father's wealth and power, and we neglect to perceive that she has any being of her own. Instead, like the light-skinned black, or the house servant under slavery, she becomes the repository of our rage against masters.

Lorraine Hansberry, in her autobiographical play, *To Be Young, Gifted and Black*, speaks of a time when she was sent to school in a poor and black neighborhood in Chicago, wearing a fur coat that her newly wealthy father had proudly purchased for her. That day on the school grounds she was beaten up by her classmates. But still, managing to cross what now was a barrier between herself and her classmates, her mind held compassion for their deprivation and their rage. She stopped wearing her fur coat. And finally, to her friends, she became only herself.

But the ordinary woman, who is perhaps married, or who was married, who has children, who must work to add to the family income, or is the sole support of herself and her children, and then at night cooks meals, cares for a house, cares for all the needs of her children, follows their homework, listens to their cries, cares for the clothing of the whole family—this woman (and now I speak from my own experience) does not have such a certain and clear relationship with the model as did the schoolchildren of Lorraine Hansberry's childhood with her fur coat. At one moment angry at this symbol of idleness, in the next the "ordinary" woman blames herself for not being that model, for not presenting herself in such a composed way to the world. Wanting to possess a grace which perhaps belongs only to idleness, she finds herself lacking. Never can she live up to the standard of these women. Their very presence in the world stands as a marshal to her consciousness, imprisoning her in self-hatred.

And now comes the greatest irony, for the image of nothingness that these women present may appear to her at times as the only idea she has of female presence. The model, after all, is photographed in a magazine. She exists in the public consciousness. Sometimes her name is even remembered. And the wealthy woman, too, is part of culture. Her activities, empty as they are, are notable. Certainly we know her name.

But of course, this nonbeing would seem by contrast to the mother, or the wife, to have a self. The mother and wife is by definition "self-less." All her activity revolves about others.* Like the pornographic images of women, the traditional images of women are of creatures without any self, who are of their nature empty.

And yet that is not the female experience of emptiness. Rather, at the heart of our condition, what we know is silence. And inside that silence, we experience what is unspoken. "Speechlessness," writes Michelle Cliff, "is not simply muteness—it is the inability to reveal." For indeed, the female self does not disappear, and, even if mortally wounded, does not die, but only exists in a state of dying. Inside our numbness, thus, is a terrible memory of pain. Inside our selflessness, a self cramped, angry, aching. Inside stillness, an aliveness battering at the walls of culture.

In *The Story of O*, when René is confronted with Jacqueline's inaccessibility and coldness, he wishes to understand her. He wants to be inside this appearance of nothingness, to see, in the language of the narrator, the "mechanism inside of a crying doll." But this is, in fact, why René, and indeed the pornographic mind itself, can never see inside female silence. For the seer sees what he looks for, what he believes to exist. And René is convinced that inside Jacqueline is a mere mechanism, a man-made object. He does not look for a real self, but only for the inner workings of a shell.

A human being cannot be nothing, nor can she experience nothingness. Therefore, one might say, why do we not simply reject the image of female nonbeingness? But the nexus between image and actuality is not simple. One cannot by an easy effort of the mind reject the image that another has of oneself. Rather, the child, wishing to be accepted, first by her mother and father, then by her teachers, her classmates, will attempt to be what others think she is or ought to be. To move away from society's metaphors of identity is to move away from society itself. The images of who we are form a kind of

---

* After the death of his mother, Henry James writes to us of this life: "It was the perfect mother's life—the life of a perfect wife. To bring her children into the world—to expend herself, for years, for their happiness and welfare—then, when they had reached full maturity and were absorbed in the world and in their own interests—to lay herself down in her ebbing strength and yield up her pure soul to the celestial power that had given her this divine commission." Cited in Tillie Olsen, *Silences* (New York, 1979), p. 215.

language by which we live. Because of language, as Simone Weil tells us, "we are related to someone else's thought as if it were our own." The very love we feel for others, our wish to participate in the life of another, our desire for closeness and knowledge of another being, compel us to wish to speak the common language.

And yet the common language culture assigns to female existence is a language impossible to actualize. One cannot *be* the pornographic culture's idea of woman, for such an idea cannot exist. One cannot *be* a nonbeing. Thus, out of her desire to be a part of culture, out of her very erotic nature, the female child must learn to act; she must learn to impersonate "the female."

But now let us make a necessary digression. We have heard that those without an identity, out of a desperate search for an identity, will often become actors. And we know there is a truth in this that extends into the life of every mind. Seeking being, we act at being. Wanting to know the life of another's mind, we actually move ourselves to feel what the other feels, by first imagining and then performing. Even an audience watching an actor does this, and this is in fact the value of a great performance. Through our vicarious pleasure we have entered another's soul, been different than ourselves. But in the midst of this very entrance into another's being, we have discovered an aspect of ourselves that is unexpressed and perhaps hidden to us. In the passion of a Sarah Bernhardt we experience now fully our own passion. Her performance has given us a larger self, a larger experience.

But the art of female impersonation is quite different. It runs in the opposite direction (and this is a key to why Marilyn Monroe was so disappointed by her success), for the woman who successfully imitates nothingness does not enlarge her experience but instead makes it smaller. Rather than express a new part of herself, or enter the heart of another and enlarge her being, she learns instead to repress her real self.

And here is another great irony. In this creation of the appearance of nothingness there is much labor. It is difficult to silence the self. This is a movement against nature; inside the act is a kind of sadism to the self. It is the height of discipline. One part of the self damages another part. But this effect takes concentration, skill, study, intelligence. Richard Avedon, in his portfolio of photographs of models, has captured a few moments here and there where the model is not posing. And yet she is working. She may be applying makeup, or dressing. And now we can see that she has a self. All the expression which belongs to a serious artist is on her face. Her eyes are intent, focused. To create this face which is a mask, she must be a painter. To walk in a way that suggests idleness and thoughtlessness, she must study, be artful, careful, dance. And above this irony is the further irony that because she successfully creates this image of nothingness, idleness, and vacuity, she is one of the few women in pornographic culture who can experience a sense of accomplishment and self-respect. Through this impersonation, she becomes someone. She is a model. She is taken seriously. (To culture, *her* work has gravity.)

But the nexus between being and image is more complex and has numerous permutations, and most of them do not lead to self-respect, but rather to varying degrees of suffering. One of these permutations is breakdown and madness. If we go back to consider again, for instance, the story of Deborah, the schizophrenic girl about whom *I Never Promised You a Rose Garden* revolves, we find in her history an impossible expectation. Born in a Jewish family at the time of the Holocaust, she is blond, and thus her existence has become for her family a reprieve from their own outcast status. She will be what they imagine they are not. In a sense, in their wishes for her we see the shadow of Lorraine Hansberry's father, and also the shadow of Patricia Hearst. She is the vessel of dreams, the symbol of success. And yet Deborah is not this image; she cannot be what her parents wish her to be. She is Jewish, and her classmates are anti-Semitic. Rather than the bland experience of acceptance, she carries about her character the knowledge of suffering, and this knowledge creates shapes in the body, expressions of the face, which do not become the female model of serenity. Thus a fracture exists between who she wants to be for her parents, the way they insist on seeing her, and who she really is, what her experience is. And inside this fracture is another suffering, which only serves to make the fracture greater. She is lonely. She cannot love herself. She has failed. And the more she experiences this sadness and this failure, the larger does the fracture and therefore her suffering and therefore her failure become.

But there is another sense in which Deborah fails expectations, and this, too, touches on the relationship between female image and being which brings some madness to almost every woman. And this is that in addition to Deborah as the symbol of success and acceptance, she must also become Deborah as the symbol of purity. Her father has become preoccupied with the possibility that strange men might accost her. When she is approached, he is angry at her, as if she had provoked this harassment. Here is the contradiction of the notion of purity. It is not a quality at all, but is, again, the absence of a quality. Purity in a young girl signifies both the absence of sexuality and the absence of sexual experience. When Deborah says that her father acted as if "all such men were bound by laws of gravity to me alone," she confesses a sense of guilt for not being pure. The behavior of men toward her signifies something sexual about *her* nature. Her father is frightened of men "lurking to grab me from dark streets; sex maniacs and fiends"; he imagines "one to a tree waiting for" Deborah; he shakes warnings into her: "Men are brutes, lusting without limit. . . ." When Deborah learns from her analysis that her father was afraid of his own lust toward her, which he had projected on these men, the unraveling of this meaning begins to heal her.

Underneath this knowledge another level of feeling is always apparent: Deborah's purity and the intimation of her sexuality in her attractiveness to strange men both elude her own experience. They are not her experience, this purity and this sexuality. In the first she must feel herself to be a sham—for the very idea of purity is a negation; it is not something one *can be*. In the second, in her sexuality, her feeling is far more dangerous than one of complete falsity. For this description of herself as sexual approximates her reality; it is a shoe that almost fits. As an adolescent, her body must have felt sexual desire, even been overwhelmed at times with wanting. She might have known within her imagination the possibility of "lusting without limit." And yet this lust without limit is in the imagination, as an attribute of sexual feeling, and is remarkably different in experience from the perverted desire for dominance and power that in fact the child-molester or the rapist feels. One of the by-products of the fact of rape in a young girl's life is that she learns to associate her own sexual feeling with an evil. And this is an evil directed precisely against her being, for rapists also murder, and at the very least, threaten death. This, then, is the final irony: the expression of vitality of being in the young girl's life—that is, her sexual desire—comes to be associated in her mind with her own death. Female beingness leads, then, to female annihilation.

We sense the same fear of her own being, her sexuality, her expression, her creativity, in the letters and the life of the poet Anne Sexton. It is as if her own self were too much for the world and thus for herself. She apologizes for the lack of "control" in her letters. Says that she tries hard to achieve this "control" in her poems. Yet this is not the simple poetic control which all authors might liken to grace in language. It is rather a control of some unnamed aspect of herself which is suffused with female sexuality. Of a poem accepted to be published in the *Hudson Review*, she writes to Carolyn Kizer:

> It is surely the most supercharged thing I've done and is entirely about the mother-child relationship. A feminine and directly emotional piece that will make most readers flinch and probably the men most of all. So perhaps it is a bad thing that I did get it in.

In every description of her self and her life that she renders, we sense two selves. One, rebellious, will not be respectful like the other students in Robert Lowell's class, or nod at everything he says. She lights up a cigarette despite the rule against smoking. She refuses to write the quiet, reserved poetry that looks more male, that does not make men "flinch." And yet alongside this rebel exists the controlling voice. A persona who would make her into the image of a man and a female impersonator simultaneously. And who would, in the end, have her be nothing. In the midst of a breakdown, she writes these words which chill us for their resemblance to the final thoughts of O: "I wish stupidly that someone but me would kill me and take the responsibility away."

Though most of us do not die of it, hardly any woman escapes this terrible split between two selves, one the authentic self, and another who would destroy her, both in the same being. We catch a glimpse of these two beings as they appear to the outside world in George Sand's description of her mother. "She had so much natural wit," Sand writes, "that when she wasn't frozen by her timidity, which became extreme in the presence of certain people, it fairly sparkled." Into this sparkling self, Sand tells us, came "lightning flashes of poetry."

How many of us who are writers have had mothers who in rare moments show this lightning flash, and how many of us still lapse into our mothers' shyness?

Adrienne Rich speaks to us of the same split when she writes of her early poetry:

> Looking back at the poems I wrote before I was twenty-one I'm startled because beneath the conscious craft are glimpses of the split I even then experienced between the girl who wrote poems, who defined herself in writing poems, and the girl who defined herself by her relationship with men.

For here are two beings. The one who tries to be what others see her to be. The other who exists, and who, therefore, can write poetry, can feel, can express being. Between these two, a kind of shyness *must* exist. George Sand's mother hides her real self behind this shyness.

But timidity is not a property of the real self. This is a self that has been warned into silence, that has, in effect, been silenced. For the existence of a false idea of the female is not all that renders the female self mute. Accompanying the pornographic image of female sexuality, and almost itself a part of that imagery, is pornographic culture's defamation of female being. The idea of female being is castigated. We find only one instance of this in the notion that a woman's sexuality attracts rape. Let us speak from examples. A woman, for instance, becomes a queen. During a period of monarchy and nationalism, she is a great monarch. She creates broad changes in the country, modernizations. She moves from a large vision of history. Whether or not we agree with her acts, we must all recognize that she was notable. Yet added to the accomplishments of Catherine the Great— that she brought European culture to Russia, that she established modern institutions, progress—we have a pornographic image of her life and death. We are told that she died crushed by the weight of a horse which had fallen on her while she copulated with him. Culture deals the same blow to female beingness in the Biblical figure of Jezebel. A prophet and a religious visionary, Jezebel carried on, within the Hebrew traditions, a tradition of the Great Goddess. For this, and for the fact that she preached at all, pornographic history records her as a whore. Most of us cannot recall at all that she was a prophet.

Her beingness is erased. Thus, too, a Hebrew scholar renowned for her philosophy and knowledge finally becomes most notable for an affair she had with a student of her husband.

Everywhere we look, female presence is thus defamed. The feminist movement of the nineteenth century, which had as a part of itself a philosophical notion of free love, an estimation of the importance of the erotic, a political campaign for birth control, is pictured by pornographic history for coming generations as a "prudish" movement which would censor sexual expression. History forgets that the Comstock laws, the first laws censoring literature about sexuality in America, were framed and used to imprison Margaret Sanger, the feminist political organizer who worked most of her life to bring birth control to women. Thus when female being is not defamed with the image of the whore, female presence is castigated for being asexual or "frigid."

Finally, in a pornographic magazine, accompanying photographs of women who are chained to a wall, exposed, posing, we read the words which they are supposed to have spoken. Speaking of their "girlie sex," these women are supposed to be telling us that they pretend to be "samples in a love slave market," that they set up an auction block in their basement and pretend to auction each other off under a sign that says "Sale." And now how many stories of female experience are silenced, or forced into "shyness" and timidity, by the ugliness of this image? For inside this defamation of female being is the whole history of women's love for women, female friendship, the erotic love of women for women's bodies, entire networks of female support and community. In this same defamation, the life of the black woman in slavery is also distorted, trivialized, hidden. That this woman was chained and raped against her will is clouded and obscured by this image. And finally, in this grotesque dumb show, the fact of female (or "white") slavery is driven even further from our consciousness. Thus the pornographic mind simultaneously gives us a pornographic image of women and erases any image of female existence which might contradict pornography's idea of women.

Suppose that every gesture one made—every word, every act, signal, motion, a smile, a frown, a wave of a hand, a shout, a scream, a kick, a rush of words—each and every expression of one's psyche were ignored. Suppose that in a company of people, every time one opened one's mouth to speak, one's own words were drowned out by other words. Or suppose that if one finally spoke into a waiting silence, one encountered no response, no dialogue but instead simply a stillness, as if nothing had ever been said. Along with defamation of being, this is the single most common experience that a woman has of her own real presence in the pornographic culture.

And now let us suppose that, outside of the image of nonbeing, a woman suspects that she has a being. She is, of course, timid. What else can one expect? This is a being which has been described variously as ridiculous, murderous, grotesque, overwhelming. (A being which makes men "flinch.") But even so, the force of her own soul drives her past her own shyness to some expression. She speaks. Or she acts. She does something and so, visibly, becomes herself in the world. She has been taught all her life, since childhood, that to be a woman is to be nothing. But now, despite the same voice within her, she rebels. She takes courage. She exists. And what, then, does she discover? Silence.

For this is the other way by which a woman is reduced to nothingness. She is ignored by culture. She is made invisible. Her presence is simply not recognized. In the case of an act of history (such as the fact that it was primarily women who brought down the Bastille), this act is simply not reported. It is erased from the history books. In the case of a woman who speaks, who writes, her work goes unrecognized. Thus, that Cristine de Pisan wrote a book called *The City of Women* in the Middle Ages is forgotten. And now if a woman has felt inside her the loss of self, which is a feeling of emptiness, when she acts and is not recognized for acting, she begins to believe that the pornographic mind is correct. She begins to believe that her identity is nothingness. That in her essence, she does not exist. Even her attempt at expressing herself ends by proving that she does not have a self.

Yet in this she cannot be content. For indeed, she does have a self, and speech and expression are part of that self's nature. We have from Isak Dinesen, for instance, this understanding that "without repeating life in imagination you can never be fully alive." The soul longs for a mirror. The soul longs for expression, and to be seen and to be heard. Imagination is a part of human nature perhaps more necessary to life than as yet we comprehend. But it is this, the self's imaginings in female nature, to which the pornographic culture is irrevocably hostile. And of course, if we meditate on the logic of pornography, we know why this must be true. For if a woman imagines her*self* and brings herself into being through her own images, then nature and culture not only are united again, but mirror and express one another. Now culture ceases to be a revenge against nature and becomes, instead, nature's reflection.

But we are speaking of the female experience of silence. And now of the silencing of our imaginations. For it is not enough that a false image of what it is to be a woman be taught us. Symbolic thought is a structure of the mind. And the idea of ourselves which our beingness creates by its own nature must be made mute. This is no small task. It is not easy to erase the images which come from the depths of being. To do this is like an attempt to silence dreams.

And yet this is exactly what this civilization we have inherited tried to do. During the famous period of the witch trials and burnings, women who were accused of being witches were tortured and forced into signing admissions of guilt through, among other means, sleep deprivation. When we add to this that the witches' Sabbath has a kind of dream or allegorical structure, that the witches were supposed to "fly" to this Sabbath, that this flight was preceded by rubbing a certain ointment on the body, and that ointments have been discovered which enter the skin and produce a dreamlike trance, we can begin to understand the burning of the witches as culture's attack, not only on women and nature, but also on the body's ability to dream and *imagine*. It is Ernest Jones, finally, who reminds us that the figure of the devil has the attributes of the earlier Pan, who was the bringer of nightmares. "When a woman sleeps alone, the devil sleeps with her," the proverb tells us. Thus one discovers from this period of history that our culture has a terrible fear of women's dreams.

In the wake of culture's fear of female dreams, one remembers the story of Judith Shakespeare. This was the woman of genius whom Virginia Woolf imagined in her work on this very dilemma of women's imagination, *A Room of One's Own*. Woolf demystifies for us the conditions necessary for creation—one must have space to oneself, time and money, and a certain freedom from the demands of others. But none of these conditions exist for the ordinary woman. Rather, by every material and spiritual means, culture tries to discourage female imagination. When Shakespeare's sister wants to write for the stage, she must run away from home; she is not allowed to act; and when she becomes pregnant with the child of the stage manager, she commits suicide.

This is a fantasy which, unlike pornographic fantasy, portrays a real female experience within pornographic culture: *there have been so many poets lost to us.*

And whenever we lose a female poet to obscurity, silence, or premature death, every woman loses words from her own language. So little of real female experience has ever been expressed. We have no familiar images with which to speak of our lives or our identities, or through which to voice our feelings. One writer tells us of Marilyn Monroe that because she lacked an education, she was "able to speak only from her own sensitivities" and that "she did not know how to express herself in the conventional way." But there is no educated nor any conventional way to describe real female experience. If we have felt numb, the word which culture has given to us is "frigid." If we have felt desire and longing, we are given images of submissiveness, and an idea of "sighing and simpering" with which to express this force of longing. In this sense we are like a colonized people who have been alienated from our own experience by a foreign culture.

These words from Reza Baraheni regarding the Western colonization of Iran apply also to women within a pornographic culture:

> In the process of our mystification and stupefaction we suddenly find another layer of alienation. So many values—and styles of values— have been imposed on us that we cannot be sure of any kind of indigenous roots or identities. Wherever we look we find objects, faces and values from other places, and we ask: where are our own objects, our own values and faces? Where are our identities? Where are we as human beings?

If to know oneself is to have somewhere an image of ourselves, and we have been deprived of the words and images, how are we to have our own identities?

In her *Memories of a Catholic Girlhood*, Mary McCarthy tells a story which one may take as a parable for the state of a woman's identity. Because she has scratched open a cut on one of her legs during the night, the girl Mary wakes to find that her sheet is stained with blood. When she asks Mother Slattery for a clean sheet, she is told that she can be excused from athletics for the day, and she is given a sanitary napkin. Her protests that she only has a cut on her leg are not heard. Now the girl feels constrained to live up to the illusory sense of who she is that the nun has imagined. "There was no use fighting the convent," she writes. "I had to pretend to have become a woman . . . for the sake of peace." Every twenty-eight days she reopens the cut on her leg, in order to stain the napkins which the sisters now give her regularly. Thus she writes: "There I was a walking mass of lies, pretending to be a Catholic and going to confession while really I had lost my faith, and pretending to have monthly periods by cutting myself with nail scissors."

Adding to this experience of alienation and pretense, she tells us her "basest pretense" was to accept a nickname that she did not like. "I was burdened with guilt and shame when the nickname finally found me out," she writes. For after she began her pretense of "being a woman," the other girls at the convent decided to call her C.Y.E. And while they explained to her that the letters "stand for something," they refused to tell her their meaning. Thus these letters began to embody her feeling of shame. For this name represented to her an aspect of herself she believed she could not see, yet the world did see. Thus the name came to represent and solidify her own "sense of *wrongness.*" Yet she could not separate herself from this name; the personality which the name evoked in her "stuck." So finally, she writes, "I succumbed to the name totally." She tells us that she made herself over "into a kind of hearty to go with it—the kind of girl I hated."

Pretense, if it begins as a separation from the self, drives the self even further away, and the soul into self-hatred, for one must hate oneself for lying. One feels a sham. Unworthy because untrustworthy, and not deserving of a love which is bestowed upon an image one pretends to be. But even where a conscious impersonation of an image does not take place and where no conscious lie is told, still, in almost any woman's life within the pornographic culture, a fracture occurs between her real experience and how she, herself, or others name it. The ability to accurately and precisely isolate, recognize, and name a distinct emotional state, much less to christen it, recognize it, and claim it for the first time as a new discovery for culture, is rare. Even Freud, in his pioneering work, accepted and used a whole vocabulary of emotional language colored by society's idea of sexual roles. (A woman is "hysterical," for instance, after the word root *hyster,* meaning "womb.") When one begins to know and express oneself, one uses the language given by culture for such an experience. But what if language never quite fits actual experience? What if the feeling of numbness is described as "frigidity," the feeling of frustration as "bitchiness," the feeling of loss and grief as "emptiness," a feeling of despair as "masochism," of rage as "imbalance" or "excess"? What if the only way that is available to a woman for expressing a desire to transform herself is a change of hairstyle or clothing or furniture or draperies?

In the Stanislavski method of acting, an actor, through the use of a sensual memory—say, the odor of cucumbers—recalls for herself the memory of an actual emotion in her life. Perhaps she has actually lived through the death of a father, or a friend. And perhaps she must *play* the part of a woman grieving the death of a mother, or a sister. The two experiences are not at all precisely the same. And yet grief has a commonality. Thus she brings back to herself her old experience in order to act out this new one, and uses the truth and energy of that actual grief to make this pretense real to her. We are all actors. And our feeling, of itself needing expression as urgently as the body needs to eat or drink, will seek some form through which to speak. One sees this in the fantasy life, the nightmares of schizophrenics. A rage for a mother or father will be displaced onto an imaginary figure. For by some means or another, the soul will attempt to express truth.

And yet the outside observer, and the conscious mind, which sees the inner self as an outsider does, never guesses at this truth. In this way culture destroys a woman's conscious knowledge of her own experience. Just as she is separated from other women, and from her body and her own feelings, she is, finally, a stranger to herself. *This* is her essential loneliness, her loss, her grieving, which culture sees as emptiness.

And when this self disappears, so, too, does the world. In varying degrees, more or less severe, as we lose our knowledge of ourselves, outer reality become dimmed and begins to look dead. Of that most severe and emblematic of female conditions, the life of a prostitute, Jeanne Cordelier writes: ". . . being a prostitute is like living through an interminable winter. At first it seems impossible. Then, as time passes, you start thinking that sun is nothing more than a word thought up by men." Not only is the sun a figment, but the word "sun" becomes a fiction. Because the words used for one's own soul are false, all words become false. And all descriptions of experience, as well as experience itself, become empty.

For the truth is, the body cannot be pitted against the mind, nor the mind against the body. We are whole. When words say one thing and the body another, both lose their reality. The condition of a prostitute, in which, in order to earn a living, she must pretend to have passion and desire or even love for a man she probably finds repulsive, is an extreme example of the condition of all women. In order to survive in our bodies, to earn a living, to be accepted in society, we must sacrifice truth, we must pretend to be other than ourselves. Hence, our physical survival is pitted against the survival of our selves.

At one end of a spectrum of violence to the female soul, women are forced into the masks and costumes of the female impersonator in order to survive economically, but at the extreme end of this spectrum a woman's very physical existence is predicated on her ability to resemble the pornographic ideal. From *Tell Me Another Morning*, a brilliant and moving novel by Zdena Berger about a young woman's existence in a concentration camp, we have an account of such a condition in women's lives. Three women, Tania, the narrator, her mother, and their friend Ilse, stand together in a line. They have removed their clothing, for they are to be examined by the Nazi guards of the camp. They know they will either be chosen to live or be put to death.

"I see Mother being pulled back by Ilse's hand," Tania tells us.

> I turn slowly, back from the file. The women around me have their eyes straight ahead, as if drawn toward the man. Ilse is by the wall, searching through her clothes, her hand still holding Mother's. Mother stands there with so much patience in her face—she looks so calm, as when she would try to explain something to us and knew we would not listen or would not understand. She stands, waiting, and I know she does not know what Ilse is searching for and it does not matter.

> Ilse opens her hand and in it lies an old lipstick, the yellow metal peeled off in many places, the shine gone, but the color there, under the cap. Slowly she spreads some of the red on her finger and she takes Mother's face in her hand. The chin of my mother rests in the hand of Ilse, as if she was waiting to be kissed. The red spreads on Mother's cheeks and Ilse smooths the last touches. Mother looks younger now and rosy.*

And what we are moved by in this account, in addition to the fact that we have finally encountered here a truthful portrait of a female experience, is the fact of female survival. It is not only that the canniness of the use of makeup in this scene is courageous which makes us want to weep. But it is the fact that in this scene the pornographic mask used to hide women is transformed by one woman into a gift of love.

This love of self, this love between women, this courage, this canniness, is the real beauty which exists beneath the pornographic mask. A woman's beauty, so seldom recorded or given image, a beauty evidenced in countless small and daily acts, and even through all the institutions—motherhood, marriage, prostitution—which alienate women from themselves, a beauty which continues and sustains our lives despite the distorting conditions by which we live.

"What will happen to all this beauty?" we cry (as James Baldwin also cries in *The Fire Next Time*). Let us end our consideration of silence with these few observations. *Tell Me Another Morning* has fallen out of print. This essential record which tells us how the soul might survive the worst horrors of our times is in danger of becoming lost to us. And in this light, let us consider the pornographer's complaint that he has been persecuted and silenced. In 1977 pornographic films earned four billion dollars, as much as conventional films and the entire music industry combined. There are 265 pornographic magazines available currently. More pornographic books and publishers than can be counted. Twenty thousand "adult" bookstores.

And let us remember finally that we cannot choose to have both eros and pornography; we must choose between beauty and silence.

---

* Of course we know that in the Nazi concentration camps Jewish men were subjected to the same scrutiny, the same pornographic standard. But we must remember that they represented "the feminine" to the Nazi mind. Thus age (or any sign of illness or weakness) in a Jewish man would, like age in women in all pornographic societies, be threatening. For the aging of "the other" represents to the chauvinist his own mortality.

Rose of the eye of the hand of the mouth. The scent of the rose. The enrapturing scent. (The rose of the nose. The rose only the nose knows.) The soft rose. The rose of our thoughts, crossed with our ways: the rose of the war of roses, of revenge; the rose of celestial perfection or of earthly passion or of both, as in the rose of martrydom, the rose of voluptuousness, the heart center rose, the labyrinthine rose, the rose of the union of opposites, the tree of life of feminine deities of Venus of resurrection, as in the rose of the beloved. Or the blood-red rose. Which shall it be? And how shall we name the rose? *O wide rose* consummation *open, quiver pause* perfection *And close* achievement: this rose. This actual rose. The rose blooming in the early fall. In the warm days of early fall. With still a few more buds unopened. The rose as yet to come. Petals soft like the skin of the body and hidden, the green sheath pulled back to reveal: the new bloom. The astonishing beauty. The color which stuns the eyes (but not only the eyes, also the heart, the breath) dark pink at the edge, infinitely by slow degrees shading into lightness and then into brilliance into yellow; petals curled, petals embracing, rounding one another, cherishing a mouth, a blessing at the center: a flutter, a swooning motion, where the secret opens. And the fullest bloom: uncurling blown, seeded, the loose rose, the laughing rose, the spent rose, the heedless, reckless rose, the shining rose. And then the old rose. Petals brown, shrinking, dry and dying, shedding to the ground, petals the color of soil, invisible, doing their dark work. Rose of the eye of the hand of the mouth. How shall we name thee, rose. By the song like a rose on our lips, rose, who is in us, wondrous, large rose, as large as we can imagine, rose who is in us, rose that we are, partly open, blooming, bloomed.

EROS: THE MEANING
OF DESIRE

Without warning
As a whirlwind
swoops on an oak
love shakes my heart.
                    SAPPHO

The Child

At the beginning of this century, the painter Paula Modersohn-
Becker drew a portrait of an adolescent girl. The child's eyes, shadowed
and dark, at once look out to us and away from us, look downward
toward her nude body, and away, as if from shame, look inward, and
off into space, as if she wished to avoid the fact of herself. She is a
girl just before the moment of womanhood. She has no breasts, no
hair where a woman might. Her hands are clasped and raised to cover
her mouth, as if she would both protect and silence her own capacity
to be a woman.

For a woman, to look on this simple drawing is to be moved past
any pretense back to an earlier self. The simple fact of her body. The
intelligence. The sexuality without a woman's sexual body. We fear
for her. Our own dark memories live in her. She is intensity of feeling
and shame, she is sensitivity and embarrassment. She is the creature
who hides behind our masks of self-certitude, our impersonations of
self. In her posture we meet again the real feeling of our bodies.

The girl who begins to be a woman. When I look on this drawing
and remember myself as an adolescent child, I am reminded of Anne

Frank. The girl almost a woman who has become a symbol for all the innocents who were slaughtered in the Holocaust. Whose diary was filled with the sensitivities of a young girl awakening to her sexuality, and to her life in the world. In this book of hers we have been given a sensual record of the lives of those sacrificed, and therefore we are moved.

She tells us every detail, all the small dramas of the life of the body, of which the adolescent girl is so aware. We learn what it is like to sit for three days without moving or speaking. We hear her careful description of her sufferings with a flu; she tells us all the remedies brought to heal her. She tells us how each member of her family was able to bathe, of how they were able to relieve themselves when the plumber turned off the water for the day. She gives lessons in how to peel a potato. All this detail brings us home to ourselves. Anne Frank was not a document. She was not a number or a photograph. Not simply part of an abstract idea or a madman's fantasy. She was flesh and blood.

This being—just over the edge of womanhood—was the most feeling and idealistic of creatures. It is her belief in the goodness of humanity which is able to bring a heart numbed by the horrible events of the Holocaust back to its own grief. Above all, she immerses herself and her readers in the world of feelings. She tells us she likes to see a person angry because from this anger she can read character. In her dreams, an old friend she had misjudged pleads to her, ". . . help me . . . rescue me." She is filled with compassion, like all adolescent girls, for the mute and the weak.

That the adolescent girl becomes ashamed of this body which she begins to feel so powerfully. That a girl just turned woman should be the symbol of those who perished from the violence of a mass delusion. That it is another girl becoming woman, Iphigenia, who is sacrificed to the principles of warfare and violence, in our mythology, in our dreams. That now, in this late twentieth century, we see the faces and bodies of girls, their bodies barely showing breasts, in postures of seductiveness which suggest to us that these souls have already gone through a kind of rape. That the innocence and vulnerability of childhood has been sacrificed in these young women, as girls too young for sexuality promise their bodies to men.

The obsession of the pornographer with the unformed body of a child virgin. The girl kidnapped and sold into sexual slavery. The young woman accused of witchcraft and burned. In the Holocaust, babies torn from their mothers' hands and murdered, young women seduced, used, delivered of early pregnancies or dying in abortions, the child who is raped or abused.

There is a thread in the mind of this culture which ties together all these acts of violence to minds and bodies of children and young women. For the calculated use of a not yet grown woman's body in pornographic poses is part of culture's symbolic murder of all that is childlike in our souls. When we love a child, we love human nature before it has been reshaped by culture. This is what we mean by "innocence" and "naiveté"; not that the child has no sexual feeling, but that this feeling has not yet been corrupted by culture's hatred and fear of nature, and that the child's idea of self has not been reshaped to a humiliating image.

When we read the words of Anne Frank, a promise comes to us. Perhaps this is a child who might have reached adulthood with this "innocence" intact. Through what we see as wholeness in her we touch again our own wholeness. But when we see the child's body remade into a pornographic object, we witness the death of a hope in us. Here is the child's flesh stripped of meaning and the child's body fragmented from spirit.

When we seek happiness, Freud tells us, we look for the prehistoric wishes of childhood. And in our dreams, the presence of the child is like the presence of an essential self. When a child is born to our dreams, we know this is a new part of ourselves, or a very old part of ourselves reborn to consciousness. We take the child's appearance as a sign of transformation. At one and the same time, the child brings us joy and change.

Yet daily, as part of the normal rituals of our culture, we sacrifice this child in us. Since birth, we terrorize the desires of the child. What is joyful and irrepressible in our natures lies mute and still. From our fear of natural change, we murder the hope of new life in us. In our myths, Iphigenia, the young girl, on the edge of womanhood, on the edge of erotic power, is murdered, and this event is the first act in a war in which a whole generation of young men is immolated. But it is no different in our lives; through acts of violence to the soul and body, we destroy the young.

In these acts, we attempt to destroy eros. For isn't it eros we rediscover in the child's world? The beauty of the child's body. The child's closeness to the natural world. The child's heart. Her love. Touch never divided from meaning. Her trust. Her ignorance of culture. The knowledge she has of her own body. That she eats when she is hungry. Sleeps when she is tired. Believes what she sees. That no part of her body has been forbidden to her. No part of this body is shamed, numbed, or denied. That anger, fear, love, and desire pass freely through this body. And for her, meaning is never separate from feeling.

But all this is erotic and erotic feeling brings one back to this state of innocence before culture teaches us to forget the knowledge of the body. To make love is to become like this infant again. We grope with our mouths toward the body of another being, whom we trust, who takes us in her arms. We rock together with this loved one. We move beyond speech. Our bodies move past all the controls we have learned. We cry out in ecstasy, in feeling. We are back in a natural world before culture tried to erase our experience of nature. In this world, to touch another is to express love; there is no idea apart from feeling, and no feeling which does not ring through our bodies and our souls at once.

This is eros. Our own wholeness. Not the sensation of pleasure alone, nor the idea of love alone, but the whole experience of human love. The whole range of human capacity exists in this love. Here is the capacity for speech and meaning, for culture, for memory, for imagination, the capacity for touch and expression, and sensation and joy.

This is why the child in the pornographic mind must be sacrificed. She must be degraded, objectified, defiled, raped, and even murdered. For the child reminds us of our own wholeness. In our minds, she stands for physical and spiritual transformation, birth and death. She is the part of nature beyond control. But she is also meaning and culture bound up with nature. In her, nature is filled with meaning and culture expresses nature. And the child's crime is that she reminds us of eros.

Psyche and Eros

One can look at the whole history of civilization as a struggle between the force of eros in our lives and the mind's attempt to forget eros. We have believed pornography to be an expression of eros. But we find that after all, pornography exists to silence eros. That it is born from that side of the mind which would replace nature with a delusion of cultural power. Our memory of eros, of the feeling of wholeness, and our idea of love is clouded over by and surrounded with pornographic images. Even the story we know of Psyche and Eros, the first version of the myth written down, and the one most familiar to us, comes to us buried and bound up in a classic pornographic novel.

The Golden Ass of Apuleius presents for us a mirror of a culture in which eros is only a vaguely remembered dream, an idyll told to quiet a frightened girl. The story of *The Golden Ass* is simple. Wishing to learn the secrets of witchcraft, the hero, Lucius, travels to the land of witches. There he stays at the home of a witch and becomes the lover of her servant. As he watches the witch transform herself into an owl, he convinces the servant to give him the means to work this transformation on his own body. But she gives him the wrong ointment. Thus he becomes an ass.

As an ass, this hero is stolen away by thieves before the antidote, a rose, can be fed to him. Thereafter, in this animal body, he suffers a series of terrible fates. He is overworked and underfed, threatened with terrifying deaths, beaten. One of his masters cruelly sets fire to a load of wood he carries, another decides to castrate him, another plans to use him in a pornographic theater—in his ass's body, the hero will be forced to copulate with a woman on a public stage.

Here in this allegory is the story of the life of the body in a pornographic culture. The ass. The word for a part of our bodies that is erotic: the animal in us, the mute and stupid beast, the debased, the foolish, the enslaved part of our souls, the ignorant, the humiliated.

Yet we know the hero of an allegory dreams his own fate. In this tale, the hero is the narrator; he himself shapes the world which finally makes him suffer. And this is a world made after the pornographic ideology. In it, the power of women to instill desire in the body becomes a feared and evil magic. When a witch seduces a young man, she "invades his spirit." In this world, to love a woman is to be "sheathed in unbreakable bonds," and to yield to pleasure is to be enslaved to the senses. Here the power of nature to transform the body and the soul (the power of a woman to give birth, the power of a witch to engender life) is terrifying and dangerous.

This hero, who is the quintessential hero of our culture, covets the power he imagines nature and women to possess. Like the pornographer, he tells us that his greatest pleasure is to "conjure up" images of beautiful women while he is alone.

But even in a pornographic world, a memory of eros survives. When the band of thieves capture the ass, they also kidnap a young woman and hold her for ransom. Thus, in captivity, the ass overhears a story that an old serving woman tells the girl to quiet her fears. And this is the tale of Eros and Psyche.

Through this story, the old woman calms the fears of the frightened girl. For she is given a promise in this myth. And so are we, for like our dreams, our myths remind us of a knowledge we possess but which we hide from ourselves. In the midst of terror, the myth of Psyche and Eros gives us a map through our own souls back into a state of joy.

The tale begins as any love story within a pornography culture would. A virgin is to be sacrificed. And her enemy is another female, a divine woman. But this is a myth which will reverse the values of pornography and transform despair into joy. Thus in the beginning we learn that Psyche is too beautiful and that this beauty threatens Aphrodite's divinity. Aphrodite is furious that this earthly being can inspire worship. For this is a story in which the taboo against the joining of heaven and earth is broken (and in which culture and nature are eventually married).

Yet this will be no easy union. The lovers must suffer great change, for they begin in a pornographic world. Thus, just as in our world we have mistaken eros for pornography, in this myth the goddess of "love" takes on the pornographer's vision. Because Psyche is mortal, Aphrodite calls her an "excrement of the earth"; she complains that Psyche *defiles* her. And like the pornographer, she is vengeful: she exercises a cruel and arrogant power over this earthly creature.

And Psyche herself is a pornographic heroine in the beginning of the tale. She is without will; she is submissive. She never rebels, nor does she question her father's decision to follow Apollo's word and place her on top of a mountain, where she must await a hideous bridegroom who will devour her. She waits passively to be devoured. She is the terrified docile victim of the pornographer's rage.

Eros, too, at the beginning of the tale, is a pornographic character. Here he is "Cupid," inspired by passion without spirit, lust without meaning. He is the personification of cupidity. Like a rapist-soldier, he conquers woman and goddess alike. And his arrows inspire not deep love but rather jealousy and intrigue. In place of a knowledge of the body, of the soul, and of love, therefore, we begin with pornography's heritage: passivity, cupidity, and revenge.

Aphrodite has asked her son to defile Psyche by making her fall in love with the most despicable of men. (And is this not the revenge of pornography, to defile the feminine soul?) But Cupid falls in love with Psyche, and here is where the tale of Eros and Psyche really begins.

But it begins with illusion. Cupid belives he can hide his lover from revenge. He builds her a palace in which she is sheltered from any natural frustration or pain. Food and wine are given abundantly. Roses grow without thorns. There is never any bad weather. Of course, we know this world cannot survive. It is a world based on ignorance—Cupid has even forbidden Psyche to look upon him. (Thus pornographic culture tries to keep a knowledge of the soul from a knowledge of the body.) Yet it is not the nature of real love to remain ignorant. True eros reflects the whole of human experience. A lover wishes to know her beloved. Desire and meaning are not separate. Psyche wants to know.

Yes, Psyche responds to the fears of her sisters, who tell her Cupid is really a monster. And we know these fears have only awakened her own fears, and that these sisters are a voice in her, for the fear of eros is a part of the human condition which we can recognize. And we also know that distrust can destroy love. Thus Psyche's vision injures Cupid, and he is burned by the oil of her lamp.

But he is also kissed by the same lamp, for the myth tells us the lamp wanted to "touch so lovely a body—to kiss it in a lamp's way." The lover's desire to see also comes from love. Both love and fear move us to want to know.

Therefore, if Psyche is to win back her love, she must be made to travel more deeply into the realms of her own fear and at the same time free herself from this fear. This she does. Her search for Cupid leads her to his mother, Aphrodite. Now Aphrodite becomes the most extreme of pornographers; she plays out all the consequential acts of the pornographic imagination on Psyche's body: she puts Psyche on a rack, she beats her until she is black and blue, she pulls out all her hair.

And Psyche survives this revenge. But Aphrodite (and Zeus) would still keep Cupid, a sky god, from an earthly marriage. Thus she sends Psyche on a series of trials, in which Psyche must face madness (the madness of the ego) and acknowledge physical death: for which she must enter Hades, and travel in the realm of the unconscious, forgotten self.

In this tale, Psyche comes through these trials, because she listens to and trusts nature: the voice of a reed growing in the river speaks to her; an eagle advises and aids her. Through her experience she discovers a culture which reflects nature, a music which guides the self through the dangers of self-knowledge and toward Eros.

Near the end of the myth, Psyche travels back to the goddess of love bearing a box said to contain the secrets of beauty, and she has been told not to open this box. Yet she cannot resist, for she is curious; she wants to *know*. And when she opens this box she falls into a deep sleep, a sleep which must be full of human memory, but which is past consciousness, past culture.

Yet Eros awakens her from this sleep. She is revived to consciousness by love—and now this dreaming knowledge of the body and of nature can become a waking conscious knowledge. Psyche is no longer docile; she has reclaimed her own power. She is whole; she becomes a goddess. And in Cupid, passion is no longer separate from meaning. So the soul and passion are finally wed, and we are told that from this union a child is born, named Joy.

"Such was the tale told by the crazy drunken old woman to the captive young girl," the ass tells us. For when we recall eros to the pornographic mind we appear to be crazy, or drunk (or perhaps *ancient*). Yet the power of this myth, with its promise of wholeness, is very great. Shortly after the ass and the girl hear this story (as if this tale of liberation has reminded them of their own freedom), they make an attempt to escape. Yet *The Golden Ass* is pornography; their attempt ends badly. Now despair dictates events again. Because she let the two captives escape, the old woman commits suicide. For this is the fate of erotic knowledge in a pornographic culture—we kill this knowledge in ourselves. (And we live in a world fashioned by theft and brutality, our souls taken, our hearts brutalized, ourselves imprisoned by fear.) The ass and the girl are captured again. And as punishment for their escape, the robbers plan a revenge against them which would compete with the cruelest atrocity from the records of Nazi prison camps or the pages of de Sade.

The ass is to have his throat slit, one of the robbers declares, and then, "after his guts are scooped out, let the virgin be stitched up in the belly of the ass. . . . Let only the girl's head project, while the rest of her body is imprisoned in this beastly embrace. Then let the ass with the virgin in his belly be exposed on some cliff edge to the full force of the burning sun." The robber tells us that thus the girl will suffer beyond suffering. She will be eaten by birds of prey, by worms; she will be burned by the sun; she will be nauseated by the stench; and she will waste with hunger. Now once again the pornographer has punished the soul and the body, and with a special fury, for they have dared to come together, and they have dared to be free.

The two escape again. The girl returns to her lover and is married. The ass is led by the goddess Isis to a wreath of roses, and eating them, he becomes human again. But neither escapes culture's revenge against nature. For the girl's husband is murdered, and after his death she kills herself. And when Lucius becomes human again, he takes a religious vow of chastity. Thus eros is forgotten once more.

Resonance

> The only possible proof of the existence of water, the most convincing and intimately true proof, is thirst.
>
> FRANZ VON BAADER

Psyche's journey toward eros and immortality is a journey into the dark side of our mind, into the knowledge that the dark one within us which we would deny is ourselves. The hideous monster she feared was a part of her own imagination, and the "immortality" she achieves through this journey is no magical longevity but rather a capacity for understanding, which is part of all our souls. This is a knowledge that lies beyond the ego, knows your grief as my grief, resonates with all being.

For the part of the mind that is dark to us in this culture, that is sleeping in us, that we name "unconscious," is the knowledge that we are inseparable from all other beings in the universe. Intimations of this have reached us. From the physicists we learn that no physical entity has boundaries, but rather that fields of being weave together. In his later work, Freud wrote that "the contents of the unconscious is collective, a general possession of mankind." From Jung we read that the "deeper 'layers' of the psyche lose their individual uniqueness as they retreat further and further into darkness." And finally, he tells us that "at 'bottom,'" this individual psyche "is extinguished in the body's materiality" so that "the psyche is simply 'world.'"

The psyche is simply world. *And if I let myself love, let myself touch, enter my own pleasure and longing, enter the body of another, the darkness, let the dark parts of my body speak, tongue into mouth, in the body's language, as I enter, a part of me I believed was real begins to die, I descend into matter, I know I am at the heart of myself, I cry out in ecstasy.* For in love, we surrender our uniqueness and become world.

But this is no easy surrender. A part of being is alarmed, that part of us which longs to be forever unchanged. The conservator, the conservative. The invulnerable one. The one in leather boots. Stiff. The stone-lipped. The one who would stop the course of the river and determine the shape of trees. And of course we must be afraid. For the part of us we believe is ourselves, what we call the ego, always changes and therefore always dies. The soul, which is the world, is infinite only because the soul is part of change. The life of the ego is as temporal as is all life, as transient as flesh and earth.

And this is why the soul forgives and the ego blames. The soul accepts transience as part of being, and the soul is not separate from the earth. And the battle between the ego which would believe in an illusion of its own permanence and the soul is the same struggle as that between pornography and eros. The nude body of woman recalls for us our mothers, our infancy, our vulnerability, the knowledge of our body, and the meanings of nature, recalls to us our mortality. Therefore, pornography, wishing to forget all this knowledge, defames that body, ridicules it, punishes it, tries to destroy the power of its presence in our minds. It would profane this body and separate our physical longing from our soul's knowledge of love. It would prevent this body or the sight of this body from transforming us, from bringing us through our own feelings to a sense of union with all that is. For pornography is the form of resistance which the ego takes when it confronts the possibility of its own death.

What the pornographer would defame is a part of himself. And he must always lose this warfare, for what he tries to destroy is his own.

I fall in love. Even as I denounce this as a delusion, I cannot resist this feeling. I cannot resist music. I cannot resist beauty. Some part of me I cannot name seems to come alive, strains toward these sounds, this beauty, as if my eyes and ears suddenly knew their purpose. This is the sound of the Siren. The irresistible charm of Calypso. I fall into an old, barely remembered state of bliss. All I had held on to before loses its meaning for me. I give up my house. I change the way I wear my hair. I see what I had not seen before. Words change their meaning. I enter my lover's mind. See with her eyes. The world flashes, changes, moves about me, through me.

Now I am someone new. I have been taken unaware. (Without warning.)

It is the nature of love to upset the daily order of things. Just as must Romeo and Juliet, love must defy authority and ignore the lines of old enmities. For eros does not accept the order of the world which the ego needs to believe. And it is for this reason that erotic knowledge is dangerous to culture.

But of course, we know that culture need not be opposed to eros, for not all culture is delusion, and culture itself can be dangerous to the ego. It can contain and reflect the natural world and lead us back into our deepest selves.

The knowledge of the body and of a unity with all beings is a fundamental characteristic of the very forms of culture: language and image. Beneath the idea of the symbol lies an erotic understanding of the nature of reality. For the metaphor, the poetic association, unconscious slips of the tongue, similes, allegories, all contain and stand for the ultimate unity and alikeness of one being to another. Taken in its natural state, the symbol awakens compassion, engenders belief in the existence of the other as one like ourselves.

When the hero of *The Golden Ass* enters the land of witches, he tells us: "In fact, there was nothing that I saw as I walked about the city which I did not believe to be something other than it was. Everything seemed to be struck by some fatal incantation into a quite contrary image." But what he fails to perceive is that he is the teller of the tale; he is the creator of culture: he is the singer, and his the song.

And were he to acknowledge this song as his own, he would see reflected a larger self. He tells us: "I thought that the statues would step down and walk, that the pictures would move, that the walls would speak, that the oxen and other cattle would tell me strange news, and that the heavens and the sun's orb of glory would make a sudden annunciation."

For just as we are born mortal, born feeling and temporal and vulnerable, we are also all born as creators. Culture is a part of nature; we who are born of nature, who are nature, want to know nature. We are singers. And the world is a resonant place. Yes, the singer is afraid of the song, as we are afraid of eros, for within eros is annunciation. But the song will not be silent.

The Winnebago Indians tell us this story of creation. Earthmaker, they say, took a white and a blue cloud and put them together, making a new substance, and then he threw this substance on the earth. And this was Earthmaker's most important creation: a shell by whose means death and reincarnation are known. As this shell passed through all the world, it dissipated all evil, and finally was seized by the otter, the least important and most inconsequential of all beings.

If we were to name this shell we would have to call it the ineffable; this that forgives all, that touches all, that makes all equal. If we possess "a grain of wisdom," Jung wrote, we would not try to name love more than we have, but only to know it as "the unknown by the more unknown," all that we will know, that there is to know. For this is the meaning of desire, that wanting leads us to the sacred.

The Seventh Life

I would like to tell you in closing a story of an old man. This old man was very wise, and he could answer questions that was almost impossible for people to answer, so some people went to him one day, two young people, and said, "We're going to trick this guy today. We're going to catch a bird, and we're going to carry it to this old man. And we're going to ask him, 'This that we hold in our hands today, is it alive or is it dead?' If he says 'Dead,' we're going to turn it loose and let it fly. But if he says, 'Alive,' we're going to crush it." So they walked up to this old man, and they said, "This that we hold in our hands today, is it alive or is it dead?" He looked at the young people and he smiled. And he said, "It's in your hands."

FANNIE LOU HAMER, "The Special Plight and the Role of Black Women," Speech given at NAACP Legal Defense Fund Institute, New York, May 7, 1971

How can a soul be taken, and where does the soul go, and how can my soul leave me?

We never lose the soul. But we do lose knowledge of the soul: we cease to know ourselves, we become ignorant, and we cease to know others. Others cease to know us. We begin to believe the world is soulless, and our belief makes this true.

For knowledge is a part of the soul. And because the world is a resonant place, none of us escape grieving over the loss of another's soul. A woman is convinced by the pornographer that she has no soul. A black man is deprived of the knowledge of himself by the racist. Now this woman and this man are excluded from the resonance of our knowledge that we call culture.

Yet to exclude another being from this resonance is an ignorant act, committed by a creature who has lost the ability to see another being, who has lost a part of himself. It is the nature of acoustics that no sound wave exists by itself. Sound itself must "listen" to other sounds and thus be changed. There is no way a sound wave can cease to know or be affected by other sound waves. It must be alive to the world or not alive at all. And in the same way, a soul that does not acknowledge the soul of another is dead.

The image of the world created after pornography is soulless. The pornographer steals the soul of the other, and among those who believe his myths, no one remembers soulfulness. Yet a delusion is hard to believe. A memory remains and in each of us there are seeds of knowledge. If the violence of a Lawrence Singleton has crushed this knowledge, if Anne Frank has been sacrificed because she reminded us of this knowledge, both Kate Chopin and Franz Marc have left us with a record, a glimpse of another vision. And there is another life possible, different from the six lives of tragedy we have heard. There is a seventh life. A life which refuses obscenity's narrow and damaging idea of what it is to be human. And lives.

We do not know the date of the birth of Fannie Lou Hamer. She was born black and a woman at the turn of the century into a culture and society which do not recognize the value of such a birth. She was the last of twenty children born into a sharecropping family in Mississippi. For eighteen years of her life she picked cotton in the fields. She lost this work when she registered to vote. And after this time she became an organizer in the civil rights movement in the South. Later she ran for Congress. Later, with poor whites and blacks, she organized a cooperative farm, called Freedom Farm Co-op, to raise animals and vegetables. For these efforts through the years, her home was bombed more than once; she was jailed; she was severely beaten. She was the mother of two children. She died of illness in 1977.

But these are only the facts and do not do justice to her presence in the world. There is a song about her which for several choruses simply repeats her name; so powerful was the force of her soul in this world that on hearing that name sung out, chills go up and down the back, tears come to the eyes, and there is a swelling with some emotion not palpable but *there*.

Fannie Lou Hamer's life. The love was *in* her work. There could be no denying of the spirit in her flesh and blood. No denying this spirit was heard by and listened to and lived in union with other spirits, in and of the earth. No denying that this large, strong presence of a woman had a soul which could never be erased, whose clear and present effect on millions of lives stood to shame an ignorant culture and do danger to its dangerous delusions. For she touched the will to live and the will to love.

And therefore, because she existed, and others before her (the list could be as long as the book, Paula Modersohn-Becker, Rainer Maria Rilke, Lillian Smith, Olive Schreiner, each bearing parts of a memory of wholeness, Baal Shem-Tov, Master of the Good Name, Frederick

Douglass, George Sand, Zora Neale Hurston, and should include the obscure with the famous, Anzia Yezierska, Rosa Parks), we cannot say we have entirely forgotten. The heart. The circle. We have emblems. The triangle. We have knowledge. The rose. We have choice.

Berkeley, California   SUSAN GRIFFIN
Fall 1980

NOTES

References are not given for pornographic works published by firms which produce pornography exclusively; these do not remain in print long enough for use as reference material. However, I have included a list below of most of the works which I consulted. Since their authorship is (if not anonymous) most often pseudonymous, and I refer to them in the text by title, I have listed titles first here, then authors' names. These works will be donated to the reference archives of Women Against Pornography and Violence in the Media, in San Francisco.

Adultery with a Black Man's Wife by L. K. Smith
Apartment House Sex Killer by Jack Thomas
Captive Virgin by Hank Watson
Case Histories: A Study of Lesbian Practices
Chained Bride by Hugo Berine
Diary of a Lesbian Slave
Fatherly Love by Alexander Bedford
Programmed for Pleasure: Sex in the Computer Age by Gardner Frost
Teenage Sadism: A Documentary Casebook by Dean Copeland, Ph.D.
The Erotic Conquest of Mexico by Pedro Malomano
The Multiple Climaxing Woman: In-depth Case Histories by Ralph Edwardson
The Skin Flick Rapist by Al Daxter
Trapped and Tied Baby Hookers by Chuck Ramsey
Venus School-Mistress

SACRED IMAGES

Page
2 *"the poetry of oppression"*: See Judy Grahn, "Pornography as Poetry," *It Ain't Me Babe*, September 17, 1970, pp. 6–7.

3 *"the state her heart. . ."*: French pornographers cited by Benoite Groult, "Night Porters," *New French Feminists: An Anthology*, ed. Elaine Marks and Isabelle Courtivron (Amherst, Mass., 1980), p. 68 and passim.

6 *"who was essentially sold"*: Andrea Dworkin, "The Prophet of Perversion: A New Reading of the Marquis de Sade," *Mother Jones*, April 1980, p. 54. See Dworkin's *Pornography: Men Possessing Women* (New York, 1981).

8 *"untouched life of animals . . ."*: These quotations were taken from an exhibit of Franz Marc's paintings at the University of California Art Museum, December 1979. See also Frederick S. Levine, *The Apocalyptic Vision* (New York, 1979).

8 *"we are more than we know"*: H. D., "The Dancer," *The Poet and the Dancer* (San Francisco, 1975).

9 *"succumb . . . heavy"*: See Franz Marc, letter to August Macke, in Levine, op. cit., p. 57.

11 *"Love is a want"*: Mary Wollstonecraft, *Letters to Imlay* (1793–95). See Ellen Moers, *Literary Women* (Garden City, N.Y., 1976), p. 148.

12 *"in whom"*: Stefan Zweig, cited in Peter Gay, *Weimar Culture: The Outsider as Insider* (New York, 1968), p. 54.
   "downwards, like a root": Cited in Martin Green, *The von Richtofen Sisters* (New York, 1974), p. 126.

13 *"haughty still . . . worm"*: Cited in Mario Praz, *The Romantic Agony* (London, 1978), p. 65.
   "perilous beauty . . . ages": D'Annunzio, cited in Mario Praz, ibid., p. 31.
   "Woman, like the Sphinx . . . anxiety": Carl Schorske, *Fin-De-Siecle Vienna* (New York, 1980), p. 225.

14 *"Movements which have"*: Cited in Thomas Mann, "Goethe and Tolstoi," Essays, (New York, 1957), p. 114.

15 *"natural beauty"*: De Cultu Feminarium. Cited in Reay Tannahill. *Sex in History* (New York, 1980), p. 148.
   "It is good": I Corinthians 7:1, 8–9.
   "never benefited": Cited in Vern and Bonnie Bullough, *Sin, Sickness & Sanity* (New York, 1977), p. 15.
   "Crime is the soul . . . worship": Cited in Simone de Beauvoir's essay "Must We Burn Sade?" in Sade's *The 120 Days of Sodom and Other Writings* (New York, 1966), p. 28.
   "No aphrodisiac": Ibid.
   Le Bain d'Amour: Extracted in Phyllis and Eberhard Kronhausen, *Erotic Fantasies: A Study of the Sexual Imagination* (New York, 1969), p. 394.
   But to this: See Lenny Bruce, *How to Talk Dirty and Influence People* (New York, 1963); Luis Buñuel, *Belle De Jour* (New York, 1971); Jeanne Cordelier, *The Life: Memoirs of a French Hooker* (New York, 1978).

16 *"great cathedrals"*: *Thy Neighbor's Wife* (Garden City, 1980), pp. 71–2.

Page
17   *"He was quite prepared"*: Op. cit.
     "the pleasure of torturing": Ibid.
19   *"ejected from internal"*: Totem and Taboo (New York, 1950), p. 72.
     "everywhere the man": Feminine Psychology (New York, 1973), p. 135.
20   *"a miserable creature"*: Cited in H. R. Hayes, *The Dangerous Sex: The Myth of Feminine Evil* (New York, 1972), p. 183.
21   *"attacking her modesty"*: Cited in Steven Marcus, *The Other Victorians: A Study of Sexuality and Pornography in Mid-Nineteenth Century England* (New York, 1964), p. 202.
22   *"imperial couch . . ."*: Satire VI, p. 93.
24   *"more savage"*: Ibid., p. 105.
26   *"civilized woman . . ."*: Memories, Dreams, Reflections, ed. Aniela Jaffé (New York, 1963), pp. 263–64.
     women exist solely: Arthur Schopenhauer, "On Women," *Parerga and Paralipomena*, cited in Hays, op. cit., p. 199.
     women cannot comprehend: See Eva Figes, *Patriarchal Attitudes* (New York, 1970), p. 120.
     "And yet woman": Cited in Carolyn Merchant, *The Death of Nature* (San Francisco, 1980), p. 27.
27   *"Her entire appearance"*: Cited in Leslie A. Fiedler, *Love and Death in the American Novel* (New York, 1975), p. 322.
     "Everything in the profound": Cited in Mary Ellmann, *Thinking About Women* (New York, 1968), pp. 99–100.
     This tradition: See Kronhausen, op. cit., pp. 56–7.
     "nothing brings the manly mind": Cited in Bullough, op. cit., p. 23.
     "These limbs": Cited in *Not in God's Image*, ed. Julia O'Faolain and Lauro Martines (New York, 1973), p. 138.
28   *"held back by a feeling"*: August Strindberg, *Inferno/From an Occult Diary* (London, 1962), p. 113.
     miniature pipe organ: Hustler, February 1980.
     "she reminds me somehow": Tropic of Cancer (New York, 1961), p. 66.
29   *"In his mind"*: In Kronhausen, op. cit., p. 389.
31   *"are caught . . . serpents"*: Heinrich Kramer and James Sprenger, *Malleus Maleficarum* (London, 1928), p. 122.
     "Thou hast a serpent": Cited in Hays, op. cit., p. 196.
32   *"Black thou art"*: Cited in Praz, op. cit., p. 44.
     "again and again": Cited in Fiedler, op. cit., p. 320.
     "And now—I shuddered": Cited in Hays, op. cit., p. 188.
     "He is mine": Cited in Hays, op. cit., p. 207.
33   *"Strip but this Puppet"*: A Satyr Against Wooing (1698?). See Katharine M. Rogers, *The Troublesome Helpmate* (Seattle, 1966), p. 164.
34   *"In good time"*: Satire VI, op. cit., p. 121.
     "the image of everything": Arthur Adamov, *L'Aveu*, cited and extracted in Kronhausen, op. cit., p. 221.
     "She was their mental mistress": Op. cit., p. 62.
35   *"Beaver Hunt"*: See Hustler, August 1979.
     "What a picture": Alan McClyde, *The Passionate Lash*, in Kronhausen, op. cit., p. 231.
37   *"Why does Sartoris"*: Satire VI, op. cit., p. 95.
     "Oh, I hope . . . too large": Santa Barbara, Cal., 1978, p. 78.
38   *"She knows no other"*: In Kronhausen, op. cit., p. 17.

Page

"*will let herself be drawn*": Cited in Hays, op. cit., p. 207.

"*something predestined*": *Beyond Good and Evil* (New York, 1966), p. 167.

"*Made but to love*": *Don Juan*, CII.

"*Knowest thou not*": In Kronhausen, op. cit., p. 11.

40   *Even the word* "*culture*": See Julian Jaynes, *The Origin of Consciousness in the Breakdown of the Bicameral Mind* (Boston, 1976).

41   "*creative power . . .*": In Kronhausen, op. cit., pp. 384–85.

42   "*A prime collection . . . fresh Venus's will rise*": Ibid.
     La Femme Endormie: In Kronhausen, op. cit., pp. 362–84.

47   *Sadism and Masochism*: (New York, 1929).

48   "*revels in the fear . . .*": Ibid., p. 49.

49   "*Who knows how often*": *First and Last Notebooks* (London, 1970), p. 185.
     "*Whip me*": See Gertrud Lenzer, "On Masochism: A Contribution to the History of a Phantasy and Its Theory," *Signs*, Winter 1975, vol. 1, no. 1.

50   "*I'll make you work . . .*": In Kronhausen, op. cit., pp. 204–8.

51   "*For two years . . .*": Ibid.

52   "*Madame, before I have the honor*": In Kronhausen, op. cit., pp. 223–28.

53   "*You are going . . .*": In Kronhausen, op. cit., pp. 147–56.

54   "*From the small of his back . . .*": New York, 1968, pp. 86–93.

56   *Ernestine, A Swedish Tale*: In *The 120 Days of Sodom*, op. cit.
     Justine: Three Complete Novels: Justine, Philosophy in the Bedroom, Eugenie de Francal, and Other Writings (New York, 1975).

58   *Stekel tells us*: Op. cit., p. 57.

59   "*as though wounded . . .*": Cited in Praz, op. cit., p. 47.

62   *The 120 Days of Sodom*: Op. cit., p. 290.

63   *The Story of O*: Pauline Réage, trans. Sabine d'Estree (New York, 1965).

64   "*O hated herself*": Ibid., p. 80.

69   "*Be certain I'll spare*": *Three Complete Novels*, p. 191.

70   "*sick of seeing . . . her milkless breasts*": *Justine*, ibid. See Karl Stern, *The Flight from Woman* (New York, 1972), pp. 113–15.

71   "*Well known to all*": Satire VI, op. cit., p. 109.

72   "*we actually do become . . . separate*": *The Tantric Mysticism of Tibet* (New York, 1970), p. 85.

74   "*When a woman sleeps alone . . . Euphrates*": *On the Nightmare* (New York, 1951), p. 183.
     Shakti and Shakta: New York, 1978, p. 326.

75   "*And I was giddy*": Cited in Alessandra Comini, *The Fantastic Art of Vienna* (New York, 1980), p. 000

76   "*dizzy*": Op. cit., p. 191.

THE DEATH OF THE HEART

84   "*dig . . . turds*": August 1979.
     "*Anatomy will never reach*": Op. cit., p. 551.
     "*index of principled inhumanity*": "The Pornographic Imagination," *Styles of Radical Will* (New York, 1969), p. 54.
     "*when Michaelangelo wished*": Op. cit., p. 552.

Page
85   *"The sadist pictures":* Op. cit., p. 56.

    "No, you worthless trash . . . father": The Past Recaptured (New York, 1932), pp. 137–47.

86   *"arousal of a sexual response":* Op. cit., p. 54.

    "Each time the soul is moved": On Love, cited in Simone Weil, "The Materialist Point of View," *Lectures on Philosophy* (Cambridge, Eng., 1978), p. 39.

87   *"blocks . . . functionally identical":* The Function of the Orgasm (New York, 1971), p. 266.

90   *"Shut up":* The Rosy Crucifixion, Book I (New York, 1949), p. 384. See Kate Millett, *Sexual Politics* (New York, 1971), p. 306.

    "the lost rights": August 28, 1920. See Rogers, op. cit., p. 215.

91   *"You desire to live!"* Theodore Dreiser, *An American Tragedy* (New York, 1959), p. 526.

    "Deborah had gotten": New York, 1965, p. 9.

94   *"and crack":* Ibid., p. 31.

    "the violent mastery": Men in Groups, cited in Evelyn Reed, *Sexism and Science* (New York, 1978), p. 85.

96   *"There is no such thing":* "Have Only Men Evolved?" *Women Look at Biology Looking at Women* (Cambridge, Mass., 1979), p. 10.

    "The anthropological data": New York, 1976, p. 204. Fromm cites a study by S. Palmer of forty nonliterate societies and his own examination of thirty "primitive" cultures to support his statement that aggression is not common in preliterate society. See p. 204, note.

98   *"who was threatened":* Amanda Spake, "The End of the Ride," *Mother Jones*, April 1980, p. 40. In a letter to the author, Singleton wrote, "Everything I did was for survival."

    "Obsession is, of course": Michael Perkins, The Secret Record (New York, 1977), p. 86.

102   *"to go to any lengths":* Ibid., p. 87.

104   *"had something to do with":* See Where Do You Draw the Line? ed. Victor Cline (Utah, 1979), p. 226.

    "provides the critical reinforcing event": See R. McGuire, "Sexual Deviations as Conditioned Behavior," in Cline, op. cit., p. 210.

    "one exposure to pornography": Seymour Feshbach and Neal Malamuth, "Sex and Aggression: Proving the Link," cited in Pauline Bart and Margaret Josza, "Dirty Books, Dirty Films and Dirty Data," in *Take Back the Night*, ed. Laura Lederer (New York, 1980), p. 215.

    "to do what they'd seen": Diana E. H. Russell, "Pornography and Violence: What Does the Research Say?" in *Take Back the Night*.

    The sociologist Pauline Bart: Op. cit.

105   *"a hardened shell":* "Nominalized Passives," 1974, unpublished paper.

106   *"designed primarily to arouse":* Ed. Alan Bullock and Oliver Stallybrass (New York, 1977).

    "A woman has finally decided": Dominique Poggi, "A Defense of the Master-Slave Relationship," *New French Feminists*, p. 76.

107   *For each culture has a range:* See Margaret Mead, *Sex and Temperament in Three Primitive Societies* (New York, 1963), pp. 110–11. She writes that the Arapesh have no "conception of male nature that might make rape understandable to them."

    "the instrument of thought": "The Logic of Signs and Symbols," *Philoso-*

Page

phy in a New Key (Cambridge, Mass., 1973), p. 63; see also "Symbolic Transformation."

108   *In the mind, we do not distinguish:* See Jerry Mander, *Four Arguments for the Elimination of Television* (New York, 1978), p. 216.

A group of athletes: See a study by Alan Richardson on the free-throw scores of basketball players, in Mike Samuels, M.D., and Nancy Samuels, *Seeing with the Mind's Eye* (New York, 1977), p. 166.

109   *"persons themselves":* Kenneth E. Boulding, *The Image* (Ann Arbor, 1961), p. 71.

110   *"The child learns":* Ludwig Wittgenstein, *On Certainty* (New York, 1972), p. 144.

In 1972, for example: Cited in Cline, op. cit., p. 212.

In the early twentieth century: This account appears in Stekel, op. cit., p. 222 and passim.

112   *"They were very picky":* See Laura Lederer, "Then and Now: An Interview with a Former Pornography Model," *Take Back the Night,* p. 65.

113   *"They were so into":* Linda Lovelace (with Mike McGrady) *Ordeal* (Secaucus, N.J., 1980), p. 45.

115   *She earns money:* Lederer, "Then and Now," op. cit., p. 61.

She does "not want to end up . . . actress": See Art Harris, "The Making of a Porn Queen," *San Francisco Chronicle (California Living),* July 18, 1976, p. 25.

116   *We are told by a woman:* See Francis O. Sinclair, "Going for the Centerfold," *San Francisco Chronicle (California Living),* July 31, 1977, p. 10.

One agency keeps a special catalogue: Lederer, "Then and Now," op. cit., p. 60.

A former pornographic model: Ibid., p. 65.

One model speaks . . . Another woman lost . . . Actresses and actors are asked . . . In Los Angeles, a woman hired . . . : Ibid., pp. 62, 66, 69. See also Lovelace, op. cit.

117   *"he knew from his research":* Kathleen Barry, *Female Sexual Slavery* (Englewood Cliffs, N.J., 1979), p. 86.

"who take photographs": Cited in Barry, op. cit., p. 85.

"keep the actor hard . . . emotions are essential to sexual experience": Rene Bond (with Winston Hill), "Interview with a Pornographic Film Star," *Sexual Deviance and Sexual Deviants,* comp. Erich Goode (New York, 1974), p. 68.

"we hated the unending sex scenes . . . lack of tits": Ron Sproat, "The Working Day in a Porno Factory," ibid., p. 89.

120   *"He sobs as he walks":* J. K. Huysmans, *La Magie en Poitou: Gilles de Rais,* extracted in Kronhausen, op. cit., p. 25.

121   *"Rape: Agony or Ecstasy?":* Cited in Russell, "Pornography and Violence," op. cit., p. 220.

122   *"precluded masturbation . . . intercourse":* Talese, op. cit., p. 33.

"through the half-raised shade": Ibid., p. 29.

"virtually lived within the glossy pages . . . feeling": Ibid., p. 23.

123   *"Symbols appear":* On Certainty (New York, 1969), p. 132.

As Susan Sontag reminds us: See *On Photography* (New York, 1977).

124   *"Paris is like a whore":* Tropic of Cancer (New York, 1961), p. 188.

Page

"*The actual scene is a disillusionment*": Op. cit., p. 72.

"*The proposition seems*": Op. cit., p. 132.

125 *And finally, the fantasy:* See *Feminist Alliance Against Rape Newsletter,* Spring 1976, p. 2; *Women Against Violence in Pornography and Media Newspaper,* October 1978 (this issue is devoted to the famous *Born Innocent* television suit).

128 "*In order that man shall become social*": Op. cit., p. 27.

"*It is not possible*": "The Most Prevalent Form of Degradation in Erotic Life," *Sexuality and the Psychology of Love* (New York, 1974), p. 69.

129 "*I shall . . . put forward . . . a lower type of sexual object*": Ibid., pp. 63–64.

"*hideous forms . . .*": Herbert Marcuse, *Eros and Civilization* (New York, 1955), p. 184.

131 "*For in our opinion*": *Sexuality and the Psychology of Love,* p. 121.

133 "*The fear of evil instincts*": Op. cit., p. 148.

134 "*If people were told*": Simone Weil, *The First and Last Notebook* (London, 1970), p. 73.

135 "*The process consists*": *The Mermaid and the Minotaur* (New York, 1977), p. 135.

138 "*Thou owest nature a death*": *The Interpretation of Dreams,* trans. James Strachey (New York, 1961), p. 205.

140 "*Sometimes, too, just as Eve*": *Swann's Way* (New York, 1956), p. 5.

"*The mixed feelings*": Op. cit., pp. 134–35.

141 "*the Stone Age baby . . . a mad world*": *The Politics of Experience* (New York, 1967), p. 58.

"*stands between man and woman*": Op. cit., p. 156.

145 "*That boy will never amount to anything*": Ernest Jones reports this remark in *The Life and Work of Sigmund Freud* (New York, 1961), p. 15.

146 "*represents to his son*": Ibid., p. 7.

148 "*dark . . . seething excitations*": *New Introductory Lectures on Psychoanalysis* (New York, 1965), p. 73.

151 *A grown man goes to a prostitute . . . :* See Stekel, op. cit., p. 203.

"*the humiliating position*": Ibid., p. 151.

"*I cannot understand*": Ibid., p. 105.

152 *A man goes to a prostitute . . . strangles him:* Ibid.

153 *A woman who cooks . . . :* See Lin Farley, *Sexual Shakedown* (New York, 1980), p. 158.

"*deranging the senses*": See Arthur Rimbaud, "Letter to Paul Demery," *Rimbaud: Selected Verse,* ed. Oliver Bernard (Baltimore, 1962), p. 8.

154 *For after all . . . the tragedy of Oedipus . . . :* See Kenneth Burke, *A Grammar of Motives,* cited by Francis Fergusson, "Oedipus Rex: The Tragic Rhythm of Action," in *Oedipus Tyrannus,* ed. Luci Berkowitz and Theodore F. Bruner (New York, 1970), p. 187.

THE SACRIFICIAL LAMB

159 *Chester the Molester . . . In another cartoon . . . :* See *Hustler,* September 1977, August 1979.

A film called Slaves of Love: See Luisah Teish, "A Quiet Subversion," *Take Back the Night,* p. 117.

Page

"*we are the members of the master race*": "*The Jewish Presence: Essays on Identity and History* (New York, 1977), p. 221.

160 "*Pornography and propaganda*": Ibid.

"*elevated cruelty*": Hannah Arendt, *The Origins of Totalitarianism* (New York, 1962), p. 333.

"*These sooty dames . . .*": "Jamaica, A Poem in Three Parts." Cited in Winthrop D. Jordan, *White over Black: American Attitudes Toward the Negro, 1550–1812* (New York, 1977), p. 150.

"*There is nothing more intolerable . . .*" *the woman who takes a man's job*: See Juvenal, op. cit., p. 121. See also Jordan, op. cit.; and Bernard Glassman, *Anti-Semitic Stereotypes Without Jews* (Detroit, 1975).

161 "*knightly . . . steady eye*": W. J. Cash, *The Mind of the South* (New York, 1969), pp. 73–4.

"*the flesh of women . . .*": de Sade, *Juliette*, cited in Mary Ellmann, op. cit., p. 66.

162 "*One day, when passing*": *Mein Kampf* (Boston, 1943), p. 56. (The citation in the text is from another translation, the note for which I have lost, but the passage cited is the same.)

woman "*can have no part*": Cited in Figes, op. cit., p. 131.

"*devil's gateway*": Tertullian, *De Cultu Feminarum*, extracted in *Not in God's Image*, p. 132.

163 "*Ham disobeyed . . .*": See Jordan, op. cit., pp. 35–6, 41.

"*The symbol of all evil*": Op. cit., p. 324.

For example, Alfred Rosenberg: See *Race and Race History, and Other Essays* (New York, 1971).

"*a farrago of bestial sounds*": See Loren Eisley, *Darwin's Century* (New York, 1961), p. 261.

A gynecologist argues: See Barbara Ehrenreich and Deirdre English, *For Her Own Good* (New York, 1979).

164 "*Jewish art dealer*": Op. cit., p. 189.

Thus we are given a portrait of the Jew . . . [including note]: See Glassman, op. cit.

"*a woman thinks alone*": Op. cit., p. 115.

165 "*the absolute female*": Cited in Figes, op. cit., p. 129.

166 "*whom somebody . . . and the man*": See Cash, op. cit., p. 86; and Schopenhauer, "On Women," cited in Figes, op. cit., p. 121.

With satanic joy: Op. cit., p. 325.

"*women eager for venerry*": See Jordan, op. cit., p. 159 n.

167 "*She is a nice, good*": Blanche Seale Hunt, *Stories of Little Brown Koko* (Chicago, 1952), pp. 5–6.

168 "*Eternal Nature inexorably*": Adolf Hitler, *Mein Kampf*, op. cit., p. 65.

169 "*lifted a corner . . . veil*": Ibid., p. 287.

"*is quite prepared to sacrifice*": p. 461.

170 "*in its nature a masculine movement*": Cited in Figes, op. cit., p. 132.

A woman "*who engages*": Cited in Hans Peter Bleuel, *Sex and Society in Nazi Germany* (Philadelphia, 1973), p. 59.

171 "*the womb of the Third Reich*": Ibid., p. 68.

172 "*the emancipation of women*": Ibid., p. 59.

"*Semitic wire pullers*": Ibid., p. 58.

Page

"*obsession with women*": Léon Poliakov, *The History of Anti-Semitism* (New York, 1975), p. 379.

During the first centuries: See Jordan, op. cit., p. 33.

"*has more than a touch*": Cited in Figes, op. cit., p. 129.

In medieval anti-Semitic iconography: See Glassman, op. cit., p. 35.

And the Nazi ideologist: See Rosenberg, op. cit., p. 50 and passim. Also see Wilhelm Reich, *The Mass Psychology of Fascism* (New York, 1973), pp. 85 ff, for a thorough discussion of Rosenberg's symbolism.

174   "*Up until now . . . in this case a 'German' ":* p. 311.

175   "*hunger for education . . .*": Arendt, op. cit., p. 61.

"*Are you blonde?*": Headline from *Ostara*, cited in John Toland, *Adolf Hitler* (Garden City, N.Y., 1976), p. 62.

"*acquired a mass of perceptions*": Chamberlain. Cited by Leon Poliakov, *The Aryan Myth* (New York, 1974), p. 289–90.

"*If we were to divide*": p. 290.

"*The Protocols of the Elders of Zion*": Cited in Vamberto Morais, *A Short History of Anti-Semitism* (New York, 1976), p. 195.

176   "*anti-Semitic politics flourished*": *The War Against the Jews, 1933–1945* (New York, 1975), p. 10.

"*the problem of racial pollution*": Cited in Toland, op. cit., p. 62.

177   *he went . . . to prostitutes:* See Trevor Ravenscroft, *The Spear of Destiny* (New York, 1974), p. 171.

urinating . . . "he had a taste": See Robert G. L. Waite, *The Psychopathic God: Adolf Hitler* (New York, 1977), pp. 237–39, p. 42.

178   "*a conglomeration of races*": Cited in Morais, op. cit., p. 181.

"*To me the big city*": Ibid.

179   "*the original sin*": *Mein Kampf*, p. 249.

"*really significant symptoms of decay . . . body and spirit*": Ibid., p. 328.

180   *a look "of astonishment*": Waite, op. cit., p. 51.

"*The discovery of the Jewish virus*": Cited in Ibid., p. 24.

"*typical Jewish attribute*": Op. cit., p. 31.

181   *And finally, his political accusation: Mein Kampf*, p. 249.

182   "*at once took over*": p. 579.

"*tries to force a doctrine*": Ibid., p. 582.

"*the ground*": Hugh Thomas, *A History of the World* (New York, 1979), p. 499.

183   "*We shall see that all sadomasochists*": Op. cit., p. 98.

"*Here at last . . . makes history*": J. P. Stern, *Hitler: The Führer and the People* (Berkeley, Cal., 1975), p. 37.

"*by the decision to produce*": *Under the Sign of Saturn* (New York, 1980), p. 83.

184   "*an orator of genius*" Werner Maser, *Hitler* (New York, 1973), p. 259.

"*sweeping along impressionable*": Peter Viereck, *Meta-Politics: The Roots of the Nazi Mind*, p. 135.

"*its performance makes history*": J. P. Stern, op. cit., p. 37.

185   "*man's role is to overcome nature*": *Mein Kampf*, p. 287.

"*lord over other creatures*": Ibid.

186   "*The effectiveness of this kind . . .*": Op. cit., p. 351.

In Mein Kampf, he tells us: p. 287.

Page
189 *"inner collapse"*: Rosenberg, op. cit., p. 33.
A man who attempted to escape: See Eugen Kogon, *The Theory and Practice of Hell* (New York, 1980).
190 *"And I understood"*: Mme Levinska, cited in Gabriel Marcel, *Man Against Mass Society* (Chicago, 1962), pp. 42–3.
"The Germans sought": Mme Jacqueline Richet, ibid.
191 *"Most of you know"*: Cited in Dawidowicz, *War Against the Jews*, p. 200.
192 *"a moral fight"*: "The Jew in German History," Nazi Army pamphlet, 1939.
195 He says that the *"great thing . . ."*: Cited in Arendt, op cit., p. 418.
"The psyche of the great masses": p. 42.
196 *"Hitler's triumph"*: Roberts, *Hitler*, cited in Viereck, op. cit., p. 124.
"the people are really feminine . . .": See Roger Manvell and Hernrick Fraenkel, *The Incomparable Crimes* (London, 1967), p. 127.
"it was nothing": *Adventures of a Bystander* (New York, 1979), p. 162.
197 *"We carry the death head"*: Cited in Heinz Hohne, *The Order of the Death's Head* (New York, 1970), p. 24.
"National Socialism is not a doctrine": Cited in Stern, op. cit., p. 33.
198 *"this becomes all the more ironical"*: Op. cit., p. 181.
"Nothing was genuine": J. P. Stern, op. cit., p. 28.
"All in all, it is surely best": Cited in ibid., p. 34.

SILENCE

This entire chapter has been preceded and informed by the insights and work of Tillie Olsen's *Silences* (New York, 1979).

202 *"our experience"*: R. D. Laing, op. cit., p. 28.
203 *"the remarkable talents"*: New York, 1969, p. 87.
204 *"Marilyn getup"*: *Nostalgia Isn't What It Used to Be* (New York, 1978), p. 331.
205 *"Do you want me"*: *Bittersweet* (New York, 1980), pp. 40–1.
"She is a mirror": *Marilyn: A Biography* (New York, 1973), p. 44.
"I used to get the feeling": *Life* magazine, August 17, 1962.
211 female children who are molested: See Florence Rush, *The Best Kept Secret: The Sexual Abuse of Children* (New York, 1980). See also "Child Pornography," in *Take Back the Night*.
"frigid": *Marilyn*, p. 48. See also p. 44.
213 *"being able to suggest"*: Quoted in *Marilyn*, p. 149.
216 *"cruel"*: Ibid., p. 30.
"charisma": See Cindy Adams, *Lee Strasberg: The Imperfect Genius of the Actors Studio* (New York, 1980), p. 253 and passim.
"always running into people's unconscious": See *Life*, August 17, 1962.
217 *"practised precision"*: Robert F. Slater, "The Mysterious Death of Marilyn Monroe," *Hustler*, July 1980, p. 37.
218 *"an end in herself"*: *Letters*, as cited in Ellmann, op. cit., p. 132.
cured by copulation: Poggio Bracciolini, "A Frenetic Woman," in Kronhausen, op, cit., p. 47.
Earl of Rochester's Sodom: In Kronhausen, op. cit., p. 27 and passim.

Page
"the sharp-tongued spinster": *The Function of the Orgasm*, (New York, 1971), p. 133.

a desire to have a penis: See Millett, op. cit., pp. 186, 187 and passim. And Sigmund Freud, "Femininity," *New Introductory Lectures on Psychoanalysis* (New York, 1961).

"*byproduct of selection*": Donald Symms, *The Evolution of Human Sexuality,* cited in Clifford Geertz, "Sociosexology," *New York Review of Books,* January 24, 1980.

"*stud father*": *Marilyn,* p. 25.

219 "*She was no longer . . . body said no*": *The Story of O,* p. 75.

220 "*like a lesson of grammar*": Ibid., p. 73.

221 "*she lost herself*": Ibid., p. 39.
  "*There exists a second ending*": Ibid., p. 20.

222 "*What she asked of women*": Ibid., p. 98.
  "*hold back the water*": Ibid., p. 46.
  "*frozen like a butterfly*": Ibid., p. 71.
  "*composed of words and looks*": Ibid.
  "*spread-eagled*": Ibid., p. 195.
  "*bird of prey*": Ibid., p. 192.
  "*one wants to tame*": Ibid., p. 195.
  "*deaf to human language*": Ibid., p. 198.

225 "*nothing had been such a comfort*": Ibid., p. 38.
  "*the peaceful reassuring hand . . . escaping*": Ibid., p. 113.
  "*is pleased to think*": Ibid., p. 176.

226 "*She blamed the sea*": Ibid.
  Susan Sontag: See "The Pornographic Imagination," *Styles of Radical Will,* p. 44 and passim.

227 "*O progresses simultaneously*": Ibid., p. 58.
  "*the wheel and spikes* (in footnote): *The Story of O,* p. 166.

228 "*Someone was drawing water*": Helen Keller, *The Story of My Life,* quoted in Susanne Langer, op. cit., pp. 62–63.
  One who is . . . to be: For a discussion of this issue, see Weil, "The Iliad: A Poem of Might," *The Simon Weil Reader,* ed. George A. Panichas (New York, 1977), pp. 153–83.

230 "*She ate supper*": Joanne Greenberg, *I Never Promised You a Rose Garden* (New York, 1964), p. 192.
  "*began to look*": Ibid., p. 198.

231 "*the blame*": Marguerite Sechehaye, *Autobiography of a Schizophrenic Girl* (New York, 1970), p. 73.
  "*Because she was going to live*": Greenberg, op. cit., p. 198.
  Viktor Frankl: See *The Doctor and the Soul* (New York, 1973).

232 "*She tried to think*": Greenberg, op. cit., p. 163.

236 "*Speechlessness*": "Notes on Speechlessness," *Sinister Wisdom* 5, Winter 1978.
  "*mechanism inside*": *The Story of O,* p. 182.

237 "*we are related*": "The Materialist Point of View," *Lectures on Philosophy,* p. 77.

239 "*all such men*": Greenberg, op. cit., p. 111.
  "*Men are brutes*": Ibid.

240 "*control . . . It is surely*": Linda Gray Sexton and Lois Ames, *Anne*

Page

Sexton: A Self Portrait in Letters (Boston, 1977), pp. 55, 56; see also p. 82.

"*I wish stupidly*": Ibid., p. 252.

"*She had so much natural wit*": George Sand, *My Life* (New York, 1979), pp. 67–8.

241 "*Looking back*": "When We Awaken: Writing as Revision," *On Lies, Secrets, and Silence* (New York, 1979), p. 40.

242 "*girlie sex*": See Kathleen Barry, op. cit.

245 "*able to speak only*": Cindy Adams, op. cit., p. 253.

"*In the process of our mystification*": *The Crowned Cannibals: Writings on Repression in Iran* (New York, 1977), p. 83.

246 "*There was no use*": *Memories of a Catholic Girlhood* (New York, 1957), p. 134.

"*basest pretense . . . girl I hated*": Ibid., p. 136.

248 "*being a prostitute*": *The Life* (New York, 1980), p. 71.

"*I see Mother*": *Tell Me Another Morning* (New York, 1961), p. 81.

EROS: THE MEANING OF DESIRE

253 *prehistoric wishes:* Cited in Marcuse, op. cit., p. 186.

256 "*invades his spirit . . . bonds*": Apuleius, *The Golden Ass,* trans. Jack Lindsay (Bloomington, Ind., 1960), p. 53.

"*excrement of the earth*": Ibid., p. 106.

257 "*touch so lovely a body*": Ibid., p. 122.

258 "*Such was the tale*": Ibid., p. 142.

259 "*after his guts*": Ibid., pp. 146–47.

260 "*the contents of the unconscious*": *Moses and Monotheism* (London, 1951), p. 208. See Norman O. Brown, *Love's Body* (New York, 1966), p. 86.

"*deeper 'layers' . . . 'world'* ": *The Archetypes and the Collective Unconscious* (New York, 1959), p. 173.

262 "*In fact, there was nothing*": Apuleius, op. cit., p. 50.

Earthmaker: See Paul Radin, *Primitive Man as Philosopher* (New York, 1957).

"*a grain of wisdom*": *Memories, Dreams, Reflections,* cited in James Hillman, *The Myth of Analysis* (New York, 1978).

264 *There is a song:* See "Fannie Lou Hamer," by Sweet Honey and the Rock.